*For my cousin John, who first invited me
to Chiapas*

For my teacher June, who brought me back

*For the women of the Zona Galáctica,
who made me want to stay*

Lydia's Open Door

TUCHTLAN

H. AYUNTAMIENTO CONSTITUCIONAL
TUXTLA GUTIERREZ
1995 - 1998

Tuxtla Gutiérrez, Chiapas

COBRO DE ENTRADA

TUXTLA TE NECESITA
¡Participa!

ZONA GALACTICA $ 3.00

DIA _____

MES _____

AÑO _____

Nº 344031

Lydia's Open Door

INSIDE MEXICO'S
MOST MODERN BROTHEL

Patty Kelly

UNIVERSITY OF CALIFORNIA PRESS
Berkeley   Los Angeles   London

Frontispiece: Tuxtla Needs You. Participate! (Entry ticket to the Galactic Zone.)

University of California Press, one of the most distinguished university presses in the United States, enriches lives around the world by advancing scholarship in the humanities, social sciences, and natural sciences. Its activities are supported by the UC Press Foundation and by philanthropic contributions from individuals and institutions. For more information, visit www.ucpress.edu.

Parts of this book appeared previously in "I Made Myself from Nothing," in *Women in Chiapas: Making History in Times of Struggle and Hope*, ed. Christine Eber and Christine Kovic (New York: Routledge, 2003), and "Awkward Intimacies," in *Anthropologists in the Field*, ed. Lynne Hume and Jane Mulcock. © 2007 Columbia University Press. Reprinted with permission of the publisher.

University of California Press
Berkeley and Los Angeles, California

University of California Press, Ltd.
London, England

Library of Congress Cataloging-in-Publication Data

Kelly, Patty, 1968–.
  Lydia's open door : inside Mexico's most modern brothel / Patty Kelly.
      p.   cm.
  Includes bibliographical references and index.
  ISBN 978-0-520-25535-7 (cloth : alk. paper) —
  ISBN 978-0-520-25536-4 (pbk. : alk. paper)
  1. Prostitutes—Mexico—Tuxtla Gutiérrez.   2. Prostitution—
Mexico—Tuxtla Gutiérrez.   I. Title.
  HQ151.T84K44   2008
  306.74'2097275—dc22   2007028981

Manufactured in the United States of America

17   16   15   14   13   12   11   10   09   08
10   9   8   7   6   5   4   3   2   1

This book is printed on New Leaf EcoBook 50, a 100% recycled fiber of which 50% is de-inked post-consumer waste, processed chlorine-free. EcoBook 50 is acid-free and meets the minimum requirements of ANSI/ASTM D5634-01 (*Permanence of Paper*).

Let us canonize the whores. Saturday's calendar of the
    saints: Bety, Lola,
Margot, perpetual virgins, reconstituted, purveyor martyrs
full of grace, sources of generosity.

You give pleasure, oh whore redeemer of the world, and
    you ask for nothing
in exchange but some miserable coins. You don't demand to be
loved, respected, taken care of, nor do you imitate the wives
    with their
whining, reprimands, and jealousy.

Jaime Sabines, Tuxtleco poet

I have said to my clients, From this door to there [the rear wall
of her room], you can take down my pants as you wish, because
that is what I do. But outside, respect me. . . . That I will always
guard—that I ask for respect.

Lorena, Tuxtleca sex worker

They [the clients] think that we are here just to serve them, but
that's not how it is.

Bárbara, Tuxtleca sex worker

Contents

Illustrations

Preface

I

I had passed by the road leading to the place dozens of times since my
first stay in Chiapas in 1992. The sign said simply, Zona Galáctica. A large
white arrow pointed south. I had thought the Galactic Zone, located in
the bustling, lowland capital city of Tuxtla Gutiérrez, was some kind of
center for astronomical observation. Five years later I was again in southern Mexico, visiting relatives and rooting around for a dissertation topic.
I went north to Tabasco and considered working there. But the state lived
up to its name—it was really hot—and I soon returned to the cool mountains of Chiapas. There, a friend who knew of my interest in commercial
sex told me about a man I should meet—a doctor who worked at the
Comitán Center for Health Research. Days later I was sitting knee to knee
with the doctor in his cramped, book-filled office. Dark eyes flashing and
hands moving wildly, he spoke to me about sex work in Chiapas. To say
he was enthusiastic would be an understatement. He leaned forward, put
his hands on my knees, looked into my eyes and said, "For example, I am

a man and I want to have anal sex with you." He was speaking hypo-
thetically, of course, about the difficulties and risks sex workers face concerning client desires and condom use. "*Mujer*," he said, giving my thigh
a gentle slap, "There is someplace you have to see." The next day he
brought me to the Galactic Zone.

It was a side of Chiapas I had never seen before. Orderly, clean, organized—it seemed that everything was in its place. Modern concrete
buildings painted pink and blue and orange and yellow and green.
Women of various ages and appearances lingered in doorways, strolled
about, or sat and ate at one of the zone's food stands. The Galactic Zone
was not a planetarium but a brothel, and not just any brothel. It was a
fairly new, legal, and state-regulated supermodern model brothel built
with public funds and intended to transform commercial sex in the
region from an uncontrolled, informal activity to a highly regulated form
of formal service-sector employment. My decision was a visceral one,
unmarked by thoughts about the realities of career, funding, and fieldwork. Something like love at first sight, it was deeply felt and not particularly logical. I had found my field site.

I returned to Chiapas to start fieldwork a year later. Beginning the project, I went to the Palacio Municipal to meet with Tuxtla's director of public heath, a *panista* (member of the conservative right-wing National
Action Party, or PAN) and a gynecologist. He introduced me to the newly
elected mayor, also a panista gynecologist. Young, good-looking, and
charismatic, the mayor extended a hand to me and said in English, "It is
a pleasure to meet you. I am the mayor." I liked him. My fears about
working closely with members of a political party whose conservative
views on sexuality, religion, and politics were so very different from my
own all but vanished. Being a politician and gynecologist is not unusual
in Mexico; in fact, the mayor's father was Tuxtla's first panista-
gynecologist-mayor, back in the 1970s. As Maria Mies has observed, gynecologists, along with the state, are the "guardians of modern patriarchy."[1]
When gynecologists run the state, such guardianship is advanced.
Doctors and public health specialists have long been involved in political
affairs in Mexico—during the revolutionary period, such men (referred to
as *higienistas*), along with criminologists and social workers, were at the

forefront of a "social hygiene" movement that sought to control, among other things, female prostitution and sexually transmitted illness.[2]

Getting permission from municipal authorities to do ethnographic fieldwork in the Galactic Zone was easy enough. But how would things go inside the brothel? "This world [of commercial sex]," Ronald Weitzer notes, "does not offer easy access to the outsider, which helps to account for the paucity of research in many key areas; but gaining access should be viewed as a challenge rather than an insuperable barrier."[3] Once inside the zone, I found that access was not a problem.[4] Populations who are institutionalized in some way (prisoners, the mentally ill, prostitutes, or students), who are scrutinized by others (guards, doctors, police, teachers, or the state), and who are subject to what Michel Foucault calls a "normalizing gaze, a surveillance that makes it possible to qualify, to classify, to punish," are, for better or worse, easily studied by social scientists.[5] The women of the Galactic Zone were a discrete group, literally contained, and subject to question and examination by doctors, administrators, and municipal police. This disturbing fact lent a certain ease (and personal unease) to my entry into the zone as an anthropologist who would also question and scrutinize. Furthermore, given the local panista government's policy of *transparencia* (transparency—clear actions and accountability intended to create distance from the ruling party's history of corruption and impunity), along with their belief in the zone as a legitimate and important public works project, there was little reason to deny me access to the Galáctica, as it was sometimes called. They were proud of the place. I developed relationships, some casual, some close, fairly quickly and naturally with many women in the zone and with government officials. With certain others I was unable to form a relationship at all. I had concerns, stemming mostly from the potential contradictions between feminism and fieldwork and from the ways that the development of rapport in the field can, ironically, put research populations at "greater risk of exploitation, betrayal, and abandonment by the researcher."[6] Yet I found that many of the people in the zone wanted to talk and be heard. And I felt my own need to listen, to observe, to try to make some sense of what was going on in the Galactic Zone.

In the days following my introduction to the workers during a public lecture on miscarriage, various women approached me. They introduced themselves, questioned me, and told me how to do my research. I couldn't just go around asking a bunch of questions, they said. As Lorena told me, "I have something to say, and I hope it doesn't make you mad, but if you go around asking questions like 'How long have you worked here?' 'What do you earn?' 'How old are you?' 'Are you married?' no one's going to answer you." Such things, said Lorena, were better learned through friendships. Lorena and Desirée cautioned me to be careful and hinted at the divisiveness that I would later find permeated relationships in the zone.

I kept regular working hours in the Zona Galáctica, though I did not live there as some women do. A zone administrator persuaded me to give English classes to a small group of interested workers, and I did so a few mornings every week. At first, I balked—I didn't come to teach English, didn't know how, and naively thought maybe the classes would be some kind of insult to Mexican sovereignty. But I soon became known as *la maestra* (the teacher), though I was sometimes also referred to as *la güerita* (a diminutive term denoting a fair-skinned person of any national origin).[7] I purchased a white laboratory coat at the suggestion (almost insistence) of Edith, a zone secretary. All female municipal staff wore them, and, she said, it would help me *evitar manos* (literally, avoid hands) and discourage unwanted attention from clients. The lab coat helped to carve out my social role as a woman in the zone who did not sell sexual services. But I also feared it would cause workers to identify me with the staff of the zone's Anti-Venereal Medical Service and distance me from workers, so I used it selectively. Sometimes I wore it just to please the medical service staff, who would occasionally cast disapproving looks my way if I walked about the zone without wearing the marker of my status as a "decent" woman. Sometimes I wore it grocery shopping. I liked the lab coat—it made me feel safe when I strolled through the rougher parts of downtown Tuxtla (I never felt unsafe in the zone) and gave me a sense of belonging. Following the purchase of the lab coat, some in the zone began to refer to me as *la doctorcita*. To most, I was simply Patty.

The women of the zone were generous. Often when I would attempt to pay my fare when arriving at the zone by pirate taxi, I would find that

Figure 1. A surprise birthday party in the Zone.

one of the workers had already paid it. It was sometimes difficult to accept their generosity—I saw each meal they paid for as the equivalent of the hard work of sex with one client. I began to measure gifts, meals, drinks in terms of sex acts. Sex became currency. Rather than converting pesos into dollars, I began converting pesos into sex. A quick lunch was intercourse, an evening of cocktails, a blow job. The relationship between money and sex became clear for me, and sex took on a new and decidedly materialist meaning.

As an anthropologist, I am cognizant of the power dimensions of the discipline: class, gender, citizenship, ethnicity—our relationships in the field are marked through and through by inequalities. But for more than a year I was far from my Brooklyn home, and it felt good to be accepted and cared for. One warm morning in late April, I arrived to find that a surprise birthday party, the only one I have ever been given in my life, had been organized for me at Pepe's food stand just inside the main gate. Pepe brought extra plates and plastic cups. Sex workers brought an orange frosted cake decorated with the words *Felicidades Patricia* (Congratulations Patricia). Jesús, the leader of the pirate taxi drivers, brought a cake too. Juanita gave me a gold ring with a red stone, and Pepe gave me a heart-shaped ring. Viviana bought me a tank top and matching skirt that actually fit. Nobody had bought me clothes since I was a teenager. As I opened gifts, the zone's janitorial staff and police gleefully set off loud fireworks in honor of the celebration. There was some heated discussion as to whether or not I should share the cake with the zone's administrative staff; they never included sex workers in their celebrations. A group of us left the zone and spent the day drinking beer, napping, swimming, and eating *botanas* (small plates of cheese, grilled meats, and pickled vegetables) at a local *balneario* (bathing resort) along the muddy banks of the Río Grijalva. The women of the Zona Galáctica looked out for me. They kept me out of harm's way, invited me into their homes, and gave me advice on love (some of it very sound). And, they brought me a serenade.

II

I sleep on the third floor of the modern concrete house on Avenue 14 Poniente Sur in the city of Tuxtla Gutiérrez, in a bright yellow room that would be the servant's quarters, if I had a servant. I awaken to find the head of Paula peering through the window. A six-foot-tall, rail-thin, blond Canadian evangelical Christian in her late twenties, she makes an unlikely roommate, given the nature of my own work. "Do you hear 'Las Mañanitas'?" she asks. "It's for you." I hear deep, resonant voices, maybe an accordion. "Las Mañanitas" is a song traditionally sung at birthdays and other celebrations. It is not quite 5:00 in the morning and still dark outside. I stumble out of bed (a twin mattress covered with a mosquito net and balanced precariously on old wooden crates) and reach for a bathrobe. Half asleep, I struggle to unlock the multiple locks on the giant metal front door. I can hear the musicians on the other side of it, and they are loud: "Éstas son las mañanitas. . . . Inspiradas y bonitas, te las cantamons a tí . . ." [These are the songs of the dawn. . . . Inspiring and delightful, we sing them just for you . . .] It is my first serenade.

Outside is a group from the Galactic Zone, where I have been doing fieldwork for the past six months. Opening the door, I find Rafaela and Esperanza, who work as prostitutes; Roberto, a brothel janitor; a man I mistakenly assume to be Esperanza's husband; and a guitar player and accordion player. All, hired musicians included, are drunk to some degree. The guitar player's eyes are a deep sunset red. My friends hug me and tell me over and over, "¡Es tu día!" (It's your day!). In our drunken, sleepy, dreamlike state, we sit in the darkness on the curb in front of my house, singing and swaying to the music. Someone requests "Cielito Lindo," one of the few songs I know well enough to sing. *Ay, ay, ay, ay, canta, no llores.* The song begs us to sing rather than cry. Every so often Roberto's head drops, long black bangs falling over his closed eyes as he begins to nod off. Roberto came to Mexico from Guatemala several years ago, and came to Chiapas from Cancún, where he worked in the sex industry. The man I thought was Esperanza's husband is actually a client from the brothel and a schoolteacher. He stands up slowly, readying to sing. He brushes off his khaki pants, clears his throat, and takes a moment to gain his composure as if living out some secret dream of stardom right there on the lonely sidewalk in the dark. He sings smoothly and sweetly. Rafaela belts out a few long, loud, plaintive ranchero-style laughs. Her sharp, strong voice cuts through the darkness. A few lone figures begin to emerge into the early morning, shadows passing us by on their way to work. Rafaela, who, like Esperanza and Roberto, is also an immigrant from Guatemala, tells me, "We want you to have good memories of Mexico."

The sky is beginning to lighten. During a pause in the music, Roberto and the schoolteacher debate over the finale. Roberto, often melancholy, wants a sad song, while the teacher hopes for a happy ending. Happiness wins out, and then the birds begin to sing their morning songs. The musicians wander off up the hill on foot, guitar and accordion in hand, while we stay on the curb in the cool morning, chatting and laughing. Only then do I realize it is Teacher's Day, a holiday celebrated quite seriously in Mexico (and what holiday isn't?), and this is why they have brought the serenade. Giggling, Roberto says to me, "We are teachers too, but we teach sex." It is nearing 7:00 A.M. Someone hails the next passing cab. We

Figure 2. A serenade. Photo by Patty Kelly.

all embrace and they are gone. I stand on the curb, clutching my robe to my body and watch as one of the white Volkswagen Beetles that serve as taxis throughout Mexico heads down the hill toward the city center. The sun is up, the *tortillería* (tortilla shop) next door is now open and a line is forming. Women, children, and a few men wait to buy breakfast, clutching in their hands the colorful cloths in which they'll wrap their warm tortillas.

III

For one year the women (and men) I met in the Galactic Zone were my teachers. Few of them will ever get the opportunity to read these pages. Since my initial stay in Tuxtla, I have returned to the zone each year. With each new visit, I find fewer old friends. I'm never sure whether this is good news or bad. Most have by now left the Galactic Zone, having gone on to do sex work in other areas, or having left sex work behind, or in some cases, having died. Still, this book is for them, as well as for those who came before them and those who will follow. That more women will follow is not inevitable. As writer Derrick Jensen reminds us, "Things don't have to be the way they are."[8] It's simple, but we tend to forget. To thank the workers of the Galactic Zone is necessary and necessarily inadequate. Still, gracias and *mil besos* to Lorena, Esperanza, Sonia, Magda, Bonita, Adriana, Rafaela, Evita, Gabriela, Desirée, Mónica, Lydia, Flor, Juanita, Alejandra, Ramona, Bárbara, Viviana, and the rest of the women in the Zona Galáctica for their openness, kindness, wisdom, and generosity.[9] Like the song goes, they taught me to sing instead of cry. I am beyond grateful.

Many other people in Chiapas made my life and work much, much better than it would have been without them, and I am indebted. *Abrazos* and so many thanks to Polly, Diego, Magdalena, Viviana, Adriana Vigil, John and Susan, all my cousins and nieces and nephews, Leticia Belmonte and family, Lorena Ballinas Guillen, Christine Kovic, Pancho Aguelles, Stephanie Paladino, Paula Zondag, Jeanne Simonelli, Duncan Earle, Kate O'Donnell, Aracely López Trejo, Elena Calvo González, Gisella Hanley, Juan Ruiz, Maria Hart, Jan Rus, Gabrielle Vargas-Cetina, Stefan Igor Ayora Díaz, the late David Halperin, the faculty and staff of El Colegio de la Frontera Sur (ECOSUR), all the people of the Galactic Zone, Larissa Narcia, Dr. Gonzalo López Aguirre, Dr. Bayardo Muñoz, Dr. Paco Rojas, and Dr. Helmer García Mesa; and thanks to Eduardo Talavera for nearly a decade of lazy mornings in the sun. Among those in Mexico City, I thank Sara Chávez and Gabriel Orozco; and my dear María Gutiérrez for, among so many other things, lying by my side in the warm sand at Playa Roca Blanca while reading parts of this manuscript.

Immense gratitude also goes to my teachers in the anthropology program at the City University of New York Graduate Center, including June Nash (who gave me a home in Chiapas and much more), Jane Schneider, Shirley Lindenbaum, Louise Lennihan, and of course, Marc Edelman, my mentor and dear friend, who continues to advise me though I graduated long ago. I am indebted to and love you all. Also, among others at CUNY, thanks to Ellen DeRiso and the members of the dissertation writing group that Jane so wisely guided, and which included Danning Wang, Leon Arredondo, Suzanne Scheld, Carol Meyers, Kitty Clarke, and Youngmin Seo. Infinite gratitude to Roger Lancaster for his encouragement and for reading various incarnations of this manuscript. Thank you to Phil Young and Carol Silverman, from my days back at the University of Oregon. And I thank my students and colleagues, especially Cathy Solomon, Eric Bronson, and Tim Dansdill (for helping me remember what really matters, as only a poet can). Great appreciation to my editor Naomi Schneider for taking on this project and for being so beautifully supportive and real. Also at the University of California Press, thank you to Jacqueline Volin, Valerie Witte, and Bonita Hurd. Fieldwork and writing were done with institutional support from the City University of New York, the Organization of American States, and the American Association of University Women.

Love and thanks to the Bellamore and Kelly families and to my friends for keeping me together all these years. They include Angela Green, Mildred Kelly, Terry Kelly, Emma Knickerbocker, Kathy Salvas, Jesse Vendley, Kathy O'Brien, Mike Farruggia, Stacey Brass, Lorna Hanes, Doug Raneri, Elsa and Ali Bahrampour, Dalton Conley (who rescued me twice this week alone), Anna Marandi, Michael Bongiorno, Beth Dobrish, Ed Heindl, Erika Foxton, Bill James, Rory and Kian, Cressida Hatch, Barb Longo, Jen Harris (for her work on the map that appears in this book), Tyler Hays, and Dorcas and Kalam. Thank you, Brooklyn: to Sal and Al and Sal and Frankie and Jimmy and Tony and Felix and everyone from the neighborhood, and to Lydia Santos for giving me a home here. Endless gratitude to my teachers Dana Flynn and Jasmine Tarkeshi and to all my friends, fellow teachers, and students at the Laughing Lotus Yoga Center in New York City. Without you all and the teachings, I might've given up a long time ago. I thank all the teachers, kind people, gurus, swamis, mystics, muses, poets, freaks, and saints elsewhere in the world whose paths I've been lucky to cross over the years. Any good in this book, we all share; the mistakes I'll claim as my own.

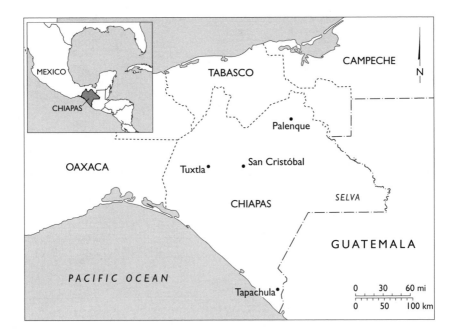

Chiapas

Introduction

The dirt road is long, seemingly isolated, and flanked on both sides by trees and tropical vegetation characteristic of southern Mexico's sweltering lowlands. During the wet season, the road is muddy. Heavy rains carve deep gashes into it, making it difficult to pass. At the height of the dry season, cars traveling the lonely road kick up a brown dust that coats the trees and bushes, leaving their foliage beige rather than green. Sometimes this dust enters the pirate taxis that travel the road, filtering through the floorboards and settling into passengers' clothing, hair, and eyes. On this road I have seen flocks of large, black vultures hopping about, looking at once joyful and sinister, picking what little flesh there is from the carcasses of unlucky dogs.

The narrow road, which local newspapers dubbed the Highway of Death following the stabbing of a taxi driver there, opens into a wide,

Figure 3. Clients and taxi drivers at the main gate to the Zona Galáctica. Photo by Patty Kelly.

unpaved clearing. A few cars and city buses are parked beneath a large sign reading Zona de Tolerancia (Tolerance Zone) in bold, black letters. It is here in the tolerance, or "red light," zone that legalized female prostitution occurs and that working-class men of the city of Tuxtla Gutiérrez and the surrounding area come to purchase sex. The tolerance zone is a brothel, and its name is the Zona Galáctica.

This is a book about women's sexual labor in neoliberal Mexico. In the following pages, I argue for a recognition of sex as work. While I acknowledge the class- and gender-based exploitation that is characteristic of female prostitution as practiced in the Zona Galáctica, it is also true that such exploitation is not unique to prostitution or to the Galactic Zone; it is found in all forms of work that poor women throughout the world must perform, as domestic services such as sex, child care, and housekeeping are increasingly commodified under advanced capitalism. What is unique in the state-regulated Galactic Zone is the stigmatization of workers, a stigmatization that is especially damaging to the human spirit and that for many women makes the work most difficult to bear. State-regulated prostitution, though legal, controls and criminalizes women who defy cultural norms by selling sexual services, and its health and social benefits are questionable at best. This book can be read as an argument for the decriminalization of prostitution and against the regulation of prostitution by the state as it exists in Tuxtla.

This book is also an ethnography of a particular place, the Galactic Zone, a legal brothel administered by the municipal government of Tuxtla Gutiérrez, the capital of the state of Chiapas. A local and regional enterprise, the zone is quite unlike the well-documented international sex tourism that occurs in countries such as Thailand and the Dominican Republic.[1] Constructed in 1991, the Galactic Zone was the creation of Governor José Patrocinio González Garrido, a member of Mexico's then ruling Institutional Revolutionary Party (Partido Revolucionario Institucional, PRI) and a close ally of *priista* (member of the PRI) president Carlos Salinas de Gortari. Both Salinas, who fled Mexico when his term ended amid scandal and accusations of mismanagement, and González Garrido, whose term as governor (1988–1993) was characterized by human rights abuses and the militarization of the state, sought to modernize the Mexican economy through the implementation of neoliberal economic policies on a local and national scale. And so this book is also an ethnography of a particular time: the neoliberal era.

Neoliberalism, as David Harvey writes, is "a theory of political economic practices that proposes that human well-being can best be advanced by liberating individual freedoms and skills within an institutional framework characterized by strong private property rights, free markets, and free trade."[2] This is a rather innocuous definition for an economic development ideology with grave and far-reaching consequences. A global phenomenon, neoliberalism represents a new, more aggressive stage of capitalism marked by financial and trade liberalization and the embrace of the global "free" market; a rejection of the Keynesian social contract, accompanied by cuts in social welfare spending; the privatization of state industries; a push toward export-led growth; and the deregulation of prices, wages, and environmental protections. Neoliberal economies are sometimes characterized by the "feminization" of wage labor related to the boom in low-wage service-sector jobs, informal work, and manufacturing employment.[3] Maquiladoras, export-oriented foreign factories seeking cheap labor in the developing world, are a central feature of neoliberalism in Latin America.[4] Neoliberalism also engenders cultural changes such as increasing exposure to advertising in daily life, rising consumerism, and the transformation of material desires into "needs."

Put more plainly, what neoliberalism means is underfunded public schools and hospitals; crumbling public housing and the growth of scattershot shantytowns lacking state-funded infrastructure such as running water or electricity; the growth of export-oriented free-trade zones where women sew lace onto panties they cannot afford to buy and where industrial runoff contaminates the local groundwater; small-scale farmers who cannot compete with cheap agricultural imports being forced to leave their rural communities to find work in cities—where they sometimes end up working in maquiladoras and living in shantytowns.[5] But neoliberalism has been good to some: there has been an increase in the number of Mexican billionaires, resulting in part from the privatization of banks, factories, and other industries once owned by the state. In 2005, this concentration of wealth earned Mexico its ninth-place ranking worldwide in number of billionaires, behind the United States but ahead of Saudi Arabia. In 2007 Mexican telecommunications tycoon Carlos Slim became the richest man in the world, fulfilling the desires of the previous titleholder, Microsoft's Bill Gates, who publicly declared in 2006, "I wish I wasn't [the world's richest man]. There is nothing good that comes out of that."[6]

The history of the Galactic Zone may be viewed as a local example of this process of global neoliberal capitalist expansion and modernization—a process marked by a widening gap between the rich and the poor, the decline of rural life, growing urbanization, exclusionary politics, decreasing state interest in social welfare, and increasing state intervention in the sexual and social lives of the Mexico's working classes. This book, then, may also be read as an argument that free trade and free markets do not make free people.

Since the foreign debt crisis of 1982 and the passage of the North

American Free Trade Agreement (NAFTA, a key feature of neoliberal policy) in 1994, Mexico has witnessed rapid economic change and increasing economic integration with the United States and the rest of the world. Yet these changes, touted as a cure for Mexico's ills, have benefited few Mexicans. Poverty has increased in both rural and urban Mexico; monthly incomes for self-employed farmers fell by nearly 90 percent between 1991 and 2003.[7] The monthly income of men working in cities dropped a little more than 16 percent between 1990 and 2000.[8] But it is poor women and children who bear the brunt of the inequalities produced under this new economic order.[9] Since the passage of NAFTA, poverty in the poorest female-headed households increased by 50 percent.[10] Between 1989 and 1998, public assistance for children living in households receiving government aid was cut by two-thirds.[11] Today, about half of all Mexicans live in poverty.

A central aim, if not *the* central aim, of this book is to make visible that which has been hidden. Specifically, to uncover and make real for readers the humiliations, despair, illnesses, and even deaths suffered because of an unjust economic system and social beliefs and practices that degrade those occupying the lowest rungs of global society. This is a story of structural violence. The anthropologist and physician Paul Farmer observes that the suffering engendered by this form of violence is produced or "'structured' by historically given (and often economically driven) processes and forces that conspire—whether through routine, ritual, or, as is more commonly the case, the hard surfaces of life—to constrain agency."[12] There is little bloodshed in this ethnography and little in the way of outright physical conflict. The violence here is diffuse, quiet, and not very dramatic. In fact, readers may at times find themselves entertained. There are descriptions of agency, resistance, and joyful occasions. There is even beauty. But the lives of the women who are the main subjects of this book have been marked by economic and social inequalities that have cheated them of a different and better life. And while they may sometimes sing instead of cry, do not forget that their moments of resistance and of happiness occur within a broader context of extreme and global inequality.

SEXUALITY, MODERNITY, AND SOCIAL CHANGE

There are certain periods in history, times of change and crisis, when sexuality comes to the fore. As Gail Rubin has written, sex may seem a frivolous topic, but during times of social upheaval, "people are likely to become dangerously crazy about sexuality. Consequently, sexuality should be treated with special respect in times of great social stress."[13] Sex, writes the historian Jeffrey Weeks, "has long been a transmission belt for wider social anxieties, and a focus of struggles over power, one of the prime sites in truth where domination and subordination are defined and expressed."[14]

Modernization projects have historically been accompanied by struggles over moral and sexual codes.[15] The late nineteenth and early twentieth centuries were characterized by rapid economic and social change in much of the globe: industrialization, continuing colonial activity, urbanization, and a new and growing concern with social hygiene and public health were signs of the times. So was the emergence of what Michel Foucault calls *scientia sexualis*—the modern production of a singular truth of sex, in which sex became a question, a suspect interrogated, an object of study, and eventually part of "an ordered system of knowledge" intricately linked to relations of power.[16] Sex itself was newly divided, into the "normal" and "abnormal," the "moral" and "immoral."

Sex, it seemed, was suddenly everywhere. But it was hard to grasp, and the question of definition became paramount. Sex was (and is) simultaneously personal and political; rebellious and conservative; provincial and modern; threatening and fulfilling. During the period about which Foucault writes, sexuality began to generate a qualitatively new kind of social anxiety as well as new discourses and social policies. From the Old World to the New, laws were passed calling for the sanitary inspection of prostitutes, the moral reform of bourgeois women and their dangerous sexual passions, and the punishment of individuals involved in the "white slave trade" (which did not involve human trafficking but was actually a widespread moral panic stemming from the occurrence of white women who had intimate relations with nonwhite men).[17]

As elsewhere during periods of political-economic transformation, in

Mexico gendered and sexual practices and beliefs have often been politi-
cized, inspected, and contested. Examining the practice and regulation of
prostitution enables us to see just how this happens. Concern with the
lives and work of *mujeres publicas* (public women) intensified in the years
preceding and following the Mexican Revolution (1911–1917). During
the liberal regime of dictator Porfirio Díaz (1876–1911), the state pursued
modernity through economic liberalism and advocated a social order
characterized by eradication of vice and inculcation of values such as
family, thrift, and hygiene.[18] Power was maintained through political
strategizing, intimidation, and sometimes, force. The Porfiriato, as the
period came to be known, was steeped in a political program based on
rationalism and science. Not unlike in neoliberal Mexico, during the liberal era industry and foreign investment grew (aided in part by an 1883
agrarian law that opened rural lands to foreign companies). The shift
from subsistence to commercial farming compelled many men and
women to seek better fortunes in rapidly industrializing cities. The costs
of modernization, then as now, were steep for many Mexicans, rural and
urban, who were increasingly impoverished by the excesses, brutality,
and social upheaval that marked the Porfiriato. For poor women in urban
Mexico, prostitution was sometimes an answer.

During this period, the medical and governmental establishments
constructed the female prostitute as a sexually promiscuous deviant
beyond redemption, while male clients who purchased their services
were seen as engaging in normal behavior expected of men. The
Reglamento para el ejercicio de la prostitución en México (Regulation for
the exercise of prostitution in Mexico) subjected women over the age of
fourteen who worked as registered prostitutes to medical and legal surveillance.[19] The Reglamento was intended to protect the citizenry from
debilitating venereal infections like gonorrhea and syphilis. Women suspected of working as clandestine prostitutes were subject to arrest and
forced medical inspection and registration. Porfirian values of female
honor and purity did not extend to the poor women who worked in the
streets, brothels, and hotels of urban Mexico. While predicated on
notions of modernity and hygiene, the enforcement of the Reglamento
and the prostitute's presumed moral degeneracy were not untouched by

religion; Catholicism's sexual morality and patriarchal *doble moral* (moral double standard) all but guaranteed the marginalization of women who sold sex.[20]

The Porfiriato bred not only marginalization but also dissent. The Mexican Revolution left more than one million Mexicans dead; exiled to Europe, Porfirio Díaz was not among them. The revolutionary state that eventually replaced the Porfirian one took a somewhat different approach to commercial sex and those who practiced it. Early visions of a "modern" and "revolutionary" Mexican society included an eventual end to state-regulated prostitution, seen as a distasteful and archaic legacy of the Porfiriato. The prostitute was now constructed as a victim of poverty, male vice, and Porfirian false modesty, one who, as historian Katherine Bliss writes, could be redeemed through the application of revolutionary principles: "Legislators, public officials, and private citizens alike invoked the 'redemption' of 'fallen women' as their *cause celébre*, promoting legislation to ban procuring, to train women to work in alternative occupations, to persuade clients to restrain their tendency toward sexual promiscuity, and to abolish the Reglamento itself."[21]

To be sure, the revolutionary 1926 Reglamento para el ejercicio de la prostitución was still rooted in previous beliefs about acceptable male promiscuity and enforced female purity (prostitutes withstanding); it continued the medical and legal surveillance of female prostitutes in the name of public health. But in contrast to the Porfiriato, revolutionary social reformers hoping to create a modern nation also sought to transform *male* sexual promiscuity, rehabilitate public women, and recast sexuality as a scientific rather than moral issue.[22] Revolutionary social reformers, writes Bliss, "had long deplored prostitution because of what they perceived to be its negative implications for economic development and national progress."[23] Debates concerning state-tolerated prostitution, along with the activism of both feminists and eugenicists, eventually led to the abolition of the Reglamento in 1940. But the suspension of state-regulated prostitution did not, as she notes, put an end to prostitution.

In contemporary Mexico, legal and regulated prostitution exists in thirteen of the nation's thirty-one states. In Chiapas, the Galactic Zone was created in 1991, a time of shift and crisis, a period of rapid economic change, cultural transformation, simmering political hostilities, and the militarization of civil society. Unlike the social reformers of revolutionary Mexico, political elites like Governor González Garrido viewed state-regulated prostitution in neoliberal Chiapas as a path *to* modernity and development. Yet there is great ambivalence about the prostitute herself: she is stigmatized by those who seek to control prostitution (and by society at large) but also viewed, in many instances, as capable of redemption and, as I heard many times, "reintegration into normal society." The nature of prostitution remains a controversial issue in modern-day Tuxtla, even within the municipal government itself. I recall the panista mayor, during a conversation with political leaders in the Palacio Municipal one afternoon, calling prostitution an "economic and a moral problem," while his panista colleague, the director of public health, disagreed vehemently, insisting that morality had nothing to do with it, that for sex workers it was purely a socioeconomic issue.

A CHANGING ECONOMY AND SOCIETY

In 1938, following a lengthy dispute between Mexican laborers and international oil companies, President Lázaro Cárdenas (1934–1940) expropriated Mexico's U.S.- and European-owned oil resources and nationalized the oil industry. During his years in office, Cárdenas also embarked upon an unprecedented implementation of agrarian reform as promised by Article 27 of the 1917 Constitution, redistributing more than 49 million acres of land, much of which had been illegally taken from campesinos during the dictatorship of Porfirio Díaz. The majority of the lands were redistributed as *ejidos*, communally held lands that could not be bought, sold, or traded. Such redistributive and revolutionary reforms incorporated rural populations into the state, giving new legitimacy and power to the federal government.

In the decades following the revolution, the Mexican economy was characterized by state-directed economic growth mixed with the growth of private enterprise. During this time, the oxymoronically titled and long-ruling Institutional Revolutionary Party maintained political control through a combination of corruption and cooptation. Labor unions functioned not independently but under the auspices of the ruling party. "Democratic" elections were a farce, as the autocratic PRI took the presidency for seventy years straight.

What precipitated the massive shift in Mexican political ideology and economic policy in the 1980s? Recession in the United States, coupled with the 1982 foreign debt crisis in Mexico and other developing nations, was followed by a shift in Mexico's political-economic ideology and practice, toward neoliberalism.

By the early 1980s, poor countries of the developing world were economically vulnerable to neoliberal restructuring for a number of reasons. Third World nations owed more than US$700 billion to U.S., European, and Japanese banks that had been making loans with variable rather than fixed interest rates; by the late 1970s, soaring international interest rates increased debtor countries' annual debt payments by hundreds of millions of dollars, leaving many nations unable to pay.[24] At the same time, these nations were also losing important export earnings as a result of the worldwide recession. The crumbling economies of the developing world provided an opening for increased insertion of poor nations into the global marketplace at their own expense. A Witness for Peace publication explains the transformation: "The solution [to the debt crisis] proposed by economists in Washington, DC, was to 'deregulate' poor countries' economies—removing all barriers to trade and letting the private sector take over as the 'engine of growth.' According to this solution, hard currency—desperately needed to pay down the massive external debts— could be brought into poor countries through increased foreign investment."[25]

These changes were achieved in part through a process known as structural adjustment, in which global financial institutions such as the World Bank and International Monetary Fund disbursed *more* loans to Third World nations. These new loans were earmarked for paying off older debt, but, unlike previous loans, which flowed freely, structural adjustment loans came with strict conditions intended to make the struggling economies more "efficient." Among the conditions were reductions in government spending and in wages, removal of trade barriers and of restrictions on foreign investment in industrial production and financial services, and the privatization of state-owned industries and a loosening of government oversight of prices, wages, and protections in favor of the "free" market. During the 1980s, more than seventy Third World nations submitted to neoliberal structural adjustment, effectively putting their economies into the hands of bureaucrats in Washington, D.C.[26] A new era of economic globalization (and what astute observers would call a "recolonization" of the developing world) had begun.

Mexico's history with neoliberalism began during the presidency of José López Portillo (1976–1982). López Portillo's term ended at the onset of the debt crisis, as a worldwide recession and declining oil prices left Mexico unable to pay international debt incurred following the discovery of new oil resources in the 1970s, when the country was considered a low credit risk by international lending institutions.

By 1982, Mexico's foreign debt had grown to fifty-eight billion dollars, an almost ninefold increase since 1972.[27] The country declared bankruptcy. The debt crisis led to implementation of structural adjustment policies, first by López Portillo and then by his successor, Miguel de la Madrid Hurtado. Pressured by the International Monetary Fund and the World Bank to adopt neoliberal stabilization policies in exchange for new loans, the state began to implement reforms associated with structural adjustment programs, such as the encouragement of the private export sector as *the* vehicle for new economic growth and an increase in foreign investment in Mexico.[28] In essence, the "bailout" of Mexico by the International Monetary Fund and World Bank was less debt "relief" than forced immersion into neoliberalism and an intensification of ongoing unequal North-South relations that have existed since colonization.

And so, during the 1980s, the Mexican economy underwent profound changes. In 1986, the priista president de la Madrid (1982–1988) began to privatize some sectors of the state oil industry, once a great source of national pride.[29] His successor and former policy advisor, priista Carlos Salinas de Gortari, halted land redistribution and endangered existing ejidos by sponsoring the reform of Article 27 of the Constitution and signing onto NAFTA. In so doing, he relinquished much state-directed economic activity, ceding ground to national and international capitalists.

The country was beginning another major period of economic liberalization that in some ways paralleled Porfirian efforts of a century earlier.

The Harvard-educated technocrat Carlos Salinas was the man who institutionalized neoliberal policies. Salinas believed that by doing so he was presiding over Mexico's modernization and subsequent entry into the "First World." Though Salinas's reforms were initially considered to be a success by many neoclassical economists, during this period the gap between the rich and poor grew even wider. By the end of Salinas's term in 1994, the poorest 20 percent Mexico's population were earning only 3 percent of the total income nationally, while the wealthiest 10 percent received 50 percent of the total income.[30] Neoliberalism brought rising unemployment and reduced social welfare spending. By 1995, the minimum wage in Mexico was lower in real terms than it had been in 1980.[31] In Chiapas, only slightly more than one-third of the employed population earned the daily minimum wage or more.[32] Particularly hard hit were rural populations and those dependent on small-scale agricultural production. Salinas's neoliberal policies did not ease poverty but institutionalized it.

In order to ameliorate some of the unintended consequences of the neoliberal program, Salinas founded Solidaridad (Solidarity), an antipoverty program that provided federal funding for local and regional community-based development projects and for national programs such as tortilla distribution to families officially certified as "needy."[33] While hardly a successful attack on poverty, Solidarity was a useful tool of political and social control—funds were often strategically disbursed in an effort to undercut opposition parties, garner support for the PRI, and further concentrate presidential power.[34]

Still, political discontent grew, as much of the Mexican population suffered increasing immiseration. While the PRI could still gain party loyalty through the promise of individual economic rewards, the politics of neoliberalism are rooted less in cooptation than in exclusion and sometimes force.[35] Small landholder populations unable to compete in a global economy characterized by large-scale agribusiness increasingly migrated to urban centers in Mexico or to the United States. Others mobilized politically, breaking away from state-sponsored unions. The hegemony of the ruling PRI was beginning to crumble. In the 1980s, many Mexicans organized around Cuautémoc Cárdenas, a former priista and the son of Lázaro Cárdenas. Disillusioned with the PRI, Cárdenas broke away from the party, unsuccessfully running for president against Salinas in 1988 under a left-of-center banner. Many political analysts believe that Cárdenas actually won the election, which was fraught with irregularities.[36]

The PRI began to lose control as governorships and mayoral races throughout the nation were won by opposition parties such as the conservative PAN and the center-left Democratic Revolutionary Party (Partido de la Revolución Democrática, PRD). Though the PAN is known for its embrace of neoliberalism and extreme social conservatism, particularly on issues of gender, sexuality, and religion, voting for the conservative party in a nation ruled by the priista one-party system for decades became a radical act. In 1991, Tuxtla Gutiérrez had not yet fallen to the PAN, though it would in 1995.[37] By 1997, the PRI would lose their majority in the lower house of Congress as well, and lose the important mayorship of Mexico City to the now vindicated leftist Cuautémoc Cárdenas. The nation would follow suit in 2000, electing panista and former Coca-Cola executive Vicente Fox. Later that same year, the PRI would lose Chiapas to the Alianza por Chiapas, a surprising alliance of the right-wing PAN, the leftist PRD, the Green Party, and the Workers Party.

Just as the inequalities of the Porfiriato had bred the dissent that led to the Mexican Revolution, diverse social movements resisting the neoliberal plan were erupting throughout Mexico. Opposition was simmering throughout the country in the years preceding the 1991 construction of the Galactic Zone; by the mid-1990s, popular protest movements would be sweeping the nation.

At the time of the Galactic Zone's birth, the Zapatista Army of National Liberation (EZLN), a small guerrilla army of mostly Mayan male and female peasant farmers, waited in the Selva Lacandona (Lacandón jungle) of eastern Chiapas and planned for the moment it would make itself known to the world.[38] This moment came on January 1, 1994, when nearly three thousand well-trained, armed, masked, and uniformed indigenous women and men emerged from the eastern lowlands, seizing nine towns and smaller villages throughout the state. Taking the name of the murdered revolutionary hero Emiliano Zapata, the Zapatistas declared war against the "illegal dictatorship" of Carlos Salinas and the neoliberal policies that threatened their way of life. After skirmishes that left more than seventy rebels dead, the Zapatistas retreated back into the Selva Lacandona, where they remain active today, building autonomous, democratic Zapatista communities.[39] Though the battle lasted less than a week, the Zapatista struggle continues. The conflict remains one of low intensity, marked by intermittent dialogues with the government and occasional violence against Zapatista supporters by government-sanctioned right-wing paramilitary groups.[40] It was no coincidence that the EZLN chose the first of January as the day of their uprising. It was precisely on this day that NAFTA was inaugurated, and the Zapatistas knew well the threat represented by the trade agreement and the broader neoliberal economic plan of which it was a part.[41]

The diverse demands and goals of the Zapatistas reflect the heterogeneity of social movements in Mexico and the new forms of political culture emerging throughout Latin America. Along with their call for "work, land, housing, food, health care, education, independence, freedom, democracy, justice and peace," the rebels sought revolutionary changes expanding the rights of women and indigenous peoples.[42] They were inclusive, inviting all of Mexico to support their struggle: students and street kids, workers and the unemployed, urban populations and rural, gay and straight. The EZLN created a new political opening in Mexico, one that was quickly filled by mobilizations of disenfranchised populations of every stripe. Much of the nation, identifying with the Zapatistas' struggles and weary of nearly seventy years of corrupt PRI rule, responded positively to the uprising. Subcomandante Marcos, the EZLN spokesperson, took on superhero status both at home and abroad; T-shirts, ashtrays, and even condoms emblazoned with the image of the masked crusaders of southern Mexico were soon for sale in plazas throughout urban Mexico.

The Zapatistas were not alone. In the southern states of Oaxaca and Guerrero, guerrilla movements also erupted in the countryside. The Popular Revolutionary Army announced itself in 1996 at a memorial service for seventeen activist farmers who were murdered when police opened fire on their truck in the state of Guerrero.[43] Among the Popular Revolutionary Army's demands was an end to corrupt PRI rule. In the state of Jalisco, once-prosperous communal and middle-class small-scale farmers now facing land repossession formed El Barzón, a debtor's alliance whose actions have ranged from debtor's strikes to the tarring and feathering of a money-lending banker in drought-stricken Chihuahua. Now a nationwide movement, there are an estimated five hundred thousand to one million members of El Barzón.[44]

The EZLN uprising and the subsequent collapse of the peso in 1994 tarnished Carlos Salinas's image as the man who would bring modernity to Mexico. His reputation was further tainted by the arrest of his brother Raúl on charges of both corruption and murder after he was accused and convicted of masterminding the killing of José Francisco Ruiz Massieu, PRI secretary-general and former brother-in-law to the Salinas brothers. The 1994 assassination of priista Donaldo Colosio did not help matters much. Colosio was to be the next president, chosen less through the farce known as general election and more by *el dedazo,* a PRI tradition in which the next president is appointed, or "fingered," by the outgoing president. During a public appearance, Colosio was shot in the head at close range on national television in a murder that many Mexicans believe was planned by PRI insiders who felt he had strayed from their agenda.

Carlos Salinas has lived in various countries under a self-imposed exile since 1995, though there has recently been some discussion of a return to Mexico. My last sighting of the fallen president was on Mexican television in 1998. The once-dapper technocrat was in a decrepit concrete room somewhere in Mexico, unshaven, wearing a ratty, stained tank-top, maintaining a hunger strike in a vain effort to get his brother Raúl released from prison. He has since written a book, appropriately titled *Un paso difícil a la modernidad* (A Difficult Step toward Modernity).

MAKING CHIAPAS MODERN

Chiapas holds an unenviable position as one of Mexico's poorest states. Yet the poverty of Chiapas is uneven and sometimes difficult for the casual visitor to see. During my first visit to the region in 1992, I spent a month in Palenque, a hot lowland town best known for its spectacular Mayan ruins. It was not until I left Palenque town for the *selva* that I witnessed the extreme poverty that shapes the lives of rural and indigenous Mexicans and that spurred the Zapatistas to action. The memories are faded now: village after village lacking running water and electricity; a near empty *casa de salud* (health center) furnished only with a table, a small pile of used, pus-filled gauze, and a single wooden bench; a young man overtaken by tuberculosis—violent coughs wracked his body and practically shook the flimsy walls of the one-room house he shared with his parents and siblings.

Nearly 25 percent of Chiapas's population over the age of five speaks an indigenous language;[45] Tzotzil, Tzeltal, Tojolobal, and Chol are the most common ones, and they reflect the diversity of Mayan identity in the state. Though linguistically diverse, the indigenous people of Chiapas have long shared the common experience of poverty and oppression. Since the arrival of the Spanish some five hundred years ago, the vast majority of indigenous Chiapanecos have lived under almost serflike conditions. Some Maya retain small parcels of land they farm as their ancestors did. Integration into the global market has not proved easy for these small farmers; for instance, the steep 1989 decline of coffee prices in the world market slashed by two-thirds the incomes of many in Chiapas who had invested in coffee, one of the state's main agricultural products.[46] Others must labor for the wealthy, sometimes as migrant laborers who leave home to work large tracts of land, growing corn, coffee, and cattle for little pay. Poor health and a lack of access to health care are, as the Zapatistas note, poverty's loyal companions:

> The health conditions of the people of Chiapas are a clear example of the capitalist imprint. One-and-a-half million people have no medical services at their disposal. There are 0.2 clinics for every 1,000 inhabitants, one-fifth of the national average. There are 0.3 hospital beds for every 1,000 Chiapanecos, one-third of the amount in the rest of Mexico. There is one operating room per 100,000 inhabitants, one half of the amount in the rest of Mexico. There are 0.5 doctors and 0.4 nurses per 1,000 people, one-half of the national average. . . . Fifty-four per-

cent of the population of Chiapas suffer from malnutrition, and in the highlands and forest this percentage increases to 80%. A campesino's average diet consists of coffee, corn, tortillas, and beans.[47]

In an effort to quell dissent among the poor, who might object to living under such bleak circumstances, Governor González Garrido revised the state penal code upon entering office in 1988, broadening the definition of rebellion and effectively criminalizing both political opposition and public protest. New and harsher penalties would be imposed on individuals found guilty of "rebellion," "civil disorder," and "conspiracy."[48] The governor often used a military model of social control to resolve social problems and contain any elements, agrarian activists in particular, who resisted his efforts. Years of absence from the Mexican political system have not softened González Garrido. In a July 2005 interview with the newspaper *Cuarto Poder*, he stated, "Nice people are no good for governing a country."[49] Rancho Nuevo, the large military base constructed on the outskirts of San Cristóbal assured a constant military presence in the Central Highlands. Repression was increasingly used to keep counterhegemonic visions in check.

As a gubernatorial candidate, González Garrido espoused Salinas's discourse of *concertación*, "consensus building across the political spectrum,"[50] but during his governorship a new politics of exclusion and clientelism emerged in Chiapas. Both cooptation and force were used to ensure stability as the neoliberal project was put into play. Though Chiapas received more Solidarity funds than any other state, these were insufficient to reverse the extreme poverty endemic in rural indigenous areas and exacerbated by neoliberal austerity measures that cut public spending. These funds were also tightly controlled by the governor, as well as by loyal priista mayors and *caciques* (local power brokers). As Subcomandante Marcos bitterly observes, "Among the constructions accomplished by Solidaridad [Solidarity] are the Cereso [Prison] Number Five, the jail in San Cristóbal, the barracks in Rancho Nuevo, the other jail in Yajalón, the one in Tila. Jails and barracks are what were built by Solidaridad."[51] In Chiapas, Solidarity was less an effective means of diminishing poverty than a symbol of the continued presence and power of the state and the unequal distribution of power. Solidarity slogans were painted on walls statewide, often on schools and clinics left unstaffed due to the lack of funding.

José Patrocinio González Garrido had many dreams. He dreamed of modernizing Chiapas, a place that much of the country viewed as backward because of its poverty, large indigenous population, and seemingly feudal economic system. In keeping with economic reforms happening at the federal level, the governor implemented policies to modernize economic exploitation in Chiapas. Among González Garrido's contributions to neoliberal policy in Chiapas were the decrease of state supports such as loans and credit for grain and coffee production, the promotion of large-scale export agriculture, and the privatization of state industries.[52] As these policies accelerated the decline of rural life, urban areas began to experience unprecedented growth when rural workers headed to cities seeking employment. In 1970, almost 28 percent of Chiapanecos lived in urban areas; by 1995 this figure had risen to 44 percent.[53] At nearly half a million people, Tuxtla Gutiérrez is one of the state's fastest-growing cities. I often heard the mayor worry aloud about how to handle the large influx of new arrivals who came fleeing rural poverty.

The politically ambitious Governor González Garrido also dreamed of modernizing sexual commerce in Chiapas.[54] As in liberal Porfirian Mexico a century earlier, in contemporary neoliberal Mexico we see an economic modernization project and a concomitant concern with sex and social order. As the state withdrew from other sectors of the economy, such as agriculture, it sought greater control over commercial sex in Chiapas through the 1989 Zona Rosa Project. The Zona Galáctica was a central feature of the governor's project. It is not unlikely that this effort, spearheaded by González Garrido, was linked to the militarization of the state and a form of preparation for dealing with the coming uprising, along with other social tensions, such as uncontrolled population growth in the city. Among the goals of the project were the relocation of brothels to "appropriate" sites "outside the perimeters of the city," far from private homes, schools, government offices and churches; the registration and strict medical examination of female sex workers; and the supervision of sex workers and clients by municipal authorities in order to prevent alcohol abuse, and drug use and distribution, within the confines of the brothel.[55]

Governor González Garrido played an unusually large role in the creation of the municipal Zona Galáctica, provoking a great deal of gossip about the governor and his sexual habits. As one official in the State Department of Public Health told me, "That guy was *really* interested in prostitution," which is ordinarily a matter of municipal, not state, concern. Local gossip suggested that González Garrido's interest in prostitution stemmed from his own sexual activities with the male transvestite prostitutes of Tuxtla. Whether true or not, his interest in controlling prostitution was clearly related to his political interest in modernizing Chiapas and quelling dissent in alternative cultures, be they agrarian activists or sex workers.[56]

By regulating and controlling prostitutes, long associated with crime and deviance, the state hoped to discipline sex workers and bring into the formal modern market a sexual-economic activity that had formerly existed outside its control. In an era marked by globalization and privatization, there has been much discussion about the weakening power of the state.[57] Popular mythology and certain theorists of globalization alike assert that economic globalization is engendering a "stateless" and "borderless" world in which national governments will become all but obsolete.[58] But neoliberalism is less about the withdrawal of the state from public life than about the shifting of arenas of state interest and intervention. Under neoliberalism, the state is responsible for creating and maintaining structures, institutions, and laws that support the free market.[59]

What is evident in the case of the Galactic Zone is a redirection of state energies toward the symbolic and social control of disenfranchised populations.[60] Drawing on social theorist Karl Polanyi, who viewed governmental control as crucial to market economies, sociologist Gerardo Otero concurs that, "far from minimizing or reducing state intervention in the economy, the self-regulating market requires intervention to create markets and sustain them."[61] Withdrawing state support from small-scale agricultural producers while promoting free trade policies forces farmers unable to compete with cheap imports to enter the labor market on terms favorable to elites; creating the infrastructure to corral and control female prostitutes who previously worked independently or informally (or as farmers) also serves elite interests by creating an ordered urban environment and highly regulated workers and consumers. Regulating prostitution and confining prostitutes makes them "legible," allowing the state to see them, administer them, and control them.[62]

And so in December 1991, Governor González Garrido, along with priista city officials, inaugurated the Galactic Zone. Such ceremony is commonplace in Mexico, where political officials of all levels, from the president of the republic to the mayor of a small village, preside over the openings of schools, bridges, highways, and in this case, a brothel. These festivities, which often include the cutting of ribbons, live music, and speeches, are a validation of both government authority and benevolence. They make the power and generosity of the state visible through public spectacle. Smaller government successes too, such as the installation of a streetlight or placement of public trash cans, do not go uncelebrated. A new lamppost in a low-income neighborhood in eastern Tuxtla is dwarfed by a large sign advertising the current municipal administration's program for providing lighting. In the Galactic Zone, the presence of the state is everywhere felt. Trash cans installed years earlier still bear the insignia of the previous priista municipal government. On an outside wall between the men's toilets and the Anti-Venereal Medical Service is a large plaque celebrating the state's creation of the Galactic Zone. The entry tickets that clients must purchase at the main gate bear the panista administration's slogan, "Tuxtla Needs You. Participate!"

GENDERS AND SEXUALITIES IN MEXICO

It is sometimes difficult to understand gender inequality, even when one has studied, witnessed, and experienced it. The doble moral, as well as women's vulnerable position in Mexican society, was finally driven home for me during a late-night, beer-fueled conversation in the apartment of friends in Tuxtla who were not affiliated with the Galactic Zone. We had been discussing a man who had entered my house from a neighboring roof a few nights before while I was in bed. Though he had left before the police arrived, I was fairly certain that the man was the same one who slept on the roof of the flower shop right next door. Conversation soon turned to stories of robbery and rape. Joel, young, middle-class and college-educated, launched into a story about a bricklayer he knew who had raped quite a few women. He laughingly told me, his sister, and his girlfriend, about how the man had raped a Mexican teenager who had been out for a walk with her boyfriend. He had also raped a *gringa* (Western woman) as she was waiting beside her broken-down car on the highway. The gringa, Joel said, was "older" and "ugly." While the story, intended to entertain, continued, the other women in the room listened, unfazed. Maybe they were even amused. On the other hand, I was horrified. Seeing the look on my face, Joel said, "Oh, well, you have to hear him tell it." Would hearing the rapist tell the story actually make it funny? "Somebody like that ought to be locked up in Cerro Hueco [the local prison]," I said. Cecilia, Joel's girlfriend, gave me a pitying look that suggested I was incredibly naive and said, "But Patty, it's very difficult to prove rape." Of course, she was right. In Mexico, rape is prosecuted at the state level. Government statistics estimate that a girl or woman is raped in Mexico every four minutes, though surely, due to underreporting, this figure is much, much higher.[63] Throughout Mexico, women and girls who report rape to the police are often viewed with suspicion and aggression and blamed for the crime, while rapists themselves receive impunity. Furthermore, while all states criminalize sexual violence, sanctions imposed often depend on the "chastity" of the victim: in Chiapas and in ten other states, there remain old laws in effect regarding *estupro* ("intercourse with an adolescent girl through seduction or deceit, as opposed to force"), which is not punished if the perpetrator marries the young victim.[64]

Over the years, I had been subject to occasional and sometimes extreme gendered harassment in Mexico. Generally, I shrugged these incidents off. At the time of this conversation, I had spent *months* inside a brothel. But hearing Joel's story and seeing the women's responses to it, I really felt for the first time that I understood the inequality that continues to mark women's lives there.

Still, gender equality is on the rise in Mexico.[65] Contemporary Mexican men of all classes, including the working class, may do housework and care for children. Women increasingly work outside the home, become political leaders, and divorce their husbands.[66] But Mexican culture, like many cultures, is generally a patriarchal one in which women are subordinate to men. It is still important to examine the impact and power of cultural ideals about gender and sexuality upon women's and men's lives and bodies. *Gender* here refers to the historically determined and socioculturally constructed character of femininity and masculinity. Gender, like class and ethnicity, plays a central role in the workings and expression of power.[67]

Despite a canon that, by its very nature, seeks a more homogenous expression of gender and sexual practice, heterogeneity prevails in Mexico, where belief and practice are marked by class, ethnic, and regional variation, and where stereotypes are manipulated, shaped, and reshaped. Virgin brides, though still desirable, are a rarity in urban Mexico.[68] Formal marriage itself, though considered a source of social legitimacy, particularly for women, is not the only option, as couples choose to live in *unión libre* (civil union) and divorce becomes more common. In Chiapas, 18 percent of the adult population live in unión libre, a close second to the state of Nayarit, where almost 19 percent live in similar conditions.[69] Homosexuality is stigmatized (nongovernmental organizations report that fifteen homophobic murders are committed each month) but has also become more visible. Mexico City's gay pride parade drew more than thirty thousand participants in the year 2000, while only five years earlier fewer than a thousand people attended.[70]

In contemporary Mexico, gendered and sexual beliefs and practices are diverse, at once contradictory and cohesive, often straying far from cultural myths about strong men and pure women. In the following pages we will meet women who simultaneously defy and embrace cultural ideals about gender and sexuality and whose views on such issues, while often outwardly contradictory, have their own internal consistency. My good friend Nanci is a young college-educated professional and, though an ardent supporter of the conservative PAN, lives in unión libre with her divorced partner, much to the dismay of her parents, who for a time stopped speaking to her. Silvia is a young, college-educated daughter of socially conservative parents; she often has romantic relationships with foreign men who pass through the tourist town in which she lives. Deeply religious and active in the Catholic church, Esperanza works in the Galactic Zone but lives with her husband. They have been trying to conceive a child for some time now. Lorena works as a prostitute in the zone too, engaging in heterosexual sex for pay, but shares a home with her female partner and their four children. In contrast to Lorena's outspokenness about her sexuality and other matters while in the brothel, her children do not know that their same-sex parents are in a romantic relationship.

Researchers and civil society alike have shown that "traditional" gendered and sexual beliefs and practices in Mexico have shifted and transformed in recent decades.[71] What we see in neoliberal Mexico is a sexual culture marked by contradiction and uncertainty—a contrary mix of resurgent conservatism alongside a new sexual liberation and experimentation. Roger Lancaster has written of capitalism's schizophrenic cultural character, its "tendency toward innovation and cosmopolitanism" that vies with its "need for order and discipline."[72] This tension is evident in Mexico and in the Zona Galáctica, where tradition and modernity, control and freedom, uneasily coexist and compete. Such transformations of the gender-sex system in Mexico are linked to changes precipitated by the economic crisis, such as middle-class women increasingly finding work outside the home and a rising incidence of female-headed households. But these changes, as we will see, have not necessarily brought gender parity.

In his study of masculinity in a working-class neighborhood in Mexico City, Matthew Gutmann discusses a cultural transformation that he refers to as "degendering," in which certain beliefs and activities, such as alcohol consumption and housework, are disassociated from a particular gender identity and linked with other social sectors, such as youth, the working class, or particular ethnic groups.[73] It is true that, in many sectors of Mexico, gender roles and gendered activities have been undergoing rapid transformation. It is also clear that there exists in Mexico a multiplicity of gender identities; the fact of this multiplicity is easily masked by stereotypes of the Mexican macho and the *mujer abnegada* (self-sacrificing woman).[74] "Why," Gutmann asks, "shouldn't the study of gender in Mexico similarly reject specious conclusions about ubiquitous (national) machos and *abnegadas*, and replace these stereotypes with descriptions and analyses of the diversity of changing gender identities in Mexico at the end of the twentieth century?"[75]

This ethnography of the Galactic Zone examines the diversity of changing gender identities and gendered activities. But it also examines the persistence of both men's domination of women and the fact that beliefs and activities surrounding sex—and stigmatized commercial sex in particular—have not undergone this process of degendering that Gutmann describes.

By acknowledging and exploring gender inequality, I am not trying to promote essentializing formulations of gender in Mexico or adhere to former simplistic, ahistorical stereotypes of the Mexican *macho* and the passive, sexually pure, and self-sacrificing woman. It was Octavio Paz who set forth this classic, stereotypical formulation of Mexico masculinity and femininity in his widely read *Labyrinth of Solitude*.[76] Paz's ideal women are virtuous, the embodiment of motherhood. Those who are not constitute a familial and societal shame and are stigmatized. Men are powerful and endowed with a right to experience this power and their sexuality. What Paz writes about are archetypes embodied by few living, breathing beings. Many researchers have already shown that such simplistic formulations are untenable, since cultural ideals are historically produced and differ from the realities of actual behavior.[77] In addition, such models are differentially ascribed, applied, adhered to, and resisted according to the particulars of class, ethnicity, and sexual orientation.[78] Along with social movements of the poor and politically disenfranchised, there has emerged in Mexico an increasing awareness of the inequalities of gender and sexual orientation, accompanied by the growth of feminist and gay rights movements seeking to address and transform those inequities.

Gutmann's claim that "the *macho mexicano* stereotypes are today largely inappropriate and misleading" is an important corrective to earlier pervasive images.[79] There are few men in the following pages who conform in full to the modern idealized image of the Mexican macho, that is, a domineering, independent, tough, womanizing, hard-drinking man. Nor do many resemble less contemporary notions of machos as "honorable men" who use their power wisely.[80]

Yet nearly all the men who appear in the following pages visit prostitutes and/or seek to control and regulate the activities of women (and men) who engage in prostitution. This may tempt some readers to identify them as stereotypical macho *mexicanos* who exploit and dominate women. But as I argue in this book, the relationships and distribution of power in the Galáctica are far too complex to be reduced to a problem of machismo. Despite this complexity, whether they are clients or government officials or *ejidatarios* (land reform beneficiaries), these men generally share a sense of sexual entitlement and of standing on the moral high ground in relation to the sex workers of the zone.

Whether practiced, believed, contested, or not, the moral double standard, men's sexual entitlement, women's subordination, and the stigmatization of certain women all make their mark on society in a variety of ways. For instance, women's entry into wage labor is at odds with cultural ideals that emphasize a woman's domestic role as wife, mother, and daughter. Women who work outside the home have historically been stigmatized in Mexico. One of many Spanish words for prostitute, *meretriz*, has its root in the Latin *merere*, meaning one who earns;[81] the link between women who earn money and perceived immorality has deep roots. Even today, domestic servants are often viewed as outlets for male sexuality within the household, particularly for teenaged boys.[82] More recently, the sexual morality of female factory workers has been held up to public scrutiny. As the northern border region began to industrialize in the 1960s, Mexican women began to enter factory work in the export-oriented maquiladoras. With the passage of NAFTA, the whole of Mexico became a free trade zone, and even more women entered into factory work. Women, who account for some 60 percent of all maquiladora workers, were hired because they were presumed to be submissive, highly exploitable, and less expensive than their male counterparts.[83] Perceived as a threat to a social order marked by gender inequality and female economic reliance upon men, female workers are often associated with promiscuity, immorality, and even prostitution. As one factory worker told the anthropologist María Patricia Fernández-Kelly, "Many people, especially men, treat you differently as soon as they know you have a job at a *maquiladora*. They think that if you have to work for money, there is also a good chance that you're a whore. But I assure you that my friends and I are decent women."[84]

The vulnerability and precarious social position of women workers is evident in the northern border city of Ciudad Juárez, where poor young women and teen girls from throughout Mexico travel to work in one of the city's hundreds of internationally owned factories. Since 1993 nearly four hundred young women, often far from home and family, have been found murdered. If the morality of a woman who simply works outside the home may be suspect, one can imagine the suspicion that accompanies the transgression of a woman who works outside the home selling sex.

ORDER AND PROGRESS: ETHNOGRAPHY
AND NEOLIBERALISM

> Chaos should be regarded as extremely
> good news.
>
> Chögyam Trungpa Rinpoche

This is the story of the modernization of the sex industry in the city of Tuxtla Gutiérrez during the neoliberal era. It offers a view from above: of politicians, bureaucrats, city workers, campesinos, and an anthropologist as they interact within the world of sexual commerce. And it is a view from below: of sex workers and their clients who directly experience prostitution in a multitude of ways. It is a local story that is culturally specific, where women and men enact, contest, and reimagine gendered and sexual cultural norms within a regional economy in which sexuality is bought and sold. But it is also a global story in which these very women and men struggle to negotiate their places within a rapidly changing cultural system and within an increasingly global political-economic system in which modernity, democracy, and neoliberal capitalism have become dangerously synonymous. And even as structural forces and governmental policies separate peasants from land, parents from children, citizens from country, and sex from pleasure, even amidst all this separation, movement, migration, and dissolution, there emerge other sorts of connections, strange and surprising encounters and engagements between disparate groups—for instance, between peasants and prostitutes and politicians.

There have been, among activists, academics, and sex workers, many bitter and divisive polemics about commercial sex. Some have argued that all prostitution is patriarchal exploitation and female victimization and does not constitute "work."[85] Others discard terms such as *victimization*, focusing instead on agency, the social construction of sexuality, the variety of female experience in sex work, as they call it, and sometimes even its liberatory potential.[86]

When framed in terms of debate, contrasting patriarchy with female power, the complexity of the multiple power relations embedded in the practice of prostitution is obfuscated, reduced to a simple question of gender inequality. In this book, I view prostitution as a form of labor experienced differently by different women, rejecting the false dichotomy of exploitation/liberation.[87] The heterogeneity of sex work is visible in the zone, making it difficult to formulate grand generalizations about prostitution. I am not alone in placing myself in the sex-as-work camp. Recent writings by sex workers, academics, and activists has shifted away from reductionist celebrations or denials of female power and instead illustrates the complexities and contradictions of sexual labor.[88]

In an effort to distance myself from polarizing debates, I have chosen to use the terms *prostitution* and *sex work* interchangeably.[89] Prostitution, defined here as the exchange of sexual services for money, is one form of sex work, different from erotic dancing, phone sex, and participation in pornographic films or still photos. There are other reasons too for using both terms. Along with the modernization of the sex industry, there has developed in Tuxtla a modern vocabulary of sexual commerce that now includes words like *sexoservidora* and *trabajadora sexual* (sex worker). The terms *prostituta* (prostitute) and *puta* (whore) continue to be used throughout Tuxtla, but sex workers and zone administrators alike increasingly use the term *sex worker*.[90] Some Western feminists and sex workers make much of the terminology used to describe women who sell sex. Antiprostitution feminists continue to use the term *prostitute*, believing it conveys a sense of the exploitation and coercion found in commercial sex, while those in the pro-sex-work camp use the term *sex worker* to legitimize sex work as a form of work. Yet in Tuxtla, terms like *sexoservidora* and *trabajadora sexual* do not suggest greater acceptance of sex as legitimate work or diminished stigmatization of the women to whom these words are applied. Though sex workers themselves may prefer these labels to others, in contemporary Tuxtla these terms are only another way to sanitize and modernize commercial sex in Mexico; they are not a true legitimation of prostitution as work.

It would seem obvious that, in studying and writing about prostitution, one would be informed by feminist theory and gender studies. And so I am. Because sexual commerce is about much more than gender and sexuality, I also rely on theories of space and place, social control, and political economy. But more than anything, I make use of ethnography. I rely most on the lived experience of the people I came to know during my twelve months in Tuxtla, as well as on my own experiences.[91]

I do not intend to rehash here the academic debates about reflexivity, representation, self and other, power differentials, polyvocality, objectivity, and so on. This is not because I do not think such dialogue has been worthwhile or productive. Critiques of anthropology's colonial history, feminist concerns with the inequalities found in fieldwork and ethnographic writing, and postmodern discourses on partial knowledge and experimental writing, all have contributed to a more ethical discipline less bounded by artificial notions of objectivity and slightly less constricted by ideas about what constitutes academic writing.

An old poet once told the Uruguayan writer Eduardo Galeano, "Those who make objectivity a religion are liars. They are scared of human pain."[92] Scholarship has long demanded distance, sterility, and professionalism. Even within anthropology, one of the few academic disciplines that displays some tolerance for difference within its ranks, there is little room for playful exploration, for intimacy instead of distance, messy tangibility rather than sterility.

I have tried to bring texture and feeling to the pages that follow, drawing the reader into rhythms of the Galactic Zone and giving a sense of what Daniel Bradburd refers to as "being there."[93] In his book about poor white sharecroppers in rural Alabama, James Agee writes, "This is a *book* only by necessity." He continues, "If I could do it, I'd do no writing at all here. It would be photographs, the rest would be fragments of cloth, bits of cotton, lumps of earth, records of speech, pieces of wood and iron, phials of odors, plates of food and of excrement."[94] Ethnographers are equipped only with words, and in many cases we do our best to do what Nancy Scheper-Hughes calls "good enough" ethnography while recognizing the flaws and challenges of the anthropological endeavor.[95]

Still, feeling and textures aside, there are knowable facts: A government-run brothel was built in the capital of Chiapas in a time of social change and economic turmoil. Fifty percent of the Mexican population lives in poverty. Despite social gains, women continue to suffer gender inequality in Mexico; poor women are doubly marginalized. Poor women who work as prostitutes are marginalized *and* stigmatized. Call these women indigenous and their marginalization only increases. An old friend likes to remind me during moments of crisis or depression, "Feelings aren't facts." This kind of self-help cliché annoys me. Facts—women who sell sex are stigmatized in Mexico—engender feelings: I'm afraid my children will find out what I do for a living. Let fact and feeling mix and we come closer to the totality of lived experience. As Galeano tells us, "Why does one write, if not to put one's pieces together? From the moment we enter school or church, education chops us into pieces; it teaches us to divorce soul from body and mind from heart. The fishermen of the Colombian coast must be learned doctors of ethics and morality, for they invented the word *sentipensante*, feeling-thinking, to define the language that speaks the truth."[96]

As the modern neoliberal project requires a certain taming of chaos, of populations and ideas that threaten the production of hegemony, so too academic writing unfortunately demands the management and control of sometimes unruly data. Writing ethnography requires the shaping of disorderly and wonderfully jumbled human experience into linear and orderly knowledge. Writing good ethnography requires doing so without sacrificing the contradictions of human experience or compartmentalizing social facts simply for the sake of analytical coherence.

So, this book is organized in the following way: Chapter 1 situates the city of Tuxtla Gutiérrez and its Zona Galáctica within neoliberal Mexico. In telling the recent history of the city, describing its transformation from lowland backwater to modern metropolis, I illustrate the ways in which recent patterns of consumption and urbanization in Tuxtla, with its service economy, U.S. franchises, shopping malls, and modern brothel, fit squarely within the neoliberal model of development. The creation of the Zona Galáctica, I explain, is part of a broader state effort to cleanse the city and remove visible and undesirable evidence of neoliberalism's failures.

Chapter 2 explores municipal efforts to contain and control the unregulated and therefore illegal prostitution that takes place beyond the confines of the state-controlled Galactic Zone, in Tuxtla's streets, bars, and hotels. The raids against street sex workers are rituals of purification, having less to do with protection of public health than with enforcement of "public morals" and with cleansing urban space of the social disorder that unregulated visible prostitution is believed to represent. The rounding up of female and male transvestite prostitutes in Tuxtla's streets also makes clear the unequal application of the law (male pimps and clients go free while women and gay men do not); and it makes clear that the raids, despite the resistance of sex workers, reinforce gender, sexual, and class inequality.

Chapter 3 examines the strict medical, spatial, and social supervision of zone workers. While the regulationist system of prostitution, as practiced in the zone, has some unexpected benefits for workers who receive condoms and adult education, the health benefits of regulated commercial sex are proven to be questionable, if not outright nonexistent. In addition, the surveillance and mistreatment of zone workers by zone staff serves only to reinforce cultural codes that designate the prostitute as both expendable and dangerous. Women's resistance to the restrictive regulationist system, including the 1996 strike in which the workers took the brothel administrator hostage, prove that resistance, even among such a divided and divisive population, is always possible.

Chapter 4 is an unlikely story of agrarian conflict, party politics, prostitution, and the public good. The efforts of communal landholders to reclaim their ancestral lands upon which the Galáctica now stands reveal not only a centuries-old conflict between indigenous Mexico and "modern" Mexico, between communal landholding and private enterprise, but also the multiple, overlapping, and intertwined inequalities, conflicts, and convergences between and among sex workers, communal farmers, landlords, politicians, and citizenry.

Chapter 5 interrogates the circumstances under which women enter the sex industry, and how factors such as citizenship and marital status affect a woman's work patterns, consumption habits, and even reputation. In examining these circumstances, we see that women enter prostitution in a variety of ways for a variety of reasons, and that sex work, neither wholly oppressive nor liberating, is constantly being shaped and reshaped by historical circumstance and cultural practice.

In analyzing the negotiation of prices and services in the Galactic Zone, chapter 6 dispels notions of prostitution as the "easy life," as it is so often called by Tuxtlecos. Sex workers are service workers in a new global economy in which gendered household activities such as cooking, cleaning, child care, and sex have been increasingly commodified. In their work, prostitutes must be skilled arbitrators, exacting cash from clients, teaching them about condom use, and sometimes enduring verbal and even physical abuse. Clients, for their part, through their visits to the zone, learn and reinforce masculine desire and privilege in the Galáctica.

In chapter 7, I describe the zone as a place of freedom from hegemonic norms of gender and sexuality, where women transgress moral norms by exchanging sexual services directly for cash, and gay male food vendors openly express their sexuality. But the zone is also a place of restriction, where sex workers, though their work is legal, are highly stigmatized. This stigmatization is key in inhibiting workers from demanding their rights and the remuneration they deserve for their labor.

The final two chapters revisit both some of the questions posed by this book and the women of the Galactic Zone. Chapter 8 critiques neoliberal capitalism and state-regulated prostitution, examining alternatives to the system in place in Tuxtla. In the epilogue, I provide an update on the lives of some of the women of the zone, including their creation of new lives and, in a few instances, their deaths.

ONE Modern Sex in a Modern City

> Tuxtla is not a place for foreigners—the new ugly
> capital of Chiapas, without attractions. . . . It is like
> an unnecessary postscript to Chiapas, which should
> be all wild mountain and old churches and swallowed
> ruins and the Indians plodding by.
>
> Graham Greene, 1939

Anthropologists and other social scientists have been at work in Chiapas for more than half a century. Most research has centered on the indigenous Maya peoples of the Highlands region; the Zapatista uprising in 1994 extended researchers' field of interest both thematically and geographically.[1] The rich work produced by scholars over the decades has generated a particular image of a Chiapas that is agricultural, indigenous, impoverished, and deeply conflicted over issues of ethnicity, land, class, and politics. Chiapas is all these things, but it is also urban, *ladino* (nonindigenous), and for some, a place to seek economic prosperity. This aspect of Chiapas has received less attention from Western anthropologists, who historically have come to southern Mexico to study indigenous peoples.[2]

A VERY NEW CITY

As capital of the state known as the birthplace of the new Mexican Revolution led by the EZLN, Tuxtla Gutiérrez is perhaps not what many imagine. Located in the hot lowlands of Chiapas, Tuxtla, home to the Galactic Zone, is a city of nearly half a million people. If Chiapas is, as it came to be known after the uprising, "the other Mexico—backward and left behind," then Tuxtla is, in many ways, the other Chiapas.³ In 1892, Governor Emilio Rabasa transferred the capital of Chiapas from San Cristóbal de las Casas to Tuxtla with the hopes of ridding the state government of the provincialism and corruption found in the Highlands government, as well as to effect the "geographic reorientation of Chiapas," turning it away from Guatemala—the state was a Guatemalan territory until 1824—and toward Mexico City.⁴ The young Rabasa (he became governor at age thirty-five) was less an elected official than an appointed one: he was chosen by President Porfirio Díaz to implement the very values (economic liberalism, modernization, and positivism) for which the Díaz regime stood. Rabasa played a key role in the political modernization of Chiapas.⁵

More than a century later, heavily touristed San Cristóbal, with its cobblestone streets and outdoor indigenous markets, is still plagued by a reputation of provincialism, while Tuxtla prides itself on its image as a modern city. Where San Cristóbal makes much of its colonial roots, Tuxtla showcases its modernity. In a document written by municipal authorities, Tuxtla is portrayed as a city without a past, an antidote to San Cristóbal, with its indigenous population and colonial architecture, both of which are considered distinctly premodern: "Outside of the museum, the visitor to Tuxtla will search in vain for signs of the colonial era and vestiges of the Spanish epoch. Tuxtla is like that, it is a very new city, its ancient traces having disappeared with modern urbanization and it would be useless to hope to still find here an atmosphere of centuries past."⁶

Tuxtla is, in this account, cleansed of its colonial past and freed from its late-nineteenth-century reputation in San Cristóbal as a lowland backwoods town lacking amenities. But in 1930, the capital of Chiapas still lacked both a drainage system and paved roads; only the central block had running water, and only four medical doctors were available to serve the entire population of Tuxtla and its hinterlands.[7]

Finally, in the 1940s the state intervened, augmenting Tuxtla's infrastructure "in order to consolidate it as the worthy capital of the state of Chiapas"; this coincided with the beginning of the state-led development of Mexico on a national scale.[8] During this period, many of Tuxtla's old and colonial-style buildings were demolished, along with parks, aging hospitals, and decaying markets, all replaced by modern structures. The image of the city was changing. The state widened principal roads in order to accommodate automobiles, the "symbols of modernity."[9] The construction of the Pan-American Highway was completed in 1942, facilitating Tuxtla's communication with Mexico City and its expansion, and new settlements sprang up in the east and west along the highway's edge.

Yet not until the middle of the twentieth century did Tuxtla truly begin to develop the infrastructure characteristic of a modern city. By the 1960s, the city had a new airport and its first automatic traffic lights. Fountains and monuments, symbols of the consolidation of state power, were built throughout the capital. Tuxtla's main thoroughfare, called Avenida Central in the eastern half of the city and Boulevard Belisario Domínguez in the west, was widened. New residential neighborhoods were constructed. Some of these neighborhoods were private *fraccionamientos* (subdivisions), while others, like Colonia Bienestar Social, were sites for state-sponsored public housing. Tuxtla's wealthier residents tended to live in the western half of the city (as they still do), while poorer Tuxtlecos (residents of Tuxtla) lived in eastern Tuxtla (also the location of the Zona Galáctica). Tuxtla is very much a city divided by class—even its movie theaters (like sexual services) are class stratified, ranging from the more expensive, cleaner, air-conditioned cineplex of the central plaza to poorly maintained, cheaper theaters with sound systems that barely function.

Tuxtla's population surged during the 1970s following the arrival of poor rural migrants, families from the neighboring city of Chiapa de

Corzo displaced by an earthquake, and workers from as far away as Guatemala who had come to build the dam at nearby Chicoasén, part of a massive, state-sponsored hydroelectric complex. Between 1970 and 1980 the number of residents doubled, reaching nearly 167,000.[10] Many of these new migrants settled on uncultivated lands in the foothills in the northern and southern sections of the city.

During the 1980s and 1990s, Tuxtla was one of Mexico's most rapidly growing cities. As the debt crisis and economic chaos engulfed Mexico during the 1980s, massive public works projects were undertaken in Tuxtla. During this time, growing economic, social, and political strife besieged rural Chiapas: croplands continued to fall into the hands of large landholders, many of whom raised cattle; and authorities jailed campesinos protesting the loss of lands, as the newly militarized state and judicial police repressed dissent. Nearly eighty thousand Guatemalan refugees poured into eastern Chiapas, fleeing the murderous military regime of General Efraín Ríos Montt. Government authorities worried about the possibility of insurrection in Chiapas.

During this period, despite austerity measures implemented throughout the nation, the state government in Tuxtla began a campaign to construct a new capital showcasing state power and advertising the successes of urbanization. Public funds were used to remodel the downtown center and construct the Unidad Administrativa, two massive buildings housing many of the offices of the state government. The Museum of Anthropology, the City Theater, and the Libramiento Sur, a wide highway that traverses the city's southern edge, were all built in this period of economic decline and social crisis. When seen in the context of demographic shifts, economic crisis, and political turmoil, it is little surprise that the idea for constructing a site for state-regulated prostitution that would control marginal populations emerged during this time.

In many ways Tuxtla stands apart from the agricultural and indigenous Chiapas represented by social scientists who bypass this often-maligned city on their way to the Highlands. Graham Greene's 1939 characterization of the "new ugly capital" still holds true for many tourists, social scientists, and Chiapanecos alike. Tuxtla has no ruins, most of its churches are modern in design, and there is little indigenous presence in the city. Its high annual population growth rate of 7.3 percent, due largely to internal migration, worries public officials, who wring their hands as shanties continue to sprout in the southern hills overlooking the city. Unlike the whole of Chiapas, where some 60 percent of the economically active population is employed in primary-sector activities such as agriculture, fishing, or cattle raising, nearly 75 percent of Tuxtlecos earn their living in the commercial and service sectors; only 4.3 percent are engaged in agriculture.[11] Some Tuxtlecos are still landholders, however: many of the city's wealthy families earn money from rural landholdings and maintain ranches in the countryside surrounding the city, a status symbol for local elites.

Consumer culture, much of it service based, thrives in Tuxtla more than anywhere else in the state. Middle- and upper-class consumers from San Cristóbal and throughout Chiapas come to Tuxtla to purchase items and receive services (particularly medical care) unavailable in their home communities. Tuxtla's western and wealthier half is home to American big-box stores like Office Depot and Blockbuster Video that reflect neoliberalism's reach into southern Mexico. U.S.-based fast-food chains such Domino's Pizza, McDonald's, and Kentucky Fried Chicken dot the landscape; the latter two have drive-through windows, making consumption as fast and easy as possible. U.S. influences permeate consumption in Tuxtla and elsewhere in Mexico. Some Mexican urban and suburban landscapes have changed so dramatically in recent years that they are nearly indistinguishable from their northern neighbors, at least to some. The author and activist John Ross writes of a group of undocumented workers who paid *polleros* (smugglers) in Tapachula, Chiapas, five thousand dollars apiece for passage to the United States. The migrants, mostly from Guatemala, were dropped off in front of a mall containing a "Wendy's, a KFC, even an Applebee's, and the ten-plex 'Hollywood Cinema' in suburban Chihuahua City, a good 100 miles from the U.S. border. The workers believed they had arrived in the U.S., as one worker told a local newspaper, 'It looked just like how it looked on television.'"[12]

American venues have made some concessions to local culture: the

Figure 4. Tuxtla's newest shopping mall. Photo by Patty Kelly.

"No Shoes, No Shirt, No Service" mantra of U.S. fast food restaurants does not apply in Tuxtla's McDonald's; small barefoot children belonging to middle- and upper-class families tear through the restaurant and its adjoining playground while their parents order McMexicanas—hamburgers with avocado and salsa. At Kentucky Fried Chicken, now called KFC, the colonel, whose cultural symbolism would be lost on most Mexicans, has been replaced by a happy cartoon chicken with robust pectoral muscles. Directly behind McDonald's is the newly opened Sam's Club, a Wal-Mart-affiliated price club. During the Christmas season, it offered shoppers pine trees shipped from the United States. The nonunion Wal-Mart currently owns 687 superstores and subsidiaries throughout Mexico (though they go by various names: Superama and Bodega Aurrera, to name two), including one built in central Mexico within sight of the two-thousand-year-old pyramids of Teotihuacán (dubbed Teotihualmart by writer and social critic Carlos Monsivais).[13] A few blocks farther west is Plaza Cristal, an upscale shopping mall with a food court where local middle-class teens gather while their younger, darker-skinned, poorer counterparts bag groceries in Chedraui, the large modern supermarket that is one of the mall's anchor stores.

Increasing commoditization and United States cultural influences also permeate sexuality in Tuxtla. Though the city has long had its share of sex workers and even a soft-core pornographic movie theater located within sight of both the municipal and state government headquarters, daily newspapers that ten years ago had perhaps one or two small ads for *edecanes* (hostesses) who provide sexual services now contain pages and pages of such advertisements. The ads often picture blond Hollywood actresses (Mira Sorvino is a favorite) and thin Western fashion models, who have come to define new cultural standards of beauty and sexiness.

Before the arrival of the Spanish, what is now Tuxtla was sparsely populated by indigenous Zoque Maya, who cultivated corn and beans. Today, the city is primarily ladino. While more than 25 percent of all Chiapanecos over the age of five speak an indigenous language, in Tuxtla this figure is just 2 percent.[14] Immigrant Tzotzil and Tzeltal speakers from indigenous Highland communities such as Chamula and Zinacantán now outnumber the few hundred Zoques remaining in Tuxtla. The three groups frequently work as day laborers, informal workers, service workers, and vendors in local traditional markets, selling fresh flowers, vegetables, and traditional foods.

While Chiapas is one of Mexico's most impoverished states, Tuxtla is

one of the nation's least impoverished municipalities.[15] The distribution
of wealth and misery in Chiapas and all of Mexico is complex and
uneven, and marked by regional and ethnic differences. In Chiapas,
indigenous residents of the Highlands and the selva suffer poverty the
most. The infant mortality rate in Tuxtla is 3.8 percent; nationwide this
figure is 4.9 percent, while in some Chiapas municipalities, such as the
indigenous town of Chamula, this figure is as high as 16.8 percent.[16]
Tuxtla boasts the highest rates of literacy in the state and the largest number of prisons or, as they are called, Centers for Social Rehabilitation.
While one-third of all homes in Chiapas lack electricity, despite the continued operation of the massive hydroelectric complex mentioned earlier,
in Tuxtla this figure is 3.2 percent; nationally, 12.5 percent of Mexican
homes do not have access to electricity.[17] And Tuxtla also boasts the
Galactic Zone, considered by its administrators to be one of the most
modern brothels in the nation.

And so, while Chiapas may be "the other Mexico," in many ways
Tuxtla is "the other Chiapas," contrasting in most respects to the indigenous Chiapas observed by anthropologists over the past five decades
and by the international media since the EZLN uprising. Yet Tuxtla and
its Zona Galáctica are not separate from the political economic trends
that gave rise to the Chiapas that has become so well known, but rather
were born from these same trends. The policies that contribute to rural
poverty and underdevelopment also engender increasing urbanization.
Nearly two-thirds of the high population growth in the city is a product
of immigration from other parts of southern Mexico. Despite the city's
prosperity, however, there are plenty of impoverished Tuxtlecos who
are unemployed, or underemployed in the booming informal economy
that flourishes in Tuxtla's streets, homes, and brothels. Those living in
the shanties in the foothills above the city watch the prosperity from a
distance. In the city center below, hundreds of poor people line up each
evening outside the public regional hospital, waiting for medical care.
The police crime pages report stories of robbery and violence, and the
private security guard industry flourishes. It may be the other Chiapas,
but Tuxtla is still Mexico.

Figure 5. The road to the Zona Galáctica. Photo by Patty Kelly.

MODERN SEX

The Zona Galáctica lies four miles from Tuxtla's bustling city center, down a lonely, bumpy dirt road flanked by vibrant green vegetation, the *flamboyán* trees blooming bright orange in the springtime. One does not arrive at the zone by chance: one must seek it out. Its location is a testament to the current status of commercial sex throughout much of Mexico: available, yet, ideally, invisible.

The dirt road leads to the large, open, unpaved lot outside the main

Figure 6. A microbus. Photo by Patty Kelly.

gate to the zone. Directly in front of the visitor, behind a tall chain-link fence kept gated and locked during the day, is the King Kong, one of the area's two nightclubs where some sex workers perform striptease. To the right are two small refreshment stands that flank the entry to the Galáctica; one of them is rarely open. In front of the stands is a line of microbuses and Volkswagen Beetles that provide transportation for zone clients, workers, and staff. (Most zone clients, working-class men, do not own their own transportation.) The *micros,* as they are called, cost four pesos (US$0.47) and make many stops between downtown Tuxtla and the zone. They provide little anonymity for sex workers and clients, who share the bus with others making shorter trips within the city. The Volkswagens, known as *piratas* (pirate, or unlicensed, taxicabs), charge five pesos (US$0.59) and proceed directly to the zone once they are filled. This mode of transport is generally considered more desirable because it is a quicker and more discreet way to arrive at the Galáctica, though if the taxi does not fill up at the taxi stand it will slowly cruise one of Tuxtla's main thoroughfares with a sign in the window that reads "ZONA," decreasing the anonymity of both workers and clients riding in it.

Outside the main gate, on the large sign that reads Zona de Tolerancia, the Coca-Cola insignia that once appeared on each side of the sign has been spitefully painted over, following a dispute with the local Coca-Cola distributors over a monetary donation to the zone Christmas party (the distributors refused the request for funds). Beneath the large sign is a smaller hand-painted one stating the many rules of the zone. Lingering outside the gates are clients and workers who are waiting for transportation back to the city center. Female municipal staff rarely wait in this manner, remaining inside their offices, since they generally prefer not to interact with sex workers and clients. They usually exit their offices only when they hear the horn of the pirata or the nasal calls of the teenage boys who collect bus fares: "*Centro. Centro.* There's still room!" Carlos, a Tzeltal Mayan who looks to be only nine or ten years old, stands outside the main gate selling gum, candy, and cigarettes. I was shocked to find that he was actually fourteen; owing to poor nutrition, many indigenous people appear far younger than their actual age when they are children. As adults, hard work takes its toll, and they often appear older than their actual years. Javier, another teenager, sells flavored shaved ices from a bright blue wooden cart. Like the boys that they are, Carlos and Javier can often be found wrestling and play-fighting in the mornings as they ready their carts for a long day of work at the main gate.

The zone is open from nine o'clock in the morning until nine in the evening. The two clubs outside the main gate open only at night. The hours of the zone's operation reflect municipal concerns with social order and the zone as a place for contained and orderly sexual practice. As Héctor Carrillo writes in his study of sexual culture in Guadalajara, the night is a transgressive time, one of diversion and sexuality.[18] In the darkness, anything can happen. By keeping the zone open during regular and "respectable" business hours, it retains a symbolic sense of order and safety. Many zone women prefer to work only during the day; keeping "regular" working hours lends workers the sense that they are operating within cultural norms in some way, despite the stigmatized nature of the work.

Clients must purchase a ticket for three pesos (US$0.35) at the main gate before entering. Clients who purchase sex in the Galactic Zone are doing their civic duty, consuming sexual services in the least transgressive and most orderly manner possible rather than contributing to the growth of the informal sexual economy found in Tuxtla's streets. Municipal police briefly search the client at the entry gate, and if he is found to be sober (enough) and free of potential weapons, he will be allowed to enter. Inside the gate are eighteen *módulos* (units), barracks-style buildings each containing ten rooms. Though the city administers the zone, each unit is independently owned. Most owners come to the zone only to collect rents, preferring to leave the daily administration of their unit to a hired hand. A few, including the well-liked Doña Mari, prefer a more hands-on approach. Doña Mari's módulo is clean, colorful, and filled with lush flowering plants.

The landlady Doña Esperanza actually lives in the Galáctica, although she is unpopular with many zone women; sex workers say that even Doña Esperanza's own daughter hates her, and that she lives in the zone because she has nowhere else to go. With her curly gray hair, glasses, and housedress, Doña Esperanza putters around the zone in a seemingly perpetual state of grouchiness. The gossip about Doña Esperanza is revealing: it is not only sex workers who are stigmatized, but also women who do not maintain family ties. Single women, women living alone apart from family, prostitutes, young female anthropologists—all are subject to scrutiny.

The eighteen buildings are organized into three rows with wide concrete pathways in between. Each building is constructed to facilitate client browsing as well as surveillance of workers: the three sides of the unit open into a central open-air courtyard through which clients may

Figure 7. Doña Mari's módulo. Photo by Patty Kelly.

stroll while "shopping." There are no dark corners or invisible spaces in the zone. Everything is within sight, within reach.

Just inside the main gate are two administrative buildings. The northernmost building houses the Servicios Médicos Anti-Venereos (Anti-Venereal Medical Service). It is staffed by three medical doctors, two nurses, a chemist, a cleaning lady, and a secretary. The interior of the building is spartan and has a bureaucratic feel to it: a few desks and plastic chairs, and in a small room off to the side, a table for gynecological examinations, a desk, and a chair. Posters and pedagogical diagrams advertising birth control and safe sex are taped up here and there, along with handwritten signs instructing workers to bring their worker identification cards with them when they come for their weekly gynecological exam. A few plants cling to life in the corners. During the Day of the Dead celebrations, old X-rays were cut up in the shape of bats and hung from the ceiling with strings by someone feeling unusually festive; they remained hanging for months, creating an atmosphere that was more macabre than cheery. The zone administrator, El Contador (the Accountant—there is a great love for titles in Mexico) is the primary occupant of the other building. This building also contains a room where municipal police sometimes eat their lunch, and two small jail cells that are used to detain "troublesome" clients and workers. Just outside the cells is a large room with two long tables and a few chairs, used for classes in adult education. Here we find a Foucauldian nightmare, a strange trio of disciplinary institutions: a brothel, a prison, a school, all in one.

Aside from prostitutes and municipal staff, many other Tuxtlecos earn their income in the zone. Scattered throughout the Galáctica are small stands where vendors sell food, refreshments, toilet paper, bleach, candles, and music cassettes. Nearly all the food vendors are gay men, who find that the Galáctica, being a tolerance zone where hegemonic norms of sexuality and gender may sometimes be challenged, is one of the few public spaces in the city where they can express their sexual orientation as they choose without fear of excessive harassment or abuse.[19] Many of these workers wear earrings and aprons.

Others who earn income in the zone are the visiting ambulatory vendors and shoe-shine boys, who must receive permission and pay a fee in order to work; middle-aged mustachioed twin brothers with kind eyes who form the zone's municipal janitorial staff, and privately hired janitors who work for the owners of the buildings and perform errands for the workers. Roberto and an older man nicknamed Snub-nose for obvious reasons are two such privately hired janitors. Small and thin, dwarfed by the enormous T-shirts he tends to wear, the endearing Snub-nose has a disoriented, exhausted, disheveled look about him as though he had just washed ashore after days at sea. He is sometimes subject to teasing, and tricked into showering and shaving by being told the mayor will be making a rare visit to the zone.

While the ways in which the work of the female prostitutes of the zone supports their individual kin are readily apparent, less visible is the way the prostitution of zone women has become entrenched in the local economy, generating a flow of material resources that families throughout the city rely on for economic survival.[20] Though it represents only a small part of the city's booming service sector, the economic opportunity offered by the zone is crucial for many Tuxtlecos.

Commodified sexual relations have a lengthy history in Mexico; ask any Tuxtleco about prostitution and he or she is likely to comment, "It has always existed." But referring to prostitution as "the world's oldest profession," as the tired expression goes, dehistoricizes sex work, failing to account for how the practice changes and the ways it is shaped by time, space, and culture. Prostitution becomes essentialized, inevitable, homogenous, and unchanging. While it has a long history in Mexico (historical evidence suggests that commercial sex existed in pre-Conquest times), how it has been practiced, regulated, and perceived has varied in space and time. It is constantly being shaped and reshaped by politics, economy, and culture.

Not surprisingly, the modern tolerance zones in Mexico emerged during the Porfiriato, a period (not unlike the current one) in which the state was known for its economic liberalism, its conservative views regarding sexuality, family, and alcohol consumption, and its embrace of science, positivism, and modernization. Regulating the prostitute through health inspections, registration, and confinement was considered indispensable to conserve order and protect public health.

The first tolerance zones, known as district zones, were located on the borders of tourist and shopping districts, most commonly in northern Mexico. Prostitutes were removed from the city center streets, bars, and cafes and subjected to increasing regulation and control. Today compound zones, like the Zona Galáctica, are located far outside the periphery of the city, invisible to the citizenry. Compound zones began to appear as early as the 1940s as a response to resident and government concerns about social hygiene and public image in the eyes of tourists.[21] As in Tuxtla, these zones often coexist with the clandestine, unregulated, and illicit prostitution that occurs in streets, hotels, bars, and private homes throughout urban Mexico. The existence of such zones depends on state and local politics, with zones opening and closing as local political conditions change.

The Zona Galáctica was an effort to materialize Governor González Garrido's dream of modernizing sex work in Chiapas. Women and men still exchanged sex for money in bars and houses throughout Tuxtla, and the city's previous red-light district, El Cocal, was considered anything but modern. Located in southwestern Tuxtla, El Cocal had been operating informally since the early 1980s, when private landowners began to build rooms to house prostitutes on a piece of land that was at the time on the outskirts of the city. El Cocal grew in a disorderly fashion. Landlords built poorly constructed rooms when finances permitted, and the district took on a shantytown appearance. Many workers remember it as an ugly place that was poorly lit and sometimes felt unsafe. As in the current zone, the clientele consisted mostly of men of the laboring classes, along with some lower- and middle-class white-collar workers and teenage boys from well-to-do families. There was no police presence and little municipal intervention in El Cocal; it functioned as a wholly private enterprise. Workers were supposed to register with the city's Department of Public Health and travel to the city center to receive medical examinations, but there was no on-site administration to enforce such rules.

With Tuxtla's rapid expansion, El Cocal was soon engulfed by urban growth. It became increasingly visible to residents of Tuxtla. City officials and complaining residents alike considered the situation unseemly. In 1991, the priista municipal government, acting in conjunction with González Garrido's priista state, expropriated the land beneath El Cocal, demolished the buildings, and created a new district. The new, municipally administered Zona Galáctica was discreetly located out on the old road to Cupia, far from the city center and invisible to the public. Tuxtla's current director of public health told me that the Galáctica was built in order to "decrease rape and street crime and to decrease the number of sexoservidoras in the city."

Sitting in Pepe's open-air food stand inside the zone one afternoon, Doña Blanca, a former landlady in El Cocal and current owner in the Galáctica, recalled the city's actions there, bitterly describing the way she had been given only seventy-two hours to vacate her premises. The wrecking crews, she said, demolished one of her rooms before she was able to remove the contents. Pepe, busy behind the counter preparing tacos, threw his hands up in the air and chimed in (as he was prone to do), "And they haven't even built anything on that land. It's a dump!" It was true. Many times, I had passed by the vacant lot that was once El Cocal.

The destruction of El Cocal and its replacement by the Zona Galáctica transformed organized prostitution in Tuxtla from a largely private, unregulated and uncontrolled industry to a public-private partnership operated both by the city and private landlords. Many of the landlords who purchased buildings in the Galáctica were formerly landlords in El Cocal. This new arrangement effectively gave the city control over commercial sex and those who practice and profit from it. It also freed the city from accusations of *lenoncinio* (pimping). By maintaining private ownership of the buildings in which the women worked, the city was able to keep its distance from pimping, an activity considered deplorable by nearly all Tuxtlecos (while prostitution is not considered a crime, the pimping of sex workers is). Building owners do not, of course, refer to themselves as pimps, but they are referred to as such in many city documents, as it is they who directly earn money from the sex workers by collecting exorbitant rents of up to US$4.70 a day. The city, on the other hand, earns three pesos (US$0.35) for each client who enters and one peso (US$0.12) for each automobile, and collects rents from vendors and worker payments for medical laboratory fees.

City officials claim the Galáctica is not a great source of revenue; the expenses of administering the zone, they say, are relatively high. Upon showing me their accounting books, one administrator was careful to tell me that under the PAN there was only one set of books in the zone. Under the PRI, he claimed, there was such corruption and graft that multiple sets of books were necessary. While I couldn't be sure about what happened under previous administrations, my own examinations of their accounting books, along with my calculations of incoming funds, seemed to support the claim that the zone did not generate large amounts of cash for the city. The benefits of the Galáctica for the city and state, then, relate less to revenue earned than to social hygiene and control of the poor and "deviant," providing a showcase for modernity and state power in the capital of one of Mexico's poorest states.

The site chosen for the Zona Galáctica was four hectares of land on the city's eastern edge, part of the ejido Francisco I. Madero.[22] In early

September 1991, a deal was struck between the city, the state, and the ruling body of Francisco I. Madero, the Comisariado Ejidal (Ejido Commission). Documents in the municipal archives describe the deal as an exchange of land for "works of infrastructure, consisting of the construction of a recreational park, expansion of the water and drainage systems, the paving of one road, and the construction of a bridge."[23] Documents emanating from the Ejido Commission describe the deal as a donation of land to the priista municipal president Esquinca Méndez and Governor González Garrido. This land exchange plays a crucial role in understanding the Zona Galáctica and its place in modern Tuxtla (see chapter 4).

Though the city government is entirely responsible for the day-to-day operations and administration of the zone, the state played a crucial role in opening and naming the Galáctica. It is said that Governor González Garrido gave the Galactic Zone its name, and tales and jokes regarding his reasoning abound. One city official suggests to me that the name has something to do with women's breasts: "Galactic. Lactic. Milk. Breast milk. Breasts. Get it?" I don't—his logic is not convincing. A doctor jokes that it has something to do with the former governor's rumored homosexuality; *puto*, a word used to describe both gay men and male prostitutes, rhymes with Pluto, the planet. Pluto is part of the solar system, hence the name Galáctica. Again, not very convincing. But the word *galactic* itself, with its futuristic sensibility, conveys a sense of the modern, conjuring up space-age imagery of futuristic worlds.

Whatever the reasoning, the name is fitting: the Galactic Zone is in many ways otherworldly. Like military bases, brothels are, as Cynthia Enloe suggests, "artificial societies created out of unequal relations."[24] Upon entering the zone, one is struck by how sharply it contrasts not only with Tuxtla but also with Chiapas as a whole. There are elements in the zone that one would find in any Mexican city: street vendors, the occasional shoe-shine boy, a few stray, lactating dogs (though I never saw their puppies), men and women coming and going, music playing, and the scent of tacos in the air. But certain features are missing: the sight of ongoing construction projects—rusting rebar stretching hopefully skyward, so common in urban Mexico, is absent. Every building is painted: red, beige, light blue, bright blue, hot pink and red, yellow and green, orange and black, or some equally unlikely combination of colors. This contrasts greatly with Tuxtla's poorer neighborhoods that are the grim gray of concrete or dull brown of scavenged wood. There are no street children begging or blind men playing musical instruments. And the place is exceedingly clean: there is little stray garbage to be found anywhere. A "city" of sex run by the state, the zone, as a place, is unlike most places. It is a public-private enterprise where men come to spend money, learn desire, and enact cultural ideals with respect to gender and sexuality. The women of the zone come to earn money while acting simultaneously within and outside the boundaries of acceptable behavior.

Yet despite the utopian tendencies and aspirations of the Galáctica, the zone is a real place troubled by real problems. During its first years (1992–1995), the Galáctica, administered by the priista municipal government, was plagued by problems. The atmosphere, in Bárbara's words, was "a drag." She tells me I would not have liked it and would have been unable to conduct my research unmolested, as I generally did. Perhaps these early years established the zone's reputation among city residents as an "ugly place," though I found the Galáctica could often be pleasant, particularly on slow, warm mornings when groups of us would gather at Pepe's food stand, sipping sugary-sweet black Nescafé and eating papaya freshly picked from one of the nearby trees.

During the priista period, alcohol was sold in the zone, which conflicted with the initial proposals of González Garrido's 1989 Zona Rosa Project. Some workers recall those days fondly, remembering how clients would often buy them drinks. Immediately after the Zapatista uprising, trucks full of soldiers sent to stop the insurrection would arrive with pesos to spend on drinks for both themselves and the workers. But some workers, along with landlords and zone administrators, felt the consumption of alcohol was excessive and that it often led to violence and arguments among and between both workers and clients. On April 7, 1994, Enrique López Peña, the zone administrator, sent a letter to Municipal Secretary Hermann Hoppenstedt Pariente asking that something be done about El Pollo Galáctico (The Galactic Chicken), a restaurant within the zone that was "selling alcoholic beverages in excess to all clients that frequent the place as well as to the prostitutes that work here, and they violate the dry law [which prohibits the sale of alcoholic beverages on election day and other national political holidays] and the rule of no serving after 6 p.m."[25] The city government did not consider the problems of the Galáctica a priority, and two weeks later, López Peña sent another, slightly more desperate letter, stating, "We have not had an answer from you and the [Galactic Chicken] continues violating the rules of this administration."

Governor González Garrido's dream of modernizing and controlling commercial sex in the state was not fully realized in the Galáctica. The city's initial efforts at making sex safer by providing condoms to clients, for example, were not terribly effective. In the early days, men received a condom at the main gate when purchasing their entry ticket. Clients were given neither instructions nor incentive to use the condoms, which often ended up unused in municipal garbage pails or were turned into toys, blown up like balloons.

Nor did the opening of the Galáctica cleanse the city center of sex workers. Clandestine prostitutes, male and female, continued to work throughout the city, and the number of rooms in the zone was insufficient to house all the displaced *cocalitas* (women who worked in El Cocal).[26] In its early years, the Anti-Venereal Medical Service lacked furnishings and medical equipment and, most interestingly, a gynecologist. As noted in the municipal archives, "The boss of the Anti-Venereal Medical Service of the Municipality is not the proper person to perform this job. Said position is occupied by dentist Richard Cruz Coello." Of course, many of these problems were resolved with time, and the dentist, whom many of the workers remember fondly (Mónica smiles to show me the work he did on her teeth), was eventually replaced by a medical doctor.

During the period of my fieldwork, the panista municipal government managed the zone, as it had since 1995. The administration entered office in 1998 and was led by a gynecologist, Dr. Paco Rojas. This administration, it would seem, was designed to run the zone. Many policy changes came with the conservative PAN: alcohol was banned entirely in the zone, and following a strike by sex workers (described in chapter 3), condoms were given directly to the women rather than to the clients.

Yet despite the efforts of the city to control and regulate prostitution (and in doing so, further cleanse and modernize the city) by constructing the Zona Galáctica, clandestine or unregulated sexual commerce continued throughout the city. As population growth and poverty challenged municipal attempts to decrease visible prostitution in the city center, authorities intensified their attention to the men and women who worked selling sex in Tuxtla Gutiérrez.

TWO Hidden in Plain Sight

It is not a witch hunt.

Bayardo Muñoz, Tuxtla's director of public health,
on raids against street prostitutes

It sounds like a witch hunt.

Joe Pisido, undergraduate anthropology student,
on the criminalization of prostitution

It is 12:30 A.M. on a Saturday, and the municipal Department of Public Health, working in conjunction with the municipal police, is readying to hold an *operativo* (raid) against the unregistered prostitutes who work the city center, beyond the confines of the legal Galactic Zone. Municipal officials have invited me to come along and observe the raid, an event one doctor from the zone described as "fun." Atop a hill overlooking the western half of the city are two new red pickup trucks that belong to Public Health and two official police vehicles. I sit in one of the trucks, napping and occasionally waking to chat with people participating in the raid. We are parked along a back road leading to Camino Real, the city's finest hotel, which boasts a swimming pool surrounded by a lush garden with a waterfall. Also along this road is the popular upscale nightclub La Uno. On weekend nights, the dark road is usually lined with parked cars;

groups of young people who cannot afford to get drunk inside La Uno sit on the hoods of their cars, drinking beer.

Tonight the road is crowded with vehicles, yet few people are out drinking by their cars. The authorities seize only a few cases of Dos Equis and a couple of bottles of rum from young drinkers. The owners of most of the cars are inside La Uno because of the evening's special event: through the fogged glass walls of the club, I can see the dancing, flesh-colored shadows of nearly nude men, their muscular torsos twisting and hips gyrating. They are surrounded by the darker shadows of women who stand below them, arms outstretched, screaming with glee. "For Women Only," a traveling male striptease show, has arrived in Tuxtla. While the PAN is generally known for its conservatism regarding issues of gender and sexuality, there is a great deal of regional difference in how the party operates. Panista authorities in Tuxtla expressed little concern about the presence of the Chippendales-like show (though some male officials I spoke with said they didn't want their wives to attend). Around this time, more conservative local panista authorities in the city of Guadalajara banned a similar male striptease show there.

As the Tuxtlecas inside the nightclub express sexual desire and fantasy in a socially sanctioned way, the caravan of municipal vehicles begins speeding down the hill. We are headed toward the San Remo, a nightclub known for commercial sex, on Boulevard Belisario Domínguez, Tuxtla's main thoroughfare. Three women are standing at the bus stop across from the club. Jacobo, a city health inspector whose girlfriend, Flor, works as a prostitute in the zone, slams on the brakes of the pickup we are in; the other city workers jump out of the bed of the truck and run toward the three women, who also begin to run. The other vehicles in the caravan have stopped too; police and health inspectors dash across the street to the San Remo. All traffic on the boulevard has come to a halt. Police and health inspectors round up suspected sex workers, all women on this evening, putting them into police vehicles and the backs of the pickup trucks. Some women are crying. Others look confused. The man-ager of the San Remo is taking photographs. A young man from the municipal Office of Social Communication is videotaping the entire scene. In recent months, some street workers have filed complaints against the new administration with the Centro Estatal de Derechos Humanos (State Commission for Human Rights, CEDH); local government officials hope the videotaping will protect them from further accusations and future legal troubles. The manager of the San Remo hopes his photographs will provide proof of abuses.

The women rounded up are brought to the Centro Reclusorio para Faltas Administrativas (Jail for Minor Offenses; a *falta administrativa* is similar to a misdemeanor offense, such as public drunkenness or disorderly conduct), where they are registered and put into a holding cell for the evening. We then head back to La Uno to wait for the next raid, which will take place when the San Remo closes and customers and sex workers spill out onto the boulevard to make last-minute arrangements. There is anticipation in the air. I am surprised and ashamed to find that, though I strongly disapprove of the rounding up of street workers, I share this anticipation. It is a powerful force, not unlike what Foucault calls the "pleasure that comes of exercising a power that questions, monitors, watches, spies, searches out."[1] Police and health inspectors coordinate with one another via radio. A broken siren, the sort that plugs into the lighter, sits quietly on the dashboard of the truck I am in. The inspectors were fiddling with it earlier in an effort to repair it. They seem boyishly excited about the raids. One government official, a medical doctor, has dressed in black for the occasion, as though he were a jewel thief or commando. He takes particular pleasure in communicating with his colleagues via walkie-talkie, saying things like "copy" and "over and out." At three o'clock in the morning, we once again speed down the hill to the San Remo.

Despite the lack of a siren, the scene outside the nightclub is loud and chaotic. Women are taken by the arms and walked to city vehicles. No male transvestite prostitutes are arrested on this night. Prospective clients as well as men simply out for the evening stand around watching. Journalists, most likely tipped off by the city in order to have their efforts well publicized, have arrived and are snapping photographs and filming. The women in the back of the pickup trucks are visible and unprotected. They duck their heads and try to cover their faces. One woman walks by me with an inspector holding her arm and a rose in her hand. Were it not for the rest of the police activity around them, it would look as if they were on a date. She asks sadly, "Why me?" A man who is likely a pimp lingers about, asking where the women are being taken.

The disciplining of women who subvert social norms by selling sex in the streets begins not in the holding center but in the pickup truck, where they are filmed, photographed, and exposed, losing the anonymity associated with clandestine informal prostitution. But the raids do more than discipline sex workers—they discipline *all* women: those who would wait at a bus stop at night, those who would go to the San Remo or another nightclub for an evening out, and those who are simply walking by and could be caught up in the chaos. The trucks are now filled with women, who are prevented from jumping out by male health inspectors and police who sit on the edges of the truck bed. One woman mistakes me for a sex worker and asks suspiciously why I am allowed to ride inside the cab of the truck instead of in the back.

Rather than heading directly to the jail, the truck I am in slowly cruises east along Avenida Central; we are looking for female prostitutes and a well-known gay male transvestite prostitute who goes by the name La Aceituna (The Olive). The women must endure being paraded through town as part of their punishment. Inside the cab of the truck, the inspectors scan the dark, quiet streets, on the lookout for more suspected prostitutes. A woman in a black minidress walks quickly into a taqueria; one of the inspectors says, "There's one," but keeps driving. I find my own eyes scanning the streets, searching, and fear that if I see a sex worker, I too will unintentionally cry out, "There's one," so I place a finger across my lips in an effort to keep them closed. Still, my eyes betray me—they dart back and forth, looking. In the back of the truck, a few women are crying. But as we near the cemetery, a woman shouts out, "¡Baja en la parada!" (Getting off at the stop!—how one asks to be let off public transportation), and suddenly everyone, men and women, begins to laugh, their white teeth bright on this near full-moon night. The raids suddenly feel like a strange game and, with our laughter, its rules are temporarily suspended.

As a group, the women do not quietly accept their fate. Rather they shout, negotiate, and complain. On this outing, eighteen women have been rounded up and will be registered and fined. Waiting to be processed, the large group is gathered in a small front room of the Centro Reclusorio. A few women stand at the window, speaking to a small group of men who are on the street outside. These are likely their pimps, who have come to pay their fines and get them released. Not all women have pimps; one woman gives me her address and asks me to go to her house to notify someone there of her situation. By the time I get there, I will find she has already been released. A man outside the window offers to pay my fine. I politely decline his offer, but wonder what I would owe him were I to accept. The group of detained women is loud and angry. Though I don't feel unsafe, an inspector takes my arm and leads me away a few feet, warning that they may hit me. The press arrives and begins to take pictures of the women trapped inside this cramped room. There is nowhere for them to hide. One woman appears very pregnant. Somebody is calling for cold water. Some scream about the presence of the reporters, who are then asked to leave. Others threaten to file a complaint with the local human rights commission.

Many of these women are keenly aware of the law and their rights. Despite this knowledge, the female street workers of Tuxtla are not organized, in part because of the stigma associated with prostitution—few women want to be known as sex work activists. When the English Collective of Prostitutes formed in 1975, they used a nonprostitute housewife as their public spokesperson since few workers could or would publicly declare themselves workers in an illegal and highly stigmatized profession.[2] In addition, many street workers are also unwilling to devote themselves to improving working conditions when they engage in casual prostitution only sporadically. Amalia is typical of many clandestine workers; at twenty-two, she has three children and is separated from her husband. Earnings from her day job as a secretary are not enough to support her family, so she works the nightclubs a few evenings a week after telling her family that she is going out with friends. Women like Amalia who engage in commercial sex informally and secretly are unlikely to commit to a social movement dedicated to sex workers' rights.

Yet female and male prostitutes in Mexico and elsewhere are organizing. Much of this organizing began in the 1980s and 1990s, as the econ-

Figure 8. Women detained inside the Centro Reclusorio talk
to a man on the street. Photo by Patty Kelly.

omy became increasingly globalized, global poverty deepened, and
women were further inserted into the (sexual) marketplace, providing
incentive for action and activism among sex workers.[3] Among the earli-
est prostitutes' movements are San Francisco's Call Off Your Old Tired
Ethics (COYOTE), formed in 1973 by former sex worker Margo St. James,
and the English Collective of Prostitutes, which grew out of the Inter-

national Wages for Housework Campaign in 1975. One of Latin America's oldest prostitute organizations, the Association of Autonomous Female Workers, has been advocating on behalf of sex workers in Ecuador since 1982. From Japan to South Africa to India, sex workers have been organizing around issues of labor, gender, health, and human rights. Women working in La Merced District of Mexico City have formed the Cooperativa de Mujeres Libres (Cooperative of Free Women) to denounce pimping and extortion. In 2004, independent female sex workers met with Mexico City mayor Manuel López Obrador to demand, among other things, a shelter for elderly sex workers; a social services center offering sex workers medical, psychological, and legal care; support for mothers who are the heads of households; and scholarships for their children. Of particular concern to Mexico City's sex workers is the Ley de Cultura Cívica (Civic Culture Law), in effect since August 1, 2004. It is important to note that the law is not the creation of conservative panista ideologues—the center-left PRD currently holds power in Mexico City. Sex workers view the law, under which prostitution is a *falta administrativa,* as the impetus for the increasing and sometimes violent police raids. Workers asked for the repeal of the Ley de Cultura Cívica during their meeting with *perredista* (member of the PRD) mayor Lopez Obrador; the mayor refused, though he did commit to searching for a solution to sex workers' frequent arrests.

The rounding up of sex workers is not unique to Tuxtla or to the conservative PAN. Rather it is a sign of neoliberal times, in which growing urbanization and concerns about social decay, crime, and hygiene have taken center stage in cities throughout the Americas.[4] When efforts to cleanse city streets of elements and people undesirable to urban elites fail, self-imposed spatial segregation is another option for the middle and upper classes. Increasing disparity in wealth breeds class conflict that can result in violence and crime (real and imagined), fear and suspicion. From São Paolo to Los Angeles, the wealthy who wish to remove themselves from what they perceive as a dangerous urban environment are retreating to what Teresa Caldeira calls "fortified enclaves," high-security gated and walled communities that are socially homogenous and therefore considered safe.[5] Whether elites confine themselves in high-security enclaves or cleanse city streets of "marginal" populations and confine them elsewhere, what results is the same: a spatial segregation that produces social segregation, which changes the nature of urban space, city life, and social interaction. What's left is less a city—a vibrant place marked by social diversity—and more an urban center with little contact between heterogeneous populations. Reduced social interaction, identified as loss of "contact" by Samuel Delany in his study of Times Square, has profound implications: when heterogeneous social groups become segregated, invisible to one another, there is little opportunity for understanding, love, or even compassion.[6] When viewed in this light, prostitution becomes an arena where socially heterogeneous groups can share intimate interactions, albeit in a controlled environment under police surveillance.

Back in Tuxtla's Centro Reclusorio, the detainees who have dared to engage in cross-class social interactions by selling sex are processed in a scene that is a highly gendered display of power. Each woman must answer a series of questions, revealing her name, age, address, and place of origin. The woman stands next to a desk as four men, some police, some health inspectors, sit, questioning, listening, and writing. An officer standing behind the desk searches each woman's purse and puts the contents into a clear plastic bag. I ask an inspector if the women usually carry condoms. He tells me that many workers make the client buy them, and many more, he says with a laugh, do it "au natural—it feels better." The detainee then signs a number of forms. Some cannot write, and so they stamp the forms with their thumbprint. The forms are not read to the women, nor are the women given time to read them themselves. An officer then takes the woman's photograph.

As a group, the women verbally and sometimes physically resist, but when they are processed individually, this resistance diminishes. Some refuse to look into the camera. One woman holds her long dark hair across her face as though it were a veil, leaving only her eyes visible. She removes it only to stick out her tongue at the group of police and inspectors. As she goes to sign the documents, laughing, she seats herself on the lap of one of the policemen. An inspector turns to me and says with a laugh, "Affectionate, isn't she?" Next, the detained woman is led to a

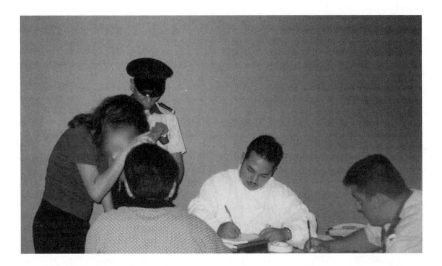

Figure 9. A suspected street prostitute being processed after a raid. Photo by Patty Kelly.

small room to be visually examined by a doctor in order to make sure that she was not bruised or beaten during the course of the raid, another effort by the local government to stave off accusations of human rights violations.[7] The woman is then walked to a common holding cell. Across from this cell is another cell for men, many of whom are drunk, singing songs, and shouting about the prostitutes. The women will pay a fine and be released early in the morning. Much to the dismay of city officials, upon their release most will return to work Tuxtla's streets and clubs.

Through the raids, power is expressed in multiple ways. There is the pure physical force of the male police and health inspectors who chase down and restrain suspected sex workers. There is the institutional power of the state and the law that allows and encourages the legal punishment of informal workers. And there are more subtle forms of power: cultural beliefs and practices that both create and condemn prostitutes, defining the unregulated prostitute as a threat to public health and social order; the power of knowledge that comes with filming, and collecting personal information about detained workers, transforming them from anonymous and clandestine to known and visible.

The raids on clandestine prostitutes and the control of prostitution in general are expressions of power that reinforce already existing inequalities of gender and class. It is working women who are subject to arrest, not their male pimps or their male clients. The raids are a reflection of the moral double standard that punishes poor women but not the men, who, either as pimps or clients, profit from or pay for their labor. Though officials claim, and even believe, that the rounding up of suspected unregistered sex workers is a means of controlling prostitution and securing public health, it is more a carnivalesque display of power. It is a way to harass poor women and men through detention and the gathering of information, and to create the illusion of the control of visible prostitution by the state, more than it is an effective means of protecting the health of Tuxtlecos.

VISIBILITY AND THE ILLUSION OF CONTROL

> Visibility is a trap.
>
> Michel Foucault

Unregulated clandestine prostitution is common in Tuxtla, and while there are no official statistics on the number of unregistered men and women working in the city's sex industry, they certainly outnumber the 140 legal zone workers. According to reports from one health-related nongovernmental organization, on any given night there could be one hundred sex workers in the San Remo alone. City officials maintain that through their raids they are not trying to eradicate prostitution or punish prostitutes, but rather to regulate and control prostitution, in the process making it less visible. As one public health official told me, "It is not that we want to punish them. What we want is to register them." Panista municipal authorities told me over and over again that it was not prostitution that they were against but *unregulated* prostitution. While city officials generally understand that most women work in the industry because of "socioeconomic difficulties," efforts to control and regulate commercial sex not only fail to address class and gender inequality but also reinforce those inequalities.

According to Tuxtla's director of public health, the primary motivation for registering street workers is public health, as the city's concerns about sexually transmitted diseases, especially AIDS, grow. Yet history has shown that programs of raids and forced registration have had little affect on the transmission of sexually transmitted disease. Writing of the origins of the Contagious Disease Acts in Great Britain (passed in 1864, 1866, and 1869 and repealed in 1886), Judith Walkowitz notes that the ostensible "goal" of the acts to control venereal disease in military men was undermined, since they were applied primarily to women suspected of prostitution and never required the medical examination of men.[8] As in Victorian Britain, the raids in Tuxtla do not call for the medical examination of male consumers of commercial sex. Furthermore, they do not (and legally cannot) require the mandatory medical testing and treatment of clandestine sex workers. Like the Contagious Disease Acts, what the raids express is "a new enthusiasm for state intervention into the lives of the poor on medical and sanitary grounds."[9] While municipal officials profess concern for the collective health of society, only a very small fraction of Tuxtla's population (poor and working-class women and male transvestites) are subject to intense medical policing.

The question of visibility is an important one. Official discourse surrounding clandestine prostitution focuses not only on health but also on the spatial regulation of prostitution. In contemporary Tuxtla, city officials approach the perceived problems of urban life (disorder, social hygiene, and epidemic disease) through arrest and confinement. Clandestine prostitutes are swept from the streets, while legal workers remain confined in the Galactic Zone, where they are visible to authorities but invisible to other citizens. I attended many government meetings where city officials again and again referred to clandestine prostitution as "out of context" while discussing the need to place unregulated workers in "appropriate places."

"Clandestine" street workers are not invisible—indeed, they are often highly visible in Tuxtla's public spaces. It is the illegal nature of their work that causes some sex workers to be classified as clandestine. Beyond the scrutiny of municipal authority, they are uncontained, unregistered, and unregulated. Though the visibility of street workers presents a problem for municipal officials and sex workers themselves, it benefits the men and women who work city streets and bars: visibility ensures that prospective clients know where to find them and also protects workers from the abuses they suffer when they work in more discreet locations.

Neoliberalism has not reduced poverty in Mexico. Its devastating impact on rural areas has sent economic refugees fleeing to cities, where they often find employment in the informal sector. The numbers of individuals working in the informal economy as ambulatory vendors and day laborers increased by 40 percent between 2000 and 2003, constituting one-quarter of the Mexican workforce; some researchers suggest the figure is closer to one-half.[10] Visible signs of poverty sometimes take the shape of human beings (street vendors, prostitutes, street children, and the homeless) who inhabit the urban landscape and challenge government officials who proclaim the successes of new economic policy. To many Tuxtlecos and the city government, visible prostitution represents social disorder, chaos, immorality, and potential disease. It is a direct challenge to conceptions of Tuxtla as a modern and economically successful city so unlike the rest of Chiapas. Street prostitution is considered a pollutant; pollution, as Mary Douglas suggests, has much to do with morals.[11] When practiced publicly, prostitution is transformed from a *mal necesario* (necessary evil) into an unclean and dangerous anomaly, into "matter out of place" or, as Douglas says, "dirt": "If we can abstract pathogenicity and hygiene from our notion of dirt, we are left with the old definition of dirt as matter out of place. This is a very suggestive approach. It implies two conditions: a set of ordered relations and a contravention of that order. Dirt, then, is never a unique, isolated event. Where there is dirt, there is a system. Dirt is the by-product of a systemic ordering and classification of matter, in so far as order involves rejecting inappropriate elements."[12]

Visible commercial sex, then, is "dirt," considered unsightly, dangerous, and wrong; it is a challenge to a pattern of "tidily ordered ideas and values" and therefore must by approached through order.[13] The raids against street prostitutes, then, are part of the effort to maintain not simply social order but also symbolic order in the city by maintaining what is "clean" and fitting while segregating or eliminating culturally defined social anomalies.

Each month the Department of Public Health receives numerous complaints from city residents. Among the list of grievances are the clandestine raising and slaughtering of pigs within private homes, street dogs, bats, *aguas negras* (sewage), septic tank problems, public urination outside of a rental hall for parties where there is only one bathroom, the unusual case of a man who defecates in the street in front of his dwelling every morning, and public prostitution.

While complaints regarding pig slaughtering, stray dogs, or aguas negras outnumber those concerning prostitution by two to one, in 1999 the Department of Public Health for the first time created a separate file for complaints about prostitution, reflecting the city's new interest in controlling clandestine sex work. Despite the withdrawal of the state from certain arenas of the economy under neoliberalism, there is continued and even growing state involvement in issues of social hygiene, public order, and sanitation; it is now the state's responsibility to cleanse cityscapes and to lay the groundwork for a social order that will support the new economic order. During my first meeting with Tuxtla's new mayor, he showed me a promotional video that highlighted some of the early successes of his administration. I was most struck by the extensive and repetitive footage of a garbage truck moving through the city at night, clearly a great source of pride for the administration. The mayor told me he was impressed with New York City's Mayor Rudy Giuliani, whose tenure was marked by the cleansing of New York's streets, often at the expense of the poor.

Complainants, both male and female, are typically concerned with visible prostitution in bars, streets, and private homes throughout the city. Complaints are generally not filed by wealthy residents of Tuxtla, who are protected from such scandal. Visible prostitution tends to occur in working-class neighborhoods and in public spaces such as the city's central plaza. In many complaints, prostitution is linked to other forms of perceived delinquency and immorality, such as the illegal sale of alcoholic beverages, noise, fighting, and scandalous behavior that endangers both minors and "public morals." Describing the teenage prostitutes who work in a clandestine bar in her neighborhood, one complainant wrote, "They come out and stand in the doorway almost nude. There are families with boys and girls that play in the street or pass by there and some even stop to look at the *chicas*. And besides, they create an uproar."

There is not one complaint in municipal archives about the Zona Galáctica or the activities there. One doctor told me that, following the opening of the Galáctica, local women would chase down the bus that traveled there, battering its sides with their fists. Today, the zone functions with little notice. In Tuxtla, prostitution is generally accepted (and sometimes valued) as long as it is confined and invisible. This confinement of people and activities deemed immoral helps, in turn, to create a city both "moral" and "modern."

In other parts of Chiapas, particularly to the east and south, where military presence has brought increasing prostitution to indigenous communities, the presence of commercial sex is alarming to many residents, disrupting gender relations and even cultural survival. Young indigenous women and girls witness and sometimes enter into prostitution—something extremely uncommon in most communities before the 1994 uprising. Some indigenous men now frequent the cabarets and brothels that opened or expanded in their communities to serve the many soldiers stationed in Chiapas to quell the Zapatista uprising. Yet unlike in Tuxtla, where citizens have organized few visible challenges to commercial sex, indigenous women have conducted their own actions against commercial sex. One day in January 1997, in Altamirano, a town governed by the PRD but living under the threatening presence of the Mexican army and conservative paramilitary groups, thirty indigenous Tzeltal-speaking Mayan women grew tired of waiting for their husbands to come home. They arrived with gasoline at the local cabaret, where their husbands spent their evenings with the *muchachas* and their *body-shows*. Matches were lit. As the cabaret burned, the women returned to their homes. According to newspaper reports, nobody dared to oppose the women, and the owner of the cabaret did not have them arrested. While the women's actions succeeded only in moving the nightclub farther from the more densely populated areas of Altamirano, the event highlights women's resistance to both machismo in their households and militarization in their community.

In Tuxtla, it is municipal authorities, not civil society, who take direct action against prostitution, and for very different reasons than did the women of Altamirano. But while the city's response to unregulated prostitution is purportedly motivated by concern for public health and social hygiene, the raids against street workers do not serve this purpose. Sex workers detained by local authorities are given neither the information (discussion, pamphlets, etc.) nor the means (condom distribution) to protect themselves. Furthermore, though the authorities aim to register female sex workers, there are few empty rooms in the Galáctica, the city's only legal zone; there are certainly not enough rooms to accommodate the numbers of individuals who work Tuxtla's streets, bars, and hotels.

The raids are, more than anything, an attempt to spatially control the activities of commercial sex workers. "Immoral" populations, lacking economic and political power, have long been confined to peripheral areas; efforts to regulate or eradicate commercial sex are often spatial.[14] In Tuxtla, in attempting to remove prostitution from public view, city officials make invisible the men and women who are "premodern" symbols of social decay and disorder, while making visible the power of the state through a well-publicized campaign against street prostitution. Just as the illusion of intimacy is created in commercial sexual relations, the state, in its effort to control those relations, builds an illusion of stability, progress, and order to counteract the disorder of growing poverty and the visible manifestations of poverty: clandestine prostitution, street vending, homelessness, the growth of shantytowns, and so on. The raids are rites, intended to purify urban space.

Furthermore, the raids are an effective means of gathering information about Tuxtla's population of commercial sex workers in an effort to transform them from casual, part-time sex workers to full-time prostitutes, from "delinquents" laboring in the informal economy to disciplined, regulated workers. For many street workers, selling sex is a casual activity that they may engage in sporadically in order to earn money in times of crisis. Some street workers work nights in order to supplement a low-paying day job or, as in the case of Ernesto, a young male transvestite prostitute, to pay for their education. Others work more frequently, but unlike the women of the zone, who may work from nine o'clock in the morning until the late afternoon, street workers often work shorter shifts. There is, then, a continuum from part- to full-time work. All the zone workers are full-time sex workers. This is less often the case for street workers.

The regulationist system, with its registration, testing, and confinement of women who sell sex, creates prostitutes. Workers in the Galáctica are women who for a variety of reasons have opted for the legal zone and to some degree acknowledge their role as full-time sex workers. In contrast, unregulated workers, particularly those who practice prostitution as a casual activity, need not recognize or concede that they are prostitutes. This creation of prostitutes through regulation and confinement is not a new phenomenon. According to Donna Guy, the regulationist movement in late-nineteenth-century Buenos Aires transformed a casual, informal economic activity into a permanent and highly stigmatized one that did little to actually improve public health or the lives of sex workers.[15] The passage of the Contagious Disease Acts in Great Britain during the same era affected poor women in a similar way, calling for medical and police supervision of workers, which "created an outcast class of 'sexually deviant' females, forcing prostitutes to acknowledge their status as 'public' women and destroying their private associations with the general community of the laboring poor."[16]

TRANSVESTITES

The role that gay male transvestite prostitutes (known as *travestis* or *vestidas*) played during this time of heightened attention to clandestine commercial sex reveals much about cultural views regarding homosexuality and public considerations of what constitutes "acceptable" commercial sex. There is a great variety of male same-sex sexual activity and identity in Mexico.[17] For example, *mayates* have sex with men, sometimes for money, sometimes substituting them for women, but do not identify as gay or display "feminine" characteristics.[18] Nor do the *masajistas* (masseurs) of Mexico City's saunas. There Ana Luisa Liguori and Peter Aggleton found that most young recent arrivals from rural Mexico seeking to earn a living through paid same-sex sexual activity were self-identified heterosexuals.[19] Derogatory words like *joto* and *maricón* are used to describe the gay, feminine, and passive partner in male same-sex activity, while a *homosexual* may be masculine or feminine, passive or active.[20] The *travestis*, generally self-identified gay men who dress as women and work Tuxtla's streets, do not represent the whole of male sexual commerce or activity in Chiapas. Rather, they are a "subculture within a subculture," a small but visible and contested presence in the city.[21]

Travestis are not allowed to work in the Zona Galáctica. According to Juana Ramos, the doctor who performs the medical examinations in the Anti-Venereal Medical Service, sex workers of the Galáctica feel threatened by travestis, who often are considered much more attractive than zone women. "They maintain themselves very well," said the doctor. This characterization of travestis as more attractive than female prostitutes is not uncommon in Mexico. In their study of travestis in Oaxaca City, Michael Higgins and Tanya Coen found that the travestis themselves felt that female sex workers "don't put enough effort into fixing themselves up and creating an attractive look."[22] Many of the transvestite prostitutes better fit the current norms of beauty in Mexico: they are all thin. Sitting in the mayor's office one afternoon, a group of us looked at photographs of a recent raid. One photograph showed a woman with curly shoulder-length hair wearing a flattering dress and light makeup highlighting the delicate features of her fine-boned face. She was beautiful. We all expressed surprise at the fact that she was a travesti and not a biological woman.

Travestis, having crossed so many cultural boundaries (in terms of dress, behavior, and sexual activity and identity), may often engage in sexual activities that female prostitutes will not perform. Their clients are often defined as heterosexual men (many are married with families). Given this fact, it is not surprising that the women of the zone view the travestis as economic competitors who are unwelcome in the Galáctica.[23]

While homosexual activity of all kinds is stigmatized in Mexico, as mentioned earlier a man who engages in anal intercourse with another man as the active, or insertive, partner rather than as the receptive partner may not necessarily be identified as homosexual.[24] In fact, men who have active sex with other men (activos) may be identified as what Héctor Carrillo describes as hombres or hombres normales (men or normal men).[25] By performing the active role, a man adheres to hegemonic norms of male dominance.[26]

Bisexuality is, in some ways, disparaged even more than homosexuality. In his study of sexual desire in Guadalajara, Carrillo found that "both heterosexual and homosexual people were strongly judgmental towards bisexuality."[27] My own conversations with Tuxtlecos support this claim. For example, both Tuxtla's heterosexual director of public health and Roberto, a gay man who does janitorial work in the zone, expressed contempt for bisexuals, suggesting that such people "don't know what they want." Roberto went further, telling me there were two sorts of people to whom he strongly objected: bisexuals and overweight people. Gordos (fat people), because they show a lack of self-discipline, and bisexuals because "they should define who they are, one way or another. . . . If God were to ever punish me," he told me, "he'd make me fall in love with a fat bisexual."

Life for travestis and others who blur social categories and sexual boundaries can be dangerous and outright deadly. Municipal authorities throughout Mexico periodically target transvestites in efforts to socially "cleanse" cityscapes. During the period of increased raids against street workers in Tuxtla, panista authorities in Córdoba, Veracruz, were also targeting sex workers, primarily travestis, claiming street prostitutes were guilty of the crime of "insulting public morals." In 2002, government officials in Tecate, Baja California, amended the city's Police and Good Governance Act, criminalizing and punishing "men who dress as women and move around public places, causing perturbation."[28] That same year, a headline in the Mexico City daily La Jornada posed the question "Vestidas Under House Arrest?" The article that followed detailed the efforts of Tuxtla's new mayor, a panista and the first female to occupy the office of municipal president, to wipe travestis completely from the urban environment. In contrast to her panista predecessors with whom I worked, who framed the prostitution problem as one of public health and order and who were relatively mild in their social conservatism, the administration of Mayor Vicky Rincón proclaimed the arrest of any transvestite in the street at any time to be part of a broader municipal program to halt "moral offenses."[29]

This was not the first time government authorities in Chiapas tried to stop men from publicly dressing as women. In 1990, priista Governor González Garrido also passed a "public health" law banning transvestism. Travestis continued to appear in public but not without repercussions. Between 1991 and 1993, fifteen gay men, mostly travestis, were murdered in the streets of Tuxtla with high-caliber weapons. Though police arrested a suspect who was sentenced to eight years in prison for homicide, many believe the case remains unresolved. According to Amnesty International, Jorge Gamboa Borraz, the special prosecutor assigned to the case, resigned in 1994 because of a "lack of cooperation" from government officials.[30] The seemingly systematic murders were committed with high-caliber weapons of the sort used only by police and the military, leading many Chiapanecos to believe that González Garrido and the state police force were linked to the killings.

The killings of gay men in Tuxtla are not isolated incidents but part of a broader cultural system that cleanses cityscapes and punishes sexual difference.[31] According to the nongovernmental organization Comisión Ciudadana contra Crímenes de Odio por Homofobia (Citizen's Commission against Homophobic Hate Crimes), there are eight homophobic murders a month in Mexico, though the number may be even higher given the likelihood of unreported cases.[32] These murders usually differ in nature from those of prostitute women—they are often more public, more brutal, and carried out by groups of men rather than by individual men. From Chihuahua to Chiapas, the bodies of gay (and often transvestite) men have been found beaten to death, run over, gagged, stabbed, and strangled.

Travestis, as homosexuals and as "nonmen," suffer multiple oppressions; as Mexico City activist Juan Jacobo Hernández says, "They are considered the buffoons of the system, products and accomplices of machismo, who reinforce all the worst feminine stereotypes. Because of that, travestis end up facing a double discrimination."[33] Consider the generally low socioeconomic status of travestis, and their oppression becomes even greater. Yet it must be noted that female sex workers too suffer multiple oppressions: as women, as economically marginalized women, and as stigmatized, economically marginalized women who transgress cultural norms by being sexually available and charging for it. Like travestis, women who work as prostitutes are also targets of discrimination, abuse, and even murder. Yet while statistics on the numbers of women or travestis murdered each month are not difficult to find, there is little information on the numbers of female prostitutes killed each month. Doubtlessly, there are many. This gap in information reveals the social status of such women—their murders have become mundane. While they may make a splash in local papers, these murders are considered unimportant enough that they generally do not elicit as much attention or record keeping from nongovernmental organizations, activists, police, and national media as the travesti murders or the slayings of young women who migrate to Ciudad Juárez to work in maquiladoras.[34]

Unlike the female street workers or the sex workers of the Galáctica, many of the male transvestite prostitutes of Tuxtla are part of an organized social movement, El Círculo Cultural Gay (the Gay Cultural Circle). This stems in part from their conscious shared identity as both transvestites and homosexuals, and in part from the repression they have suffered in the streets of Tuxtla; these men, despite their competition with one another as workers in the sexual marketplace, have created a social network that provides them with support and solidarity as gay men. Tuxtla's Gay Cultural Circle is part of a broader gay rights movement that dates from the late 1970s in Mexico, when homosexuals (mostly men) formed groups with strong politically leftist leanings, like the Homosexual Front for Revolutionary Action (Frente Homosexual de Acción Revolucionaria) and the Lambda Group for Homosexual Liberation (Grupo Lamba de Liberación Homosexual).[35] Today's gay activists focus less on leftist politics than on issues like homophobia and HIV/AIDS, though the members of the Gay Cultural Circle are actively pursuing their economic rights as workers as well.

Following months of raids on clandestine prostitutes, a group of travestis, mostly members of the Gay Cultural Circle, began dialogues with the municipal government regarding homophobia, human rights, and their right to work. On a Tuesday afternoon in June, I left the zone and headed directly to city hall to observe a meeting of the panista bureaucrats and the male transvestite sex workers. Waiting in the hallway on the second floor of the municipal palace, I watch the workers begin to arrive. They greet each other warmly and are clearly a community. Sitting on a couch are a number of travestis. Soon there are nearly two dozen men, the majority dressed as women, lining the halls of the municipal palace. Blonde hair pinned up, with bangs falling on a heavily made-up face. White leggings, white turtleneck covered with a blue, fitted blazer, and white pumps. Pert ponytails, purses, and false breasts. And then there is the lovely transvestite I first saw in the photographs of a raid. Tall and thin, she wears a long slim skirt covered with flowers and a cropped tank top. Her hair is pulled back into a short ponytail to reveal a beautiful face. As they wait, they are passed by other Tuxtlecos who have come to city hall to take care of business. An elderly indigenous woman wrapped in a shawl passes, as do campesino men in sombreros and huaraches, panista functionaries in suits, and administrative workers. Now this, I think to myself, is Chiapas. Not the Chiapas constructed by those scholars who have focused on the Highlands and the selva, but Chiapas as I have known it—an ethnically, sexually, politically, and economically diverse place peopled by Mayans, ladinos, and foreign immigrants; businessmen, bureaucrats, farmers, and politicians; panistas, *perredistas* (members of the center-left PRD), and priistas; men and women, rich and poor, gay and straight, and travestis.

The solidarity that exists among this group of travestis is not shared by their female counterparts in the streets or in the Galáctica. It is a solidarity based less on their identity as sex workers than on their self-identification as members of an oppressed sexual minority. The lack of organization among female prostitutes is in part the result of economic competition, but it is also a consequence of both male domination experienced since childhood and the stigmatization of women who transgress sexual norms. Female sex workers in Tuxtla generally seek total anonymity. Despite the transgressive nature of their work, most female sex workers accept and embrace many of the cultural ideals that shape their lives. Unlike the travestis, who, through their dress, publicly reject social norms by displaying their difference, female sex workers in Tuxtla can and generally do choose to pass for normal. As Liguori and Aggleton note, once men have made the decision to cross-dress, their options for employment are few, reduced to prostitution and vending in tolerance zones like the Galáctica.[36] Passing for normal is not an option for travestis. Though some men on this day were wary of being photographed while in the meeting, the travesti sitting next to me, upon seeing a camera, asked me, "Are they going to take photos?" and proceeded to take down her ponytail, shaking loose a head of enviably thick and wavy black hair. By arriving at city hall during the day in full female dress, the male transvestites willingly gave up anonymity and upset a social and spatial order that segregates "deviance." By meeting with the travestis, the PAN revealed that their reputation for social conservatism is uneven, at best.

The meeting between the panistas and the travestis focused on a single issue: finding a space for the travestis to work where they would not be subject to raids and constant police harassment. Importantly, despite the government's framing of the problem as a public health issue, there was no discussion of health concerns during the meeting. Tuxtla's director of public health stood up and spoke first, saying, "We don't have anything against homosexuality. What we are against is prostitution." He maintained that prostitution should not take place in "public view," and that the men should look for a building where they can put on their *espectáculos* (shows or performances) and do their work, one located far from schools and homes, not right on a main street. The travestis began to describe the places they were considering. They briefly considered one location on the Libramiento Sur, but it "did not suit us because it is too far from the city," and another, close to downtown, which they knew would be a problem because it was too "centrally located."

The travestis are caught in a complex dilemma. Though the city wants them to pursue their economic activities in an area not visible to the public, they fear that being too far from the city center will isolate them from the very members of the public whom they serve and rely on for income.

Furthermore, as one worker noted, being in public view protects street workers from abuse by clients precisely because "it is well lit and centrally located." Pushing their activities into the margins could serve to increase crime and violence against them. One man stood up and asked, "In the meantime, what are we supposed to do? We are going to continue to work, and you are going to continue the raids." The group repeatedly asked for a fifteen-day reprieve from raids in order for workers to earn the money to help rent a building, organize, and "tell clients who are accustomed to having us on Avenida Central" what was going on. They also requested that the city give them financial assistance to open their new venue. "Give the girls a break," they asked. Though city officials refused both of these requests (providing public funds for commercial sex between men, even travestis, is not a possibility, given cultural beliefs about gender and homosexuality), they said they would continue to look at the options for locating the travestis in their own venue.

Following months of raids, street prostitution did become less visible in Tuxtla, but like drug dealing in New York City in the 1990s, it became less visible simply because it moved elsewhere. One evening, after months of raids, I was driving down Avenida Central with a doctor from the Department of Public Health. He said, "Look. No prostitutes." He was right. There were no sex workers at the bus stop or in front of the San Remo nightclub. But as I looked into the car next to us, I saw two young men seated in the front and a man and woman, likely a prostitute and a client, having sex in the back seat.

THREE Inside the Galactic Zone

REGULATING SEX, REGULATING WOMEN

All this garrulous attention which has us in a stew
over sexuality, is it not motivated by one basic
concern: to ensure population, to reproduce labor
capacity, to perpetuate the form of social relations:
in short, to constitute a sexuality that is economically useful and politically conservative?

Michel Foucault

Governor González Garrido's dream was progressing nicely. The state
was investing in regulating and modernizing the sex industry. Other sectors of the economy were also being changed; state supports had been
pulled from small-scale farmers, endangering rural populations. Many
people left for cities elsewhere in Mexico or made the difficult decision to
migrate to the United States. Some, like the Zapatistas, stayed behind,
struggled, and engaged in political protest. During Mexico's prolonged
economic crisis, cities grew, as did the gap between the rich and the poor.
Known as places for the expression and experience of different forms of
sexualities, cities also teemed with new immigrants and the underemployed. But Mexico's gender and sexual hierarchy permeated urban
areas, shaping both prostitution and responses to it. While prostitution
existed before Mexico's turn toward neoliberalism, recent urban popula-

tion growth, international migration, poverty, and underemployment—coupled with the increased wealth of a small minority, social dislocation, new state attention to health and social hygiene, increased and class-differentiated patterns of sexual consumption, and enduring patriarchal sexism—all laid the groundwork for prostitution as it exists in Tuxtla today.

The Galactic Zone is a social experiment with a dual character. It is a place for exploration that defies the social order: women there sell sex to support themselves in defiance of cultural norms that would have them rely on men for support, and gay male vendors wear frilly aprons and earrings and discuss their sexual selves openly. The zone simultaneously defends the entrenched social order: women who sell sex there are stigmatized, while men enact the cultural privileges that allow them to consume commercial sex. Gay men and informal and undocumented workers considered suspect are confined there. Whereas the men and the women who worked the streets became symbols of disorder, the Galáctica, with its regulations, medical service, and location far from the city center, became a source of pride and a symbol of modern progress to government officials. Like prisons and schools—other institutions designed to contain, control, and even redeem—the brothel is a place where individuals' bodies, behaviors, and beliefs are disciplined.[1]

The surveillance and confinement of sex workers in the Galáctica disciplines and individualizes the women, making collective action or revolt challenging. Such disciplinary practices, when combined with the unbridled free market that reigns in the zone, produce a heightened sense of economic competition that further increases isolation and individualization among workers. Municipal police man the entry, providing constant surveillance in the zone. The front gate is the only entrance to and exit from the zone, allowing the movement of both workers and clients to be scrutinized and regulated. The high fence that surrounds the zone serves as a subtle form of coercion: unable to exit without the notice of a police officer, individuals are less likely to misbehave within the confines of the zone. "Discipline," writes Michel Foucault, "increases the forces of the body (in terms of economic utility) and diminishes these same forces (in political terms of obedience)."[2] The body of the regulated prostitute is then, in part (and only in part), Michel Foucault's "docile body";[3] like the soldier, the sex worker is made useful as she sells her services within a modern economy of service and pleasure.

The official document titled "Regulations for the Control and Vigilance of Prostitution in the Municipality of Tuxtla Gutiérrez, Chiapas," which dates to 1993, lays out the basic rules of the Galáctica. Unlike in the streets, bars, massage parlors, and hotels of the city that welcome all prospective workers, city regulations list the multiple prohibitions and myriad requirements for sex workers in the tolerance zone, many of which are arbitrarily enforced. Workers may not practice if they lack the health certificate supplied by the city, if they are pregnant, or if they suffer from contagious diseases. Each worker must be a Mexican citizen over eighteen years of age, "demonstrate that she is able to discern the risks of the activity," be in "full use of mental faculties and not addicted to drugs," and "carry out her activity in the tolerance zone called Zona Galáctica." Nowhere in the regulations is there any reference to the clients of sex workers, whose sexual consumption is unimpeded by municipal rules.

THE RHYTHM OF WORK

Each morning before the zone opens to the public, workers come trickling in. Pepe is often there quite early, pants rolled up, throwing buckets of soapy water across the cement floor of his food stand. Gloria, the eighty-eight-year-old woman who sells basil to ward off "bad vibrations," sits on a planter waiting for clients, long gray braids flowing down the back of her pink dress. Carlos, the young candy vendor, removes his stand from storage and begins to set up outside the main gate, stopping only to wrestle with the teenage Javier, who is readying to open his flavored-ice cart. The workers arrive in small groups, exiting the bus or one of the pirate taxis. Some arrive empty-handed; others arrive with their work clothing, food, or comic books. One woman carries a large basket that holds a head of lettuce and a white rabbit with pink eyes. Some workers will not arrive until long after the zone has opened, and others work only evening hours.

Figure 10. Galactic morning: Gloria, Javier, and Carlos prepare for a day of work. Photo by Patty Kelly.

Work schedules are flexible: workers make their own hours, choose which days to work, and come and go as they please. Sick children, dental appointments, vacations, and illness can all be accommodated. Some women, like Gabriela, work days so they can be at home with their children during the evening. Women who live in the zone may work sporadically throughout the day and evening. Some workers stay home during their menstrual periods, while others do not.[4] Women often take extended leaves, going to visit family in other parts of Mexico or Central America. During Holy Week (the week preceding Easter Sunday, Semana Santa), many give up their rooms, put their belongings into storage and leave Tuxtla for vacation, like other Tuxtlecos.

While landlords may occasionally pressure women to work more so they can collect the rent, independent zone workers experience a great deal of freedom and exercise control over their work. Aside from making their own hours, women decide what prices they will charge (though this is determined by their "value," competition, and the services they provide), what services they will offer, and what clients they will serve. As Gabriela says, "I have the opportunity to say no. Nobody forces me to go with a client if I don't want to." According to Lorena, "There is freedom here. You behave freely. You don't have a yoke around your neck, a boss telling you, 'Get up, get to work, do this, do that.' It's up to you if you work or don't work and how you are going to pay your debts. We aren't working now, and look at me, I'm calm. I know that for an hour or two I'll be charging my batteries, and that then I have to make an effort to pay the rent."

This flexibility of work ultimately depends on one factor: clients. During slow periods, workers may leave the zone, and when there are clients they return. As the women say over and over, "Hay que sacar ventaja." "One must take advantage" of the opportunity to earn money. Few workers take time off during the *quincena* (payday) and the days following it, when clients are more likely to arrive with money to spend. Flor schedules her day off on Wednesdays, a slow day, making sure to be present on busier weekend days. Political demonstrations and marches bring more clients and workers to the zone.

Slow periods are often marked by boredom, anxiety, and increased tensions between workers as competition for clients is heightened. There are days when a worker will see two or three clients at most. The women must wait. They fill this time in a number of ways: eating, socializing, watching television, sleeping, and reading comics.

Because they have no access to cooking facilities, workers depend on the vendors who sell food from one of the food stalls. Many workers are loyal to particular vendors and run long tabs with them. Unpaid tabs may lead to the end of a worker-vendor relationship, as happened with Pepe and Desirée. Pepe says she has owed him one hundred pesos (US$11.75) for more than a month, that she is sneaky, and that he will not serve her. Jealousy and rivalry is common among food vendors, who rely on zone staff and workers more than on clients, who generally buy inexpensive soft drinks and rarely purchase meals. I normally ate at Pepe's, and on the day I bought a shrimp cocktail from Doña Paula, Pepe told me I would surely become ill (I didn't). Workers have little control over what they eat in the zone, as vendors serve only one meal, along with tacos, *tortas*, and quesadillas. One vendor serves only fruit. Coca-Cola is the beverage of choice. Women emerge from their rooms on hot days and scream to Pepe, who is rather deaf and rarely wears his hearing aid, "Pepe! Coca!" He'll go running down to the rooms, toilet paper in hand, as we shout, "No, Pepe, she wants Coca!" only to return laughing when he realizes he misunderstood.

Women eat both at the food stalls and in their rooms, and often eat because of boredom or stress. Many workers are overweight, and for some, like Flor and Bonita, this weight was gained in the zone. Being overweight is not simply an aesthetic issue but also an economic one, now that cultural notions of beauty have changed and many clients prefer thinner women to the fleshier ones. Flor is extremely unhappy about her weight gain, which is substantial. Sitting at Pepe's food stand with Mónica, she lifts her shirt to show us her ample belly and complains that she is "a little fatty." We are soon joined by Bárbara, who asks Pepe what he brought. Steak, he tells her. She eats three steak tacos and asks for two more. As she goes to the counter to pick up her food, Flor and Mónica exchange a look. Neither of them is fond of Bárbara.

Just as prostitution in the zone often cleanses sex of a certain kind of intimacy, so too are conversations cleansed of intimacy and exposure of one's self. Workers pass time socializing and gossiping while waiting for clients, and conversation is often related to work. Despite the fact that their work can generate intense emotions, rarely is conversation intimate and personal. Few women care to appear vulnerable in front of coworkers, and often the women stopped private conversations with me about family or other personal matters when another worker appeared. At Pepe's, Flor and Mónica complain about the lack of business: "Yesterday, nothing, and today, nothing." Their conversation, peppered with words like *verga* (dick) and *puta*, at times becomes so animated that the two women are nearly screaming at the same time in an effort to make themselves heard. They are anxious about the lack of work. Flor speaks of having worked in other places: in Campeche, in Tabasco, and in a bar outside of San Cristóbal called Siberia. She says she would like to go back and earn *buen billete* (good money), since it is slow in the Galáctica, but that her boyfriend, Jacobo, will not let her. Mónica says she would like to go for a week and make some money, bringing the condoms she receives at the zone with her, since they don't give them out at Siberia.

Over in Verónica's room, Lorena lies on the bed wearing a tight yellow minidress, beneath a poster of Leonardo di Caprio and Kate Winslet embracing. Days before, Verónica took down the two larger-than-life portraits of her daughters back in El Salvador. Lorena moans and slowly pours a bottle of water into her open mouth. She is suffering from a hangover, having spent a good deal of money at the Gitano nightclub and having drunk, she says, "four hundred beers." Marco, the ponytailed food vendor, enters the room in a huff. Feigning anger, he complains that *gringos* are *fríos* (frigid), casting me a look. He says he once had a *gringo* lover and was not satisfied with him. He then abruptly leaves. Lorena proclaims she adores me, and I groan and tell her she is as bad as the men, maybe worse. She laughs. Conversations in the zone are like this: lots of complaining, some gossip, and lighthearted banter; a bit of camaraderie but often a certain distance.

Workers spend a great deal of time alone in their small, dark rooms, waiting for clients, watching TV, reading, primping, or in Desirée's case, playing Tetrus on her Gameboy. From time to time, a man will poke his head into a room or enter, since the doors are left open while workers are waiting. Negotiations may begin, or the client may simply look and decide to move on. Sometimes, says Mónica, a client will first tell her she is too fat or too old, and then move on. The waiting causes workers a great deal of anxiety, particularly during the rainy season, when fewer clients arrive. One worker says she needs to talk to a psychologist, as she is very upset, sits in her room, and worries. Mónica says that she was doing fine until she started spending the night in her room at the zone. She has been unable to sleep and says, "It's this place, this room, that makes me sick." Lorena suggests that the workers "are going crazy in their rooms, and the television is no good." She complains of the city's unkept promise to provide the women with a basketball hoop. The women, she says, need to get out, to jump, to scream; the rains, the lack of clients, and being trapped in their rooms is making them crazy.

Figure 11. A room in the Zone. Photo by Patty Kelly.

And so the rhythm of work in the zone is marked less by flow than by discord. The zone promises little in the way of a stable income, as slow periods of little activity are common and produce anxiety. There is a decided lack of privacy, and boredom sometimes gives way to gossip and fighting. Though work hours are flexible, hours spent in the zone are not always productive. Furthermore, though they are regulated by the state, sex workers are considered entrepreneurs and receive none of the benefits associated with being a state employee, such as health benefits and pensions.

Some nations prohibit all forms of payment for sex. Others criminalize certain aspects of prostitution, such as recruiting or living off the income of sex workers, while legalizing the act of prostitution itself. Where prostitution is legal and regulated, women who work as prostitutes are usually subject to mandatory STD testing and other medical controls. Health care for prostitutes often narrowly focuses on the treatment and prevention of sexually transmitted illness. The medical system rarely views the prostitute body as a "whole": health care for sex workers seldom reaches beyond the reproductive system. Sex workers in the licensed brothels of rural Nevada (the only region in the United States with legalized prostitution) must undergo mandatory weekly tests for chlamydia and gonorrhea and monthly tests for syphilis and HIV. Prostitution is also legal and regulated in Greece and Turkey, where women must register as prostitutes and undergo frequent mandatory medical testing. Turkish sex workers whose identification cards reveal they have not been submitting to the required testing may be taken to a state hospital by police, where they will forcibly undergo a gynecological exam. Laws passed in the Netherlands, a place long known for its tolerant attitude toward prostitution, have changed the ways Dutch prostitutes experience sex work. Before the new laws were enacted, brothels were banned there, while prostitutes themselves were not criminalized. Since the October 2000 legalization of commercial sex venues (brothels and bars), sex workers now benefit from certain occupational safety and labor laws, but lose other freedoms when licensed brothel owners require their employees to undergo medical testing. In addition, the new law now prohibits brothel owners from employing immigrants without residency permits. Given that more than two-thirds of all sex workers in the Netherlands today come from other countries (Latin American, eastern European, and African women predominate), making the work of these women illegal isolates them, driving them to work in underground locations where they may be more susceptible to abuses and less likely to seek medical care when needed.[5] Legalizing some forms of sex work while criminalizing others creates a stratified system of prostitution, a hierarchy of despair in which all workers lose.

In Tuxtla, the regulations of the Galactic Zone are shaped by cultural beliefs that designate sex workers as dangerous social elements who must be overseen by the state. The Sanitary Control Card that workers must purchase upon entering the Galáctica not only declares a woman's health status but also is one of the tools used to strip the woman of the anonymity associated with clandestine prostitution. The card declares the woman a prostitute as a matter of public record. Every three months, workers must purchase a new card for fifty pesos (US$5.90). On the back of the card is a calendar in which a zone health inspector marks the date of the worker's periodic gynecological inspections, known as *visitas*, or visits. The worker's photograph, name, room and building number, and landlord's name appear on the front of the card. Attached to the lower left corner of the card is an HIV-negative certificate, which also bears the worker's name and photograph. This certificate too must be purchased.

The worker's weekly visit to the Anti-Venereal Medical Service (SMAV) is the linchpin of medical control. Each morning, with the exception of Sundays and holidays, a group of workers enters the SMAV. They arrive in various states of dress: some ready to work, fully made-up and dressed, others in street clothes or long nightshirts and flip-flops. Those who wear complicated high-heeled shoes that must be buckled or tied often stroll in with them undone, so they may more easily slip them off when their turn comes. They stand with control cards in hand or sit in the white plastic chairs that line the hall leading to the exam room. On the wall, a handwritten note reminds workers to bring their cards.

The weekly vaginal examination includes a swabbing for any abnormalities such as vaginosis, yeast and other types of infections, and gonorrhea. During the exam, other tests may occur too: a worker is tested for syphilis every three months and HIV every four months, and she receives a Pap smear (named after its inventor, George N. Papanicolaou) twice a year. Every two weeks she receives a free box of one hundred condoms.

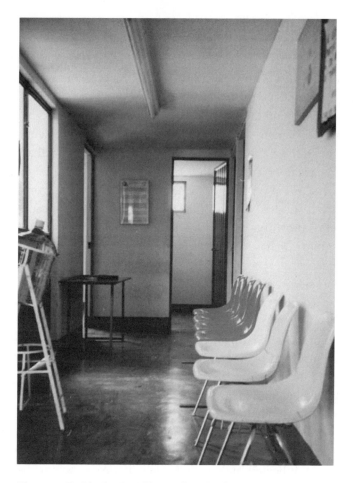

Figure 12. Inside the Anti-Venereal Medical Service. Photo by
Patty Kelly.

Workers themselves are responsible for paying laboratory fees. When a
worker tests positive for a transmissible illness or infection, she is suspended until cured. If she is found to be HIV positive, she is suspended
permanently. A worker who tests positive for illness is said to be *pon-
chada,* or "punctured," a word normally used to refer to flat tires.

The stated goal of the regulationist system of prostitution is to secure public health. Regulating prostitution and subjecting female sex workers to mandatory testing scapegoats prostitutes, implying that they are a major source of disease and that testing them will prevent transmission.[6] Yet the incidence of sexually transmitted diseases in Mexican states and other countries that regulate prostitution is no less than in places that do not.[7] That regulation does not stop sexually transmitted illness should be an old lesson: in revolutionary Mexico City, where prostitution was regulated, it was found in the late 1930s that men who had contracted gonorrhea reportedly did so from both sex workers and from women who were not prostitutes.[8] The regulationist system was abandoned there shortly after.

Furthermore, mandatory HIV testing for prostitutes is not a particularly effective way to prevent the spread of the illness, given that workers in the Galactic Zone may serve up to two hundred clients each month and there is a three- to six-month window between initial infection and seroconversion (the formation of antibodies to the virus that would indicate a positive diagnosis). Also, a narrowly focused prevention effort that targets a small sector of society (like female prostitutes) is unlikely to have a great impact on the transmission of HIV in Mexico or anywhere else.[9] In addition, the incidence of HIV infection in female Mexican prostitutes is relatively low (various studies put the percentage at between 0.5 percent and 2.2 percent).[10] The lack of intravenous drug use among female Mexican sex workers (such drug use is far more common in Europe and the United States) contributes to this relatively low rate of HIV infection.[11] Another factor is that many prostitutes are informed about HIV risk and adopt preventative measures when they can. In fact, sex workers may be more likely to know how to protect themselves than other sexually active populations such as teenage girls engaging in noncommercial sex.[12] Sex workers have a vested interest in staying disease-free that is both personal and professional; as Lorena told me, "It's like a secretary with her typewriter. I've got to keep my machine clean."

Rates of HIV infection have remained somewhat stable in Mexico over the last few years; the overall infection rate among adults ages fifteen to forty-nine is 0.3 percent, with higher rates for men engaging in same-sex sexual relations and for intravenous drug users.[13] In 2004, the

Mexican government reported 93,979 cases of HIV in Mexico, but the UN estimates that the number of cases, reported and unreported, is closer to 160,000.[14] While heterosexual transmission was initially low in Mexico, infection rates are growing among heterosexual women and youth. In Chiapas, the presence of HIV has some unique qualities. There, transmission rates through heterosexual sex are higher than the nation's as a whole; in Chiapas, for every two men who are HIV positive, there is one woman infected; nationwide the ratio is about three men to one woman.[15] In addition, given the state's border status, it experiences flows of people to and from countries like Guatemala and Belize, places with greater rates of poverty and HIV infection; some health researchers suggest that Chiapas may be the gateway for furthering or slowing the spread of HIV in Mexico.[16]

I was told there had never been a case of HIV infection in the Galactic Zone, and though I found it surprising, I naively believed this claim. But during a visit to the zone after my initial year of fieldwork was over, I found out the danger of such naïveté. Just as I had begun to wonder about HIV infection in the zone, so too had panista municipal authorities, who stopped using the medical laboratory that had been testing the blood of zone workers for many years and switched to another. Upon doing so, three women immediately turned up HIV-positive. I don't know who these women were or what happened to them. I fear they may have been women I was close to who just disappeared, like Bárbara. I don't know if they received support, counseling, and drug treatment. While treatment for HIV, including antiretroviral drugs, is available in Mexico, access is uneven: the poor and those without access to social insurance and state programs often have difficulty receiving treatment.[17]

It appears as though the laboratory was either testing the women's blood and not reporting the results or, more likely, not testing the blood at all, though it took their blood and the fees they paid. Panista city officials were dismayed but chalked the matter up to party politics. They took no action against the laboratory owner, whom, they told me with disgust, was a priista with political aspirations. In the zone, neither SMAV staff nor sex workers, who may not have known about the change in laboratories, pursued the issue. It is likely that government officials, zone staff, and sex workers alike felt they would benefit most by keeping news of the presence of HIV in the zone quiet, as public knowledge would result in slowed business and undermine the reputation of both the workers and the municipal government. This incident reveals not only the ineffectiveness of the regulated zone but also the social space occupied by sex workers, who, while deemed necessary to a functioning society, are, sadly, also expendable.

The focus on testing the bodies and controlling the activities of the female sex workers while their male clients remain free from such regulations serves to reinforce and perpetuate already existing and broader patterns of gender inequality in Mexico, where women's sexuality is relatively circumscribed and heterosexual men's is not. The privacy of clients is protected in the zone, while the private lives of "public women" are not. Though some health workers and administrators in the zone do discuss the medical exams as a way to prevent disease in sex workers for the purpose of protecting the workers themselves, the health of clients and society at large is the primary concern. Speaking of the visita, one zone administrator described its purpose as a way to "care for the clients." Glaringly absent from his discussion was the well-being of the women who serve the clients. Clients themselves receive no medical tests or information from SMAV staff regarding the sexual transmission of illness.[18]

The SMAV also offers lectures and workshops, often sponsored by a pharmaceutical company or laboratory, on various topics such as self-esteem, sexually transmitted diseases, chronic gastritis, family planning, miscarriage, domestic violence, and once, human rights.[19] In mid-March, following a lecture attended by only two workers, the SMAV staff informed the women that lectures were now mandatory: if they did not show up, they would be suspended from work for three days. Women were not compensated for the time they spent listening to the lectures, a policy that reflected the paternalism and disregard for workers that permeates many zone policies.

The marginalization of zone workers is evident in their treatment by SMAV staff in other ways too. Sex workers (much like welfare recipients in the United States and other groups in unequal relationships with state agencies) are subject to the controls and arbitrary bureaucratic whims of the SMAV. Though workers generally do not resist the required visita, viewing it as their responsibility, they do privately express many complaints about the functioning of the SMAV. Workers object to the fees they must pay for laboratory tests. Lorena complained to me that, were she to have her Pap smear done in the city center at a public hospital, it would certainly be cheaper than the sixty pesos (US$7.05) she is charged in the Galáctica, but, she says, the SMAV will not accept the results of outside tests. Other workers complain that their bimonthly allotment of condoms is insufficient. Furthermore, the medical and administrative staff often arrives late, leaving sex workers waiting for their medical examinations when they could be elsewhere, in their rooms, working, relaxing, or eating breakfast. And though there is supposed to be a medical doctor available for consultations until the afternoon, Dr. Ramos and her assistants often leave the zone hours earlier. Should a worker have a question or problem, there is no medical staff available to see her.

The decided lack of concern about the well-being of zone workers and the impunity and lack of accountability among zone doctors and lab technicians is reflected in a story told to me by Edith, an SMAV secretary. My relationships with the sex workers caused nearly all the SMAV staff to question both my moral character and good sense. Edith herself had warned me about socializing with sex workers, saying that among their ranks were "criminals and lesbians." But one day Edith came to me at Pepe's food stand, looking worried and angry. She confided that during the visita that morning, as the workers were lining up waiting, it became clear that there was no soap with which to wash the speculums. Though they should be sterilized after each use, the speculums are washed each day with soap in a large tub of water by Olivia, a nurse whose husband is a pirate taxi driver. According to Edith, upon telling the Accountant that there was no soap, and that Olivia would not be washing the speculums, he replied, "So, don't wash them." Ana María, another secretary, claimed it was not part of her job to run errands and refused to go to the city center to buy the soap. Finally Dr. Ramos exclaimed in front of a group of women waiting for their gynecological exams, "I don't care if they are washed or not."[20]

It is during the daily visits that the world and values of the Galáctica workers meet and sometimes clash with those of the SMAV staff. The SMAV building is a site of power and protest; the visita is the occasion on which the constructions of the "moral" and "immoral" city collide, despite municipal efforts to keep the two separate. While the staff views the SMAV as a place of employment that has attached to it certain middle-class behavioral norms, many zone workers, though they earn more than some SMAV staff, have their own standards of acceptable behavior within the brothel that are often quite unlike their standards of behavior outside the zone. These frequently include yelling, laughing, and cursing. Raucous behavior is one way some workers, who are sometimes told to "shut up" by SMAV staff, express their displeasure with the controls of the regulationist system. Many workers speak angrily about the rudeness of the SMAV staff. Dr. Ramos, who performs the examinations during the week, they say, is brusque. She yells at them to relax, and according to Bonita, she is rough during the exam and does not lubricate the speculum. My own experience as a patient of Dr. Ramos confirmed the reports of workers. As I lay on the examining table, she looked me over coldly. Had she a scythe in her hand, I might have mistaken her for Death himself. Many workers prefer to go for their visit on Saturdays, when the soft-spoken and respectful Dr. Felipe Otero, a man, performs the exams. Dr. Otero and Edith, in a rare and even socially dangerous show of support for the well-being of zone women, were unusual among their colleagues in their attitudes toward sex workers.

REDEMPTION AND RESOCIALIZATION

Leaving the Anti-Venereal Medical Service, I am about to head down to the rooms to see who is around. On my way I see Laura, a doctor doing some research in the Galáctica. She stops me and asks, wide-eyed with amazement, "Do you go down there?" It is rare for any of the female staff of the Galáctica to *bajar*, or go down to see, the women in their rooms or pass through the modules. The SMAV is located next to the entrance to the zone—its staff can come and go without ever having to pass by the workers' rooms. On the rare occasion that they must go down, they always travel in large groups, as if engaged in some harrowing alpine expedition in which they ought to be roped together. On this day, I take a curious Laura with me. We stroll along, running into people: Verónica has just returned from El Salvador. We kiss and I welcome her back. Bonita, dressed casually in jeans, a green T-shirt, white sneakers, and eyeglasses, is on her way to the center of town. We chat briefly, and when she leaves, Laura asks, "Is she a professional (*profesionista,* a respectable professional working person)?" and without thinking, I say yes. I soon realize what she means by *professional*—she means not a prostitute. So I say, "Well, she is a professional, but she works here."

Rarely are prostitutes viewed as workers (despite increasing use of the term *trabajadora sexual*), much less as professionals. Rather they are viewed as a deviant population that inspires curiosity, fear, disrespect, and sometimes sympathy. The behavior of prostitute women lies beyond cultural norms, a "scandalous" affront to public morals, as the complaints of Tuxtlecos about clandestine prostitution reveal.

But municipal authorities do not consider sex workers to be beyond redemption. As in revolutionary Mexico City, when the redemption of "fallen women" through vocational training and limited education became the chosen cause of social reformers and the well-to-do, the women of the Galactic Zone are not considered beyond hope or help. But some sex workers are considered better choices for rehabilitation than others. When it was decided that I would be giving English classes to zone workers, I strolled about the modules with Hector, a municipal worker stationed in the zone. We knocked on women's doors to let them know about the classes. Hector carried with him a list detailing who occupied each room and at times led me past a worker's room, claiming she would not be interested because she was too old. Age was considered a major factor in a woman's ability to rehabilitate herself. Women who had been working as prostitutes for years and even decades were believed to have fallen too far to come back to "normal" society.

There is much discussion by zone officials of rehabilitating the women of the Galáctica and preparing them to enter "normal" society. Efforts at rehabilitation include not only the lectures on physical and mental health but also occasional job training workshops in dressmaking and baking.

Zone women understand the realities of the Mexican economy. Viviana took part in cooking courses not because she wished to leave prostitution to work longer hours for lower pay in a bakery but because, in baking, she found a hobby she enjoyed and could share with her family. Vocational training prepares zone women for jobs that pay less than what they earn as sex workers, but which are considered suitable for poor women, and thus it reinforces patterns of gender and class inequality.

Courses sponsored by the Instituto Nacional de Educación para Adultos (National Institute for Adult Education) held in the Galáctica are in some surprising ways a more appropriate response to the marginality of sex workers. Primary and secondary school classes do not give women the means to find well-paid employment elsewhere. Though it is frequently poverty and a lack of education that bring women to the zone, educating sex workers does not necessarily cause women to leave prostitution; sex work offers educated women more money than they can earn using their training because of the nature of the Mexican economy, depressed wages, and their gender. What education does give zone workers is a sense of both community and self-worth. "Profe" (short for *professor*), a retiree well into his seventies, teaches the classes. Profe is a frail man with rheumy eyes and a soothing voice that sounds like bare feet walking across a gravel path. His skin hangs down from his thin face like a hound dog's jowls. When he writes on the blackboard in the makeshift classroom, his hand gently shakes, leaving behind a scrawl that looks more like an echocardiogram than like words. Profe said he was bored staying home and felt there was a need to educate the women of the zone, so that they would not be "marginalized from society." Of his eight full-time and eight drop-in students, he says they are not *malcriadas* (poorly raised). His class runs smoothly, he says, because "I respect them and they respect me."

Though located within the zone, the makeshift classroom sometimes became a space apart, where sex workers who otherwise engaged in an economic and sometimes moral competition against one another became fellow students learning together. During the time set aside for English classes, we often strayed from our lessons, talking about our love lives, our families, and Bill Clinton. (It was the height of the Monica Lewinsky scandal, and many Mexicans found the situation and the American response to it hilarious.) The classroom provided a safe space for workers to show their vulnerabilities and experience their strengths as students.

One-third of zone workers cannot read or write. This is roughly equal to the number of Chiapanecos over the age of fifteen who are illiterate (30 percent) but far greater than the 10 percent of Tuxtlecos over the age of fifteen who cannot read or write.[21] Statistics on literacy illustrate women's precarious position in Mexican society—illiterate women out-number illiterate men in Chiapas by two to one.[22] Some students have learned to read in Profe's class. When Roxana arrived at the zone, she could not read at all. Now she sat in class, struggling but proudly reading aloud: "I . . . live . . . with . . . my husband." Moving on to multiplication, Esperanza looked over Roxana's shoulder and helped her. "There are four sweet rolls in each basket. There are four baskets . . ." The two women counted together, "One, two, three, four." Some students, like Esperanza, have managed to pass through primary school and have advanced into secondary school. One afternoon I accompanied a group of students heading to the offices of the National Institute for Adult Education to pick up the results of their last examinations. Roberto was extremely nervous; he did not pass the previous round of exams and had not been able to move on to secondary school. Evita, as usual, was very quiet. This time we found Roberto had passed his mathematics examination with a high score of eight and would be moving on to secondary school. He was incredulous and exuberant, mouth and eyes open wide, "I can't believe I got an eight! I thought maybe a seven. An eight!" Evita had not passed some of the exams and looked rather dejected. I told her, "Next time," as Esperanza put an arm around her briefly in a surprising and rare show of physical affection between workers.

The programs offered to sex workers shed light on the complex inequalities that exist inside the Galáctica. While prostitute women suffer social stigma because of their profession, as well as gender inequalities, they earn more than many other zone workers. The zone classroom was an open space in the administrative building that also held a small office for the police, two small jail cells, and the office of the Accountant. Often during the English classes I gave, a few police officers would linger silently at the back of the room, listening intently and sometimes taking notes. Prior to my arrival, Profe had been doing his best to teach English, but since he neither spoke nor read the language, the lessons were often riddled with errors. One day after class, Emilio, a tall and very thin police officer in his late twenties approached me, saying politely that he too would like to learn English. But the classes were for the sex workers (though Dr. Ramos and Olivia sometimes attended class, causing some discomfort for both teacher and students). It was feared that the animosity that exists at times between the workers and the police would cause conflict in the classroom. Something about Emilio's desire to learn was heartbreaking. Municipal police officers in Tuxtla earn about thirteen hundred pesos (U.S. $153) every two weeks, while a sex worker can earn twice that amount by serving three to eight clients a day, depending on her price. Emilio's life situation seemed bleaker than that of many zone women. When I returned to the classroom days later, I found that somebody with poor penmanship, likely Emilio, had crookedly scrawled on the blackboard in English a single word: love.

SEIZING THE GALACTIC ZONE

They shut our mouths with a box of condoms.

Desirée

On the fifth day of August in 1996, two years before I arrived, sex workers of the Galactic Zone stopped working. They blocked the access road to the brothel with rocks, a fallen tree, and their bodies, secured the entrance with padlocked chains, locked Auber Domínguez, the zone's administrator, in his office, and raised a red flag as a symbol of their struggle. They were on strike.

As noted in the previous chapter, sex workers across the globe have been organizing since the 1970s. Yet there has been little social protest among the female street workers of Tuxtla, many of whom work sporadically and do not identify as sex workers, and still less among regulated workers of the Galactic Zone, until that warm summer day. What precipitated this collective action was the administration's decision to raise the price of the entry ticket that clients must purchase, from two to three pesos (US$0.24 to US$0.35). Clients had previously paid two pesos to enter the zone and another peso if they wished to use the public toilet. Some workers feared that the price increase would prevent clients from coming to the zone or make it more difficult to negotiate higher payments for their services. As Gabriela remembers, "This is why they got angry. They said that the men weren't going to come, or that there weren't going to be any people, because the entry fee was expensive and they weren't going to want to pay." Striking workers demanded that the administration lower the entry ticket price back to two pesos. Furthermore, they wanted the city to pave and install streetlights along the poorly maintained dirt road leading to the zone; decrease the price of the Sanitary Control Card; relocate the female clandestine prostitutes working the city center to the zone in order to decrease "unfair competition"; and ensure that the workers and their human rights were respected, particularly by municipal police officers in the zone.

The strike of 1996 shows that organized dissent is still possible even in the face of the fierce economic competition and individualization that characterize the entrepreneurial service work done in the zone, and despite the spatial, behavioral, and medical regulation of zone workers. Though criticized for the lack of human actors in his work and his denial of agency, Michel Foucault himself writes, "No matter how terrifying a given system may be, there always remain the possibilities of resistance, disobedience, and oppositional groupings."[23] The strike shows that the prostitute body had not been made fully docile and politically obedient.

But a deeper examination of the strike also reveals the fragmentation among zone workers, even as they engaged in collective political action, a testimony to the politically demobilizing effects of neoliberalism. In her work in La Paz, Bolivia, Linda Farthing found that the character of commerce among informal street vendors bred an atmosphere of competition, individuation, and distrust.[24] The solidarity that had existed among workers when mining, public administration, and factory work had characterized the Bolivian economy, shifted with the growth of the informal sector. Now, instead of workplace trade unionism, there was a struggle at the level of neighborhood and household, a shift from "the search for structural change to single-issue strategies."[25] As among the street vendors of Bolivia, the service sector and the entrepreneurial (though state-regulated) nature of work in the zone shapes prostitutes' views of their fellow workers, who are seen as competitors rather than as allies. The sexual nature of the work furthers this divide, as the economic competition is often accompanied by a moral competition in which workers who will "do anything" out-compete their neighbors and provoke their gossip and anger. In addition, the international character of the zone, where half of the workers are Central American, breeds divisive xenophobia and nationalism that further separates workers.

Some workers felt they were forced to participate in the strike. Gabriela, one of the zone's more politically active workers, recalls that she did not want to participate but wanted to go home and take care of her two daughters. She bargained with strike leaders, saying that she would stay for a while if they would let her go home to her daughters later. Lorena had been at home sick and was surprised to arrive at the zone to find "everything closed and the women piled up there out front." Once she entered the zone, the other workers wouldn't let her leave. Lorena supported the strike but was disturbed to find that many of her colleagues were drinking alcohol. She went to the vendor and demanded that he stop selling alcohol, warning him that under such circumstances the women could take a bottle or a knife and go after the police. The vendor complied with her wishes. Bárbara, known for her individualism and lack of political engagement, remembers:

> I didn't think it [the taking of the zone] was good. They had no reason to go meddling in that, and besides, the majority that were involved in that were foreigners, . . . and the number one person that was there, making this kind of scandal, was Desirée. She was supposedly the leader of all of them and even demanded that we didn't sleep in our rooms, but that we had to sleep outside [near the entrance], on strike. They made us stay out there and stay up late. . . . Everyone had to do it.

Though her account does not ignore the dissent within the ranks of the workers, Desirée, from Guatemala, remembers the event somewhat differently. Of the administrator locked in his office, she laughingly recalls, "He asked me to let him out and I said, "No. Ask Valentina" and she said, "No. Ask so-and-so" and it went on like that. And we didn't let him leave, and we put a lock on the door." Of the night spent outdoors, she told me:

> And we were here all night, with the mattresses out in the center and everything. . . . Some police sat down to eat with us. They supported us, put things in the street so that cars couldn't pass. The owners brought food, coffee, and didn't charge rent. It was really nice because everybody supported us. . . . The Poblanas, since they have pimps, didn't want to support us. . . . I hit one of them.[26] All of us will benefit from this. We were all united. We ate dinner together as a group, talked through the night, and stayed up late.

Following two hours of talks with Samuel Hernández Solís, Tuxtla's director of public health at the time, a partial agreement was reached on August 6, 1996. The entry fee would remain at three pesos, though there would no longer be a charge for clients to use the malodorous public toilet, which was often in a state of disrepair. Furthermore, the funds would be used to improve the road and install streetlights. Municipal authorities promised they would look for a way to decrease the cost of the Sanitary Control Card and agreed that the women could now have their Pap smears done at the public Regional Health Center, free of charge (though this new policy concerning Pap smears was never enacted).

One of the most important achievements of the strike was the fulfillment of the workers' demand that they receive condoms directly from the SMAV rather than having them distributed to clients at the main gate. This method of condom distribution both empowers workers to better negotiate condom use and saves them from having to spend their own money on condoms and charge clients extra for this expenditure. Clients would often throw the condoms out, play with them, or arrive at a worker's room claiming they had not received one. As Gabriela remembers: "I personally talked with Dr. Samuel, and I told him, 'Look, so that we don't have these kinds of problems because of the condom, provide us with the boxes of condoms every fifteen days. . . . Give them to us so that we can protect ourselves and so that there isn't the problem of the client throwing out the condom, because I already have it in my hand and it is put on him.' "

Despite some of the gains of the strike, particularly the empowering of sex workers through condom distribution, many workers viewed the event as a failure. As Desirée recalls, "I went out, and they made a deal when I wasn't there. They shut our mouths with a box of condoms." Lorena also felt that "we sold ourselves for a box of condoms."

Since this time, there has been little collective activity among zone workers, many of whom were disillusioned with the outcome of the strike or continued to resent what they felt was their forced participation. But some workers, like Gabriela, Lorena, and Flor, continued to decry the lack of unity and shared worker consciousness in the zone. Gabriela says she used to be outspoken about workers' rights. She attended health workshops and organizing meetings, and became interested in making the zone a better place to work. She supported many of the activities that the Comitán Center for Health Research undertook there. When a representative arrived and spoke to the women about forming a cooperative in order to purchase necessities such as soap and toilet paper, Gabriela was eager to take action. But nothing came of the plan, because, as Gabriela puts it, "there is no union." Gabriela's outspokenness transformed her not into a leader but into a pariah; during a workshop on sexually transmitted diseases, she actively participated and asked questions. Afterward, other women in attendance spread a rumor that she had an STD. Gabriela has come to believe that activism in the zone would be futile. "It is better I don't go out and get myself involved in problems. I work for me, and the world keeps turning, right? I can't get involved anymore. What I would like more than anything is that this [work] were something different, but it cannot be done. There are many problems here precisely because nobody wants to be ordered around. Nobody wants to have a boss."

Lorena is often one of the first workers to be involved in discussions of work issues with landlords or administrators, who sometimes describe her as "difficult." She is angry about the high rents landlords charge. "The price of gas goes up and our rent goes up five pesos." Landlords, she says, try to quell dissent by "running out" women who protest, particularly Central American women. She is concerned about the elements of control and exploitation present in the zone: domineering police, exploitative landlords, and an administration and medical staff that judge and discipline workers. "They call this place a tolerance zone? What do you think tolerance means? For me, tolerance means to put up with a lot and to permit a lot. But here they permit nothing." Despite her outspoken nature, Lorena, like Gabriela, is disillusioned by the lack of unity in the zone.

> I would like to organize, but that is to complicate matters for no reason. A group came here to speak to us, to talk to us about the union of, one could say, *chicas elegantes* throughout the republic in the Federal District. They already have a union and everything. They are better organized. So they tried to organize us too, but it was like I wanted to cross the river swimming without a life jacket or anything. Just me alone. Nobody got involved to support it. Those that are Mexican are the Poblanas, and the Poblanas are pimped. So for them, cash, cash, cash. It's the only thing that interests them. Their own well-being doesn't interest them—that in the future they are going to be old ladies. And if you want to find out more or get organized, the landlord will squash you, the city will squash you, half the world will squash you in order to put out the blaze you want to ignite. That is why I say it is like complicating matters for no reason.

The individualism among workers in the zone, and their decided lack of shared consciousness as workers, is a common characteristic of the neoliberal era throughout Latin America.[27] Unemployment, underemployment, increasing fragmentation of the labor market, growth in the informal economy, decreases in social spending, and the diminished power of unions, all consequences of recent economic restructuring, have led to the erosion of class identity among many Latin American workers.[28]

Yet along with the potentially politically demobilizing effects of neoliberalism, there are other reasons why few zone women actively pursue better working conditions in the Galáctica. Women come to the zone to earn money, and many are simply unwilling to spend costly time engaging in organizing activities. Furthermore, those who work for pimps are less likely to participate in any form of collective action, since doing so could mean punishment. Other, undocumented workers often fear engaging in political activity because of their precarious immigration status. And rivalries, gossip, and jealousies that arise while laboring under conditions of intense competition keep other workers from organizing. These workers, like Sonia, seek to avoid conflict. Finally, the stigmatized nature of the job also inhibits collective action, as women are unlikely to public identify themselves as prostitutes and take their labor disputes beyond the walls of the Galactic Zone. Yet despite this lack of political engagement, the Galáctica remains in other ways a site of protest.

FOUR Convergence

PANISTAS, PROSTITUTES, AND PEASANTS

The newspaper headlines screamed, "400 Ejidatarios Could Take Over the Zona Galáctica," "They Want to Throw Sex Workers out of the Galáctica," and "Eviction Feared in the Zona Galáctica." It was early spring in 1999, and the people of the ejido Francisco I. Madero were looking to reclaim their land—four hectares located at the end of a lonely dirt road eight kilometers east of the city center of Tuxtla Gutiérrez. The land, unfortunately, was not vacant. Rather, since 1991, the communal ejido land had been known as the Zona Galáctica. The *ejidatarios* (communal landholders) warned that if the city did not return their land by April 2, they would "arrive well armed" and evict the inhabitants of the zone, using force if necessary.

This local land struggle involving the communal landholders of the Francisco I. Madero ejido, the municipal government, and the private landlords and prostitutes of the Zona Galáctica propelled prostitution to the forefront of public discussion and government activity. It was precisely during this period of conflict that the municipal government increased its assault on clandestine prostitution in the city center and stepped up its control in the zone, while also holding press briefings to advertise the "successes" of the Galáctica.

The unfolding land conflict revealed the face of a Mexico that existed before the advent of neoliberal capitalist expansion and pursuit of what is, in some circles, defined as modernity. Even within Tuxtla Gutiérrez, the showcase for modernity in Chiapas, older patterns of thinking and being, embodied by the ejidatarios of Francisco I. Madero, continue to exist and resist. In his book *México Profundo*, anthropologist Guillermo Bonfil Batalla claims there exist two Mexicos, an "imaginary Mexico" and what he refers to as México profundo (deep Mexico).[1] The small minority of the powerful who have pursued Western models of development in Mexico for the past five centuries constitute the "imaginary Mexico," while México profundo, rooted in Mesoamerican culture, resists the "civilizational programs" of "imaginary Mexico." Formed by the majority of the population, México profundo is diverse and includes both indigenous rural populations of subsistence agriculturalists and urban populations who have retained various traits of Mesoamerican civilization. What unifies the people of México profundo is "that they are the bearers of ways of understanding the world and organizing human life that have their origins in Mesoamerican civilization and that have been forged here in Mexico through a long and complicated historical process."[2]

Bonfil Batalla's conceptualization of Mexico, as a dichotomous pair of coexisting civilizations (Western and Mesoamerican) that have not blended to create what calls a "new civilizational plan," may cry out for a more nuanced approach. But his argument nonetheless has particular resonance in Chiapas, where one finds both subsistence and neoliberal economies and, in the case of the Galáctica, both the "modern" brothel of the "imaginary Mexico" and those representatives of Bonfil Batalla's México profundo, the ejidatarios of Francisco I. Madero.

I had come to Tuxtla to work in the "other Chiapas," removed from the land and ethnic conflicts so central to the work of many others in the region, until the ejido conflict, a convergence of local, national, and global politics, exploded in the Galáctica, threatening its very existence. Despite my stubborn intention while in Chiapas to research something, anything, other than agrarian disputes, I found myself studying exactly those as México profundo emerged in the middle of the Zona Galáctica.

Conflicts over land, labor, and ethnicity are central to Mexican history. From the initial arrival of the Spanish to the Zapatista uprising and beyond, subordinated groups within Mexico have long struggled to retain their vision of and their place in the world. In Chiapas, this struggle has been especially pronounced; by the 1990s, various well-established and newer peasant organizations throughout the state, particularly in the east and the north, were actively working to reclaim land.[3] The Zapatista uprising and the actions of the ejidatarios of Francisco I. Madero are part of a broader movement in which oppressed peoples actively respond to increasing local, national, and global political economic trends that would separate them from their lands and lifeways.

LAND DEALS AND PARTY POLITICS

It is a warm May afternoon in the downtown office of the *ejidatarios* of the Francisco I. Madero. The communal landholders are the original owners of the land now occupied by the Zona Galáctica. I am sitting at a table leafing through ejido archives when a tall, imposing, mustachioed man enters the office smoking a cigarette and complaining loudly of a hangover. "It is not a headache," he groans. "It's that everything is spinning." He puts his large hands around my waist and says, "Buenos días, chaparrita" (Good morning, shorty). He is Emilio Santiago Romero, the ejido's brash and charismatic spokesperson. He launches into a tirade about prostitution in Tuxtla, questioning what the city calls "control." A secretary with startling ice-blue eyes brings him coffee, and he gruffly calls to his nephew to bring him the *Cuarto Poder*, one of the city's most widely read daily newspapers. He speaks about how only about 150 women work in the zone, and how there are many more in the streets and bars of

Tuxtla. My mention of clandestine prostitution—that is, unregulated prostitution—makes him laugh incredulously. "How can it be called clandestine? It's public!" He is right. It is regulated prostitution that is clandestine, its practitioners and clients secreted away and made invisible, while what is called clandestine prostitution is often visible to the public. But for the state, the prostitute who is unregistered, unknown, unconfined, and therefore uncontrollable is clandestine.

Santiago Romero smokes cigarettes at an alarming rate, opens the newspaper to the classified section and begins to read aloud from the many advertisements that offer sexual services. He reads, "Bored? Forget stress! How about a relaxing massage? Oriental massages." I try not to giggle at his performance and blink at the smoke searing my eyes. He pauses, looks up from the paper, takes a drag on his cigarette, and, exhaling, says to me, "And I will tell you right now, there is not one Japanese or Chinese girl in there." A group of men enter the office, and I introduce myself as an anthropologist. One man asks if I am studying ruins, but before I can answer, Santiago Romero answers for me, "Yes, the ruins of Mexican society."

The communal landholders of Francisco I. Madero are not morally opposed to prostitution. When I asked their opinion of the women of the zone, the reply was, "They are beautiful." What is at issue is the use of once communally held lands for what the ejidatarios view as a revenue-generating business for the city and the private landlords who rent the rooms to zone workers. Santiago Romero tells me the ejidatarios have donated other parcels of land throughout the city for various "good" (and nonprofit) causes, including the land beneath the Patricia Ecological Park in southeastern Tuxtla.

According to documents from both the municipal and the ejido archives, in September 1991 (during the term of priista Governor González Garrido), four months before the Zona Galáctica was officially inaugurated, a land deal was negotiated between the two parties. Ejidal documents describe the deal as an exchange of services from the priista government for four hectares "that are no longer lands of any use to the Ejidatarios of this place and that will serve for the settlement of marginal groups lacking public services." The ejidatarios of Francisco I. Madero are an urban population who have been partially integrated into the urban economy and no longer wholly depend on agricultural production.[4] Municipal archives explain the deal as an exchange of land for public works projects. In a letter addressed to the priista municipal president, Dr. Enrique Esquinca Méndez, dated September 19, 1991, a state representative of the secretary of agrarian reform approved the exchange, stating that there was "no legal impediment to the donation made by the Ejidal Assembly to the [priista] Municipal Council of this city . . . as long as the ejido receives in exchange multiple collective social benefits in their community, compensating the ejido in a fair and equitable manner." He ends the letter by advising the priista city government to legitimize the land exchange by requesting from the federal secretary of agrarian reform the legal expropriation of the four hectares.

The paperwork was never completed. As the city archives state, "In seven years the land was never formally transferred." The zone operated for seven years, and no efforts were made to reclaim the land until April 18, 1998, when the ejido community registered a claim against the city government (now led by the opposition PAN), demanding restitution for ejido lands, payment for damages to the community, and the payment of all legal expenses. It is perhaps significant that the original land deal was made with priista city and state governments, and that the challenge arose when Tuxtla was run by the opposition PAN, in a weakened position with respect to the priista state and federal governments. A week later, panista municipal president Enoch Araujo Sánchez moved to request that the secretary of agrarian reform expropriate the land in accordance with Article 93 of the Agrarian Law, which states that communal lands may be expropriated for the cause of "public utility." The lands would be used, he claimed, for a public park.

The ejidatarios soon found out about the mayor's efforts, and they too wrote to the secretary of agrarian reform, stating that the land in question was not going to be used for a park as the city claimed, but that it was "already being used for prostitution and strip clubs."[5] Along with the letter, the ejidatarios sent a videotape showing the clients coming and going at the Galactic Zone's main gate. On February 2, 1999, the city's request for expropriation was canceled by the secretary of agrarian reform, who rejected all claims of "public utility." The ejidatarios gave the city until April 2 to give up the Galáctica. By this time Mayor Araujo's term had ended. The new mayor, the panista obstetrician-gynecologist Paco Rojas, inherited the problem when he took office.

A month later the conflict was made public, and it received a great deal of press coverage. Images of machete-wielding campesinos ready to "shed blood" for their cause, and of "women of dubious reputation" who would converge upon Tuxtla's downtown were the Galáctica to close, began to circulate in the press and among the public. Both populations were considered a source of fear and danger; both sex workers and peasant activists presented a problem for the state and society. The new municipal administration was in a difficult situation. Tuxtla's new director of public health, also an obstetrician-gynecologist, could be heard lamenting the previous mayor's decision to lie about the zone, shaking his head and sighing, "He told them it was going to be a park."

This was when the well-publicized raids on street prostitutes began. Yet, as previously described, the raids served more as a display of state power than anything else, since clandestine prostitution did not become more regulated or more sanitary but simply moved to the shadows. The city's new efforts were likely in part a response to the ejidatarios and any sympathizers who would question the city's control of street prostitution and the necessity of the Zona Galáctica.

In the Galáctica, the conflict between the city and the ejidatarios had a ripple effect that laid bare the competing interests and multiple levels of exploitation present in the zone. Sex workers worried first about slowed business and the threatened loss of livelihood and, second, about potential violence. Some believed the state would resolve the problem by cracking down on the ejidatarios, but others disagreed. Doña Paula, a former sex worker who now runs a food stand in the zone, asserted that, in the wake of the EZLN uprising, the campesinos would no longer be as easily subdued as they once were. "Once their eyes have been opened," she said, "it is not so easy to shut them again." Doña Paula's assessment was an astute one; the EZLN uprising generated new and lasting political activism and awareness throughout Mexico.

While the motivations of the Ejidal Assembly (the governing body of the larger community of landholders) and the timing of their protest are open to question, many observers believed their actions were linked to Tuxtla's uneasy place within the Mexican political system. Sex worker Lorena viewed the conflict as "purely political" and asserted that the panista mayor would not receive any support from the priista state government in resolving the conflict. As she and I discussed the situation, Lorena gave me a pop quiz on Mexican politics in order to prove her point. "Who is the president of Mexico?" she asked. "Zedillo." "And what party does he belong to?" "The PRI," I answered. She continued, "And who is the governor of Chiapas?" "Albores." "And what party does he belong to?" "The PRI." "And who is the mayor of Tuxtla?" she asked. I was catching on. "Paco Rojas and he's a panista," I answered. "There you have it," said Lorena, "That's why I said it's purely political."

Hostilities also arose between the sex workers and their landlords, all of whom, except one, had removed the televisions, one of the few means for passing time, from the workers' rooms in order to safeguard their property in case the ejidatarios came. Without television, the women became bored and angry and irritable, like a group of newly sober addicts. Gossip became a primary and destructive way to kill time while waiting for clients. Workers resented the removal of the televisions, especially because their exorbitant room rates had not been lowered to reflect this change. Many women were also angered by the fact that some owners had stopped making mortgage payments to the city and paying the water and electricity bills, while still collecting rents from the women. Some sex workers, like Mónica, threatened to use the media coverage of the ejidatario challenge to publicize the landlords' exploitation of the women through exorbitant rents.[6] Landlord Don Alejandro believed that Mónica would not dare to publicly proclaim herself a sex worker, but she told him, "Oh yes, I will. Besides, Channel Five doesn't reach Veracruz [her home state]." Business was slow as clients, fearing violence or believing the zone was closed, stayed away. Inside the zone, tensions ran high.

Landlords who had bought the buildings from the city were angry that the city had failed to protect their interests. They expressed disbelief that they had been paying all these years for land that was not saleable.

Landlords banded together and wrote collective letters to the priista state governor. Drawing on the standard rhetoric, they begged for his "valuable help" in protecting them from the "campesinos" who would "spill blood" in the Galáctica. They claimed they were the "legitimate owners," and that their work in the zone was "the only source of support for our families."

Workers in the Anti-Venereal Medical Service were also concerned. The extra police protection promised by the city had not yet arrived, and April 2, the deadline the ejidatarios had given the city to vacate the premises, was fast approaching. Edith, a secretary in the SMAV, was angry about what she perceived as the city's lack of concern for zone staff. "It said in the paper they [the ejidatarios] would use violence. . . . There could even be rape!" She looked out the window into the zone's entryway and said bitterly, "They said they were going to send twenty police officers today. And where are they? I don't see them. Yes, look at all the police out there protecting us."

April 2, which was also Good Friday, came and went without incident. As it was a holiday, there was little transportation serving the zone. Clients who had come seeking pleasure were forced to walk the kilometer from the zone to the highway in 104-degree heat. I secured a ride there only by chasing down Jesús, the leader of the pirate taxi drivers, who just happened to be passing by in downtown Tuxtla. Turning onto the Highway of Death from the Pan-American Highway, I saw what looked like a group of seven or eight refugees walking slowly down the dirt road. Some were bare-chested, their shirts wrapped around their heads like turbans. Others had pulled up their shirts to reveal large, sweaty bellies covered with the orange-brown dust kicked up by the rare passing car. Of course, they were not refugees, only clients who, having given up waiting for a pirate taxi, were forced to walk to the main road to wait for a bus to take them back to the city center. As we sped past the men, our loud, rusty, red VW Beetle kicked up dust, again coating the men, who were powerless to protect themselves.

Inside the zone, it was quiet. The medical service and administration buildings appeared empty. Most of the zone staff was off for the day, and others had refused to come because of the land conflict. Extra police had finally arrived and were scattered about, leaning against the walls of the buildings, seeking shade. These men appeared not to be actual police officers but rather day laborers hired to protect the Galáctica. In contrast to the uniform-clad officers, these young men wore street clothes, a blue police-officer style cap, and carried black batons. The "police" leered and halfheartedly called out to passing women; the heat was diminishing their ability to effectively catcall. By noon many of the food vendors and sex workers who had dared to come to work decided to call it a day. Pepe, busy stacking up the white plastic chairs at his food stand, sighed, "There is nothing." I left with Lydia, going back to the small dirt-floor house where she and her sons lived in the city's southern hills. She killed a turkey for me, and we watched on live television the reenactment of the crucifixion of Jesus Christ that takes places annually in Itzapalapa. As the young man playing Jesus was actually nailed to the cross, the voiceover announced, "Ladies and gentlemen, the blood you see is real." Whether because of the holiday or the ejidatarios, there was no business in the zone.

The zone conflict continued to play itself out in the press during the weeks following April 2. The city and the ejidatarios negotiated inter-mittently, but most communication was carried out via press conferences, press releases, and letters. By mid-May, news coverage of the conflict had died down, fears had subsided, and the owners had returned the televi-sions. The ejidatarios had begun to make fewer threats, and there was more discussion of payment and of surveying the land to assess its worth. Meanwhile, the city was taking a different approach, hoping that if it could prove the "public utility" of the Zona Galáctica it would be able to legally expropriate the land.

PROSTITUTION AND THE PUBLIC GOOD

The land dispute and discussions about it by the public, press, ejidatar-ios, and city officials converted an agrarian dispute between the state and communal landholders into a broader public debate about prostitution. During this time, the media played a crucial role in fomenting public anxiety about prostitution, giving undue coverage of a sensationalized nature to the event.[7] Press reports detailed the calamities that would follow if the zone were to be closed: most important, Galáctica prostitutes would come to the city center to work. One of the state's most widely circulated papers published a large photo of a woman seated on a bench in Tuxtla's Central Park and surrounded by three municipal police officers. The caption read: "Fleeing the Galáctica, sex workers in the center of Tuxtla." Once again, visibility and space had become key issues in the discussion of prostitution in the city. Yet the threat of the sex workers of the Galáctica converging on the city center was hardly real.

Few regulated workers would leave the relative safety and legality of the Galáctica to work the streets; they fear the police, as well as abusive and sometimes murderous clients. In addition, in the zone, undocumented immigrant women work fairly freely. On the streets they might be arrested or harassed and face greater risk of deportation. Zone sex workers do not view themselves as lawbreakers but as women who respect the law. One worker even suggested that to work in public view was morally wrong, and that citizens who complained to the city about clandestine prostitution were right. "That's why we have the zone, but they don't want to come here," she said.

Zone women express a great deal of ambivalence about street workers and feel little camaraderie with them as co-workers. When a Galáctica police officer, hoping to get in her good graces, told Sonia that, when his beat was in the city center, he did not like to arrest the prostitutes there, she simply asked, "Why not?" Zone women see the street prostitutes as "unfair competition." Legal workers sometimes envy the independence and economic power of street workers—they are free from "all the rules" and generally charge more and spend less than their legal counterparts. As Flor said, "Why would they want to come here? In the street they charge two hundred pesos (US$23.50). Here twenty (US$2.35), and you have expenses to pay."

Yet despite the ambivalence and occasional overt hostility toward unregulated workers, some zone women do feel for the street workers. Both Doña Paula and Flor spoke of the abuses that the street women suffer during the raids, and how they are sometimes grabbed by the hair by those conducting the raids. Flor has warned her partner, Jacobo, the city employee who participates in the raids, that he had better not be mistreating the women. She identifies with the street workers not as a fellow prostitute but as a woman, saying of the abuse of these women, "I am a whore, but I am also a woman, and as a woman, I say it is wrong." Identifying herself as a whore silences Flor. She speaks out on behalf of other sex workers not as one herself but as a woman. As a "whore," she does not speak or demand to be heard. As a "woman," she does.

Though press reports suggested a disaster of unimaginable proportions would result if the Galáctica were to be closed (as one reporter wrote, the city would be "totally unable" to control prostitution in the streets), it is unlikely legal sex workers would have found their way to the city center to work. Many would probably have done what they do when business slows down in the zone: they would have headed for other legal zones and bars throughout southern Mexico. The photograph of the woman working the city center was not a woman from the Galáctica but one of the many unregulated workers already present there.

Other press reports highlighted not only the presence of prostitutes in the city center but also the potential threat to public health. One reporter suggested that "the prostitutes will surely be launched to the streets of Tuxtla Gutiérrez in search of earning a living, and without medical control, the venereal diseases will truly begin to wreak havoc among them and those who purchase this type of 'service.'" In short, the health and social consequences would be disastrous and the city out of control.

Women, and in particular women who sell sex, are often a source of moral anxiety for the public and a political liability for the state.[8] From Latin America to the United States to Southeast Asia, the "dangerous" sexuality of unregulated prostitutes challenges not only cultural moral codes but also the spatial ordering of society.[9] In Tuxtla, it was believed that the closing of the Galáctica and the supposed increase in public prostitution would be a health and moral nightmare. City officials and ejidatarios alike agreed with the conclusions above and promoted them in the press as much as possible in order to influence popular opinion and advance their own respective causes. The prostitute, a symbol of disorder and disease, became Stanley Cohen's "folk devil," the embodiment of deviance and wrongdoing.[10] In order to safeguard the city, her inevitable presence had to be contained and controlled, and the only way to do this was to settle the land dispute. Prostitutes, regulated and clandestine, became pawns used by both sides in the struggle over the four hectares beneath the Zona Galáctica.

As the current administrator of the zone, the municipal government had the upper hand and cast itself in the role of protector of the city.[11] Once the dispute went public, city officials launched a campaign to prove the public utility of the Zona Galáctica. City propaganda detailing the zone's social benefits appeared in the press, and television news crews were invited on-site to film, much to the dismay of sex workers.

These stories highlighted the "safety" of the zone and the "dangers" of uncontrolled prostitution. The municipal secretary suggested that, if the zone were taken back by the campesinos, this would "increase the possibility of diseases, above all of venereal types, since there could be no strict control of prostitutes." During a press conference, the mayor spoke of the return of prostitution to the city center and the serious social and health consequences of loss of city control over the zone. City officials repeatedly emphasized the importance of having a "controlled population," as in the Galáctica.

Sex with regulated workers, the city implied, would be safer. In the Galáctica, they said, the Anti-Venereal Medical Service distributed thirty thousand condoms a month to workers, who also received medical services and exams. In fact, the actual number of condoms distributed was several thousand fewer. Thirty thousand was the average number of clients who visited the Galáctica each month. The inflated figure of thirty thousand condoms wrongly gave the impression that each sexual act performed in the zone was potentially a "safe" act, thanks to the city's Anti-Venereal Medical Service. Furthermore, as noted earlier, while for some women the biweekly allotment of condoms was sufficient, for others it was not, and they had to either purchase more with their own earnings (in the pharmacy, where condoms were rather costly, or from other workers who had not used their allotment) or have unprotected sex. Municipal functionaries claimed there had not been one case of HIV in the Galáctica, and while they themselves likely believed this claim, as seen in the previous chapter it was probably untrue. City propaganda also emphasized the health-related lectures that sex workers received on topics such as HIV prevention and miscarriage. Before the land dispute became public knowledge, these lectures were voluntarily attended; only afterward, as the city increased control of prostitution both on the streets and in the zone, did the lectures become mandatory.

Appealing to the citizenry, who could be expected to (and often did) complain about public prostitution, city officials claimed that the existence of a regulated tolerance zone decreased not only prostitution but also crime and rape in the city center. Some sex workers themselves felt they were providing a public service by assisting with rape prevention, thus finding a larger purpose and value in their work. This notion of prostitution as a "social service" is not unique. Both Liz Bondi and Alexa Albert, in their studies of Scotland and the United States, respectively, found a similar discourse among the public and sex workers.[12] In the Galáctica, one sex worker spoke of clients who wanted to enact their rape fantasies with the workers, asking the women to leave their undergarments on during intercourse. It is often believed that, if such clients had no opportunity to act out their fantasies with a prostitute, they might actually rape respectable nonprostitute women. This discourse surrounding rape illustrates a widespread cultural belief that men need sex, and that some men may be prone to rape if their "needs" go unmet. Furthermore, the discourse divides women into two camps: those who should be protected from rape ("respectable" middle- and upper-class women), and those who work to protect them—prostitutes and poor women, who by virtue of their class are sexually suspect and not beholden to or capable of the same moral norms as middle- and upper-class women.

Anxiety about rape also has a strong class component. Most, but not all, zone clients tend to come from the laboring classes. In the regulated zone, it is not the sexuality of Tuxtla's upper classes that is being controlled but rather the sexuality of the working poor, which is deemed more dangerous and perhaps even violent. Struggles over sexuality are frequently not simply struggles over sexuality but are also, as in Tuxtla, struggles over class and expressions of economic power and powerless-ness. These discourses about rape and prostitution justify controlling and enclosing the sexuality of poor men acting out "natural" desires and poor "loose" women in a tolerance zone.

Of course, the entire notion that consensual intercourse with a prosti-tute is a substitute for rape is simply wrong—one does not replace the other. Rape is less about sex than it is an expression of power and gender inequality. Susan Brownmiller wrote in her groundbreaking book *Against Our Will*, "Rape is not a crime of irrational, impulsive, uncontrollable lust, but is a deliberate, hostile, violent act of degradation and posses-sion."[13] Access to a consenting partner does not stop rape, and men who rape come from all economic classes. Furthermore, many of the clients do have access to sexual partners: their wives.

Prostitution in Mexico and elsewhere has long been associated with criminal activity and other "deviant" behavior. Implicit in the city's mes-sages about the public utility of the zone was the fear of both sexually transmitted diseases and the moral and social decay associated with the possible presence of prostitutes in the city center (even though sex work-ers had been present there since long before the land dispute). What was born as a land dispute between municipal authorities and communal landholders was transformed into a moral panic fomented by the media and a dispute about public prostitution.

During this time, the figure of the prostitute was, ironically, also con-structed as a source of wealth and order. In their dealings with the media, city officials stressed the fact that the prostitution of zone workers had become entrenched in the local economy, generating a flow of material resources on which families throughout the city relied for economic sur-vival. Though Tuxtla is a large city with a booming service sector, munic-ipal authorities stressed that up to six hundred Tuxtlecos could remain without employment were the Galáctica to close. But only the legal and state-organized nature of zone prostitution made this so; the clandestine prostitution of Tuxtla's streets did not necessitate the same formal exten-sive infrastructure or give rise to the same exchange of material resources. Pervading the legal sex trade were "networks of dependen-cies,"[14] the very existence of which made legal prostitution in Tuxtla something of a family affair. Aside from sex workers, the Galáctica directly employs medical, administrative, security, and janitorial staff. Also earning their living in the zone are taxi and microbus owners, drivers, and fare collectors; the private owners of the módulos; stationary and ambulatory vendors; laundresses; seamstresses; and privately hired janitors. City officials highlighted the possible economic devastation of families dependent on the continued existence of the Galáctica.

MOTHER'S DAY

Perhaps the most fascinating effort to prove the public utility of the Galáctica was the Mother's Day fiesta the local government held for sex workers in the zone on May 26, 1999, some two weeks after Mother's Day. The festivities, to which the press was invited, were a showcase in which the municipal government could display its power to control prostitution and promote the public good. The Mother's Day fiesta gave the city the opportunity to instill middle-class values of femininity, domesticity, and maternity in zone women and provided another chance to prove the social benefits of the Galáctica. As luck (or good planning) would have it, the event also distracted zone workers from the campesinos of Francisco I. Madero, who arrived on that very day with their own surveyor in order to take measurements of the land.

And so, as a small group of ejidatarios walked about the zone dropping plumb lines and drawing tape measures, the city's official marimba band played beneath a tent put up for the occasion. Workers from Desarollo Integral de la Familia, the city's social service organization, were busy warming tamales in Pepe's food stand. Pepe himself had dressed up in dark pants and a fine lacy white shirt for the occasion. Inside the Anti-Venereal Medical Service, dark-skinned, sullen looking cosmetology students of indigenous descent, wearing red-and-white striped uniforms, cut and permed and colored sex workers' hair in an effort to "feminize" them. Psychologists were on hand for counseling. A reggae-rap band from Honduras, replete with female dancers and a male dancing dwarf, took the stage. Functionaries from the panista city government gave speeches to boost sex workers' morale and to remind them of their duties as women. One local male official compared them to Mary Magdalene. Another representative, employing essentialist notions of what a woman is, spoke to them of their roles and obligations as both women and mothers: "As women, we have much to give, and as the mothers of families that we are, we must not forget our function. This *primordial* function is to educate our children, to instill in them a love of life. . . . You must take for always the responsibility that is not simply to give life but also to watch over our children, to give them what they need, which is not just food but also love, guidance, and a good example."

Carefully avoiding any direct reference to their current employment, the speaker added that perhaps in time, with training provided by the city, the women would be able to find other (class and gender appropriate) work, as beauticians or dressmakers. The majority of zone women were mothers, and generally mothers who did not receive male economic support. My own random sampling of workers found that 70 percent were mothers. A random survey conducted by the Comitán Center for Health Research four years earlier, in 1994, found the number to be 100 percent.[15] It is sex work that allows the women to provide economically for their children, and although Lydia admits to having a child who died from neglect, most zone workers take this responsibility fairly seriously. The discrepancy between my statistics and those of the Comitán Center for Health Research may be explained by the possibility that workers lied about having children in order to avoid the greater stigma attached to women who work in the zone only to support themselves. Such women are considered less "needy" and therefore more "indecent" than mothers who work in prostitution to support their children. In using the rhetoric of motherhood to distance themselves from women who would engage in prostitution for reasons other than the support of their children, sex workers reinforce patriarchal beliefs about "good" and "bad" women that so stigmatize them. In a study of urban Oaxaca, one prostitute initially lied to researchers Michael Higgins and Tanya Coen about her status as a mother. When she later revealed the truth, she told them she thought they would be "upset with her" if they knew she had no children.[16] The words of Lorena, speaking of her own children, bear a striking resemblance to those of the city representative: "What a rich life I give them! They live untroubled, yes, untroubled and happy. And before anything else, before I give them luxuries, I give them affection, I give them education. And the tiny bit of wisdom that I have, I instill in them."

A final effort to domesticate the prostitutes during the Mother's Day fiesta came in the form of a gift whose symbolism was clear: the end of the festivities was marked by the distribution of a few condoms and by aprons inscribed: "For Mama, Compassion, Affection, Support. DIF [Desarollo Integral de la Familia] Municipal. Tuxtla Gutiérrez, 1999–2001." Unfortunately, rooms in the zone, where some women live as well as work, lack cooking facilities of any kind.

Sex workers' responses to the day's events were varied. Some were angry they had not been forewarned that clients would not be permitted to enter during the fiesta, and that they, as a result, would be unable to work. As prospective clients clung to the chain-link fence bordering the zone, peering in like uninvited guests, these women fretted about earning the money to pay their daily room fees. Others, like Magda, were excited about both the aprons and the beauticians; by day's end, her frizzy auburn hair was transformed into tight dark curls. Still others viewed the city's efforts with cynicism, commenting on the "cheapness" of the cloth from which the aprons were made. Lorena held hers up and asked sarcastically, "And what are these for? So I can be a great housewife?" Many of the workers who viewed the city's efforts with contempt attended the fiesta only in the hope of gaining an audience with the mayor's wife, who was rumored to be among the city representatives present. These workers were hoping to air their grievances about a dispute that occurred between a sex worker and a municipal police officer in the zone, which ended with the worker's temporary confinement in the city jail. The mayor's wife did not show up.

All told, the fiesta (to which the press was invited) drew attention to the zone women as a controllable population, one that was being cleaned up, groomed, and taught solid family values, and in doing so it rendered the place a training ground for transforming deviant sexualized creatures into good mothers. Recalling that the fiesta coincided with Mexico's leap into neoliberalism, it is interesting to reflect on where the state puts its energies. Clearly, ejidatarios are not considered viable economic actors in a "modern" economy, but regulated sex workers are.

The land dispute between municipal authorities and the ejidatarios, and the social anxiety about prostitution that grew out of the dispute, were the impetus not simply for the Mother's Day fiesta but also for increased control of prostitution both in Tuxtla's streets and within the Zona Galáctica. Writing about heroin use among the working class of Costa Rica in 1929, Steven Palmer suggests that moral panics about particular social issues often "hide more than they reveal; rarely are they about what they seem to be about, and inevitably, they end increasing the power of moral and repressive authorities to intervene in the lives of the less powerful, with the pretext of the urgent necessity to resolve a social crisis."[17] Triggered by the potential closing of the Galáctica, fears about public prostitution and sexually transmitted diseases, and about the social and moral decay of the city, increased municipal control of commercial sex throughout Tuxtla. Yet the ostensible aims of this increased control—the regulation of clandestine prostitutes; the prevention of crime, deviance, and rape in the city center; and the protection of public health—are not achieved through raids on street prostitutes and the corralling of a small group of sex workers into a regulated zone.

Contrary to the discourses that emerged about the public utility of the Galáctica, the presence of a tolerance zone does not guarantee the "safety" of the city. The zone is not a particularly safe place for sex— many workers do not always use condoms, clients often refuse them, and an HIV test administered only three times a year is not a very useful preventative, particularly when a worker may service more than two hundred clients a month. Furthermore, despite the raids against them, clandestine sex workers, both male and female, outnumber regulated workers. Arresting and fining clandestine workers will not prevent them from practicing prostitution, though it will make them more careful about where they practice it. In addition, of the hundreds of women arrested during raids, not one clandestine worker that I am aware of went to work in the regulated zone. Finally, sex crimes are not prevented by providing access to a consenting partner.

The discourses that emerged out of the land dispute are not just about public prostitution and sexually transmitted diseases, or only about class oppression, but also speak to and reinforce deeply held beliefs about gender and sexuality: that sex for men is not a luxury, but a need. Without access to women, they may be prone to rape, especially the working-class men who frequent the inexpensive Galactic Zone. The women available to these men are linked to delinquency, though their only crime is their transgression of moral (and sometimes geographic) borders in order to satisfy their economic need.

Though characterized by austerity measures that reduce state supports for small-scale agriculture and social welfare programs, the economic shifts of neoliberalism do not signal a withdrawal of the state from public life, but rather a shift in arenas of state intervention. The ejido conflict, the Mother's Day fiesta, and the relationship between the entrepreneurial prostitute and the communal ejidatario expose the current priorities of the state: order and modernity. The events of the spring of 1999 also signify a broader global economic shift, in which the service economy is privileged over subsistence agriculture, in which sex workers are considered economically viable while campesinos are not, in which communal lands are taken away in order to make room for greater, more modern forms of exploitation.

FIVE "It Began Innocently"

WOMEN OF THE AMBIENTE

Both in the academy and among sex work activists, many have discussed the necessity and relevance of writing about why women become
prostitutes. Some suggest avoiding the question altogether, that we "take
sex work as a given and start from there." This remark was made in a
New York City feminist bookstore-cafe by the male editor of a collection
of nonfiction essays by sex workers. The audience in attendance was a
mostly white, young, and literary crowd, as were the book's contributors.
In the United States, sex work is sometimes viewed by this same population as a decidedly fashionable way to earn money. It is an alternative
to the nine-to-five grind, a declaration of rebellion against confining
American middle-class cultural values and sexual norms. For the largely
poor, nonwhite, uneducated women laboring in the Galáctica, sex work
is none of these things. Rather it is a highly stigmatized form of employ-

ment and often one of the last options among few undesirable job choices for poor, uneducated workers. As such, sex work and the conditions under which women (and men) enter the ambiente must be interrogated rather than "taken as a given."

Others warn that inquiry should focus not on families of origin but on recent economic histories, and that "data about a woman's home life reveal only the quality of her home life; how a woman spends her earnings explains something about why she became a prostitute."[1] The question of how a sex worker spends her money does reveal a great deal about her entry into prostitution: a woman forced into prostitution generally gives her earnings to a pimp, while a woman working independently to support her children may spend the bulk of her earnings on rent, food, and school supplies. But there are multiple intertwined and overlapping social, political, and cultural factors, along with economic factors, that contribute to a woman's entry into sex work. Class, ethnic, and cultural histories are crucial to understanding sex work, or any work for that matter.

The practice of prostitution is continuously being shaped and reshaped by culture, politics, and society, as are the circumstances under which women enter prostitution. The radical feminist belief that claims *all* prostitution is sexual slavery and a form of gendered violence against women homogenizes and dehistoricizes sex work.[2] Historicizing women's lives and examining the totality of their lived experiences generates a deeper understanding of how the prostitute, as a dehistoricized stereotypical figure, is constructed, and of how commercial sexuality is actually experienced in diverse ways by diverse women through space and time. Upon entering the zone, women craft, embrace, and contest their new identities as prostitutes in a variety of ways.

HOW I CAME TO LIKE THE AMBIENTE

When I asked how she came to work as a prostitute, fifty-year-old Magda, who has done sex work for more than two decades, told me, "Well . . . it began innocently." Many of the workers' stories reflect strongly their recollections that there was a time in their lives when they did not work as prostitutes, that they *became* prostitutes. Furthermore, their stories reveal that, while all workers live within a larger framework of dependency and inequality, each woman enters sex work somewhere along a continuum ranging from choice (often among limited options) to force. The radical feminist perspective, which asserts that prostitution is not work and that women who sell sex do so as a result of male force rather than by choice, not only undermines the rights due to prostitute women as workers but also essentializes female experience, failing to grasp the differences of class and culture that shape women's lives. Researchers and activists who do view prostitution as work argue for the recognition of difference and assert that one must "see how the social context shapes it to make it distinct."[3] For sex workers like Gabriela, the circumstances under which a woman enters sex work determine much about how that woman experiences and practices prostitution.

I arrive at Gabriela's house one evening as the sun is beginning to set and the warm streets of downtown Tuxtla are growing still. It is cooler inside the house, a gentle and welcome breeze blowing the lacy white curtains every now and then. The room that serves as Gabriela's dining room and living room is painted the same antacid pink as many of the rooms back in the zone. In the center of the room is a long table covered with a plastic tablecloth and surrounded by a few plastic chairs. In contrast to the frivolity of the bright pink walls, the room is sparsely furnished, and includes, besides these items, a bookshelf holding a VCR and color television, and a large refrigerator that hums quietly. Ximena, Gabriela's eldest daughter, sits nearby, giggling from time to time while cutting out pictures of famed Mexican military leaders for a school assignment. Without my asking, Gabriela begins to tell me her story.

Thirty-four years old, Gabriela is from the state of Puebla. Speaking of her childhood there, she recalls, "I grew up like a little animal, with nothing more than luck and God." When her mother died, nine-year-old Gabriela stopped attending school in order to work. Her father, sunk in depression, took little responsibility for the care of Gabriela and her four siblings. "He would leave the house around five in the afternoon, and come back around this time, drunk," she remembers, glancing at her watch, which reads 7:30. Sometimes her father would come home with a bag of bread that someone had given him for the children, but more often he returned empty-handed. Gabriela and her siblings would beg, "Please Papi, go to work. Bring us food. We want to eat."

By age twelve, Gabriela, like many other young, poor girls in Latin America, left home to work as a servant. Along with factory workers, domestic servants comprise one of the largest categories of the economically active female workforce in Latin America.[4] They also constitute one of the most exploited and unprotected sectors of the working class,[5] with a work experience marked heavily by female-to-female subordination. "They mistreated me as well," Gabriela tells me, recalling the frequent verbal abuse by her female employer. "And the stove," she says, gesturing with her hand to just above her breasts, "was up to here! I was just a girl." She grew up like an "orphan," without guidance or advice from anyone. When her first period came, she didn't know what it was: "There was nobody to tell me, "You are a señorita now. You need to be more careful; take care of yourself."

An early marriage to an older man provided Gabriela with an escape from her life as a servant and gave her two things she longed for: a house and a family. But marriage also brought a host of new problems; her husband had a violent temper. After enduring nearly a decade of physical and verbal abuse, Gabriela decided to leave him. She saw sex work as a path to freedom from domestic abuse. Without education, a new partner to support her, or resources, and with children to support, it seemed the only way she could escape a decadelong, financially sound but unhappy marriage to a man who beat and humiliated her: "Who is going to accept you into his house with children? Nobody is going to say to you, 'Come, I accept you with the kids and everything.' So, I knew about this, that this work existed. It exists everyplace. If I was going to go, I would put myself to work, even if it was in this, in being a prostitute."

Gabriela left her husband, moved to Tuxtla, where she had an acquaintance, and became a sex worker. She could have worked as a servant, she said, but the earnings from such work would not have enabled her to pay the rent, send her children to school, and feed them properly. As noted earlier, the majority of zone women are the heads of their households.

And, as Gabriela points out, the employment options for women with few skills or little education (servant, cook, factory worker) are poorly paid. In her study of maquiladoras in Ciudad Juárez, Maria Patricia Fernández-Kelly writes "Factory work offers wages and benefits that keep women only a step removed from the circumstances that can lead to prostitution."[6] Working as a servant or cook is often even less lucrative.

The issue of male financial support figures prominently in women's entry into prostitution. Unemployment, low wages, and other structural socioeconomic circumstances imposed by neoliberalism make it increasingly difficult for men to fulfill their culturally prescribed responsibilities within the household. Women must take on increasing economic responsibility, despite cultural attitudes that continue to stigmatize them for working outside the home.[7]

Like Gabriela, many of the women of the Galáctica came to sex work in order to support themselves and often their children while simultaneously freeing themselves from abusive, unreliable, or unhappy relationships. Twenty-one-year-old Juanita moved to Tuxtla from the southern city of Tapachula in order to escape the father of her four-year-old son, who was "abusive and horrible. . . . Every now and then he would insult me, hit me, and I felt desperate. Finally, there came a moment when I woke up and said, 'Why am I putting up with this man?'" Leaving her son in the care of her financially secure mother, Juanita asked the manager of the pharmacy where she was employed to transfer her to their branch in Tuxtla in order to escape the man "who would not leave me in peace." One day while sitting in Tuxtla's Parque Central, a man approached her. "I didn't know he was a *padrote* (pimp)." She agreed that he could bring her to the zone and introduce her to one of the landlords. Following this meeting, they agreed to meet again, and that she would go to the SMAV for her initial medical exam and begin to work. Feeling both fear and shame, Juanita did not meet with the pimp the next day. She said to herself, "Ay, no. How could it be possible that I am going to work in this?" Juanita returned to her job at the pharmacy, but only for a few weeks. Then, she returned to the zone, but alone, of her own volition. Juanita had decided to enter the ambiente. The prospect of earning more money in the zone was appealing to Juanita, who describes herself as a "liberal woman" who prefers the relative cosmopolitanism of Tuxtla to what she identifies as the more conservative ethics of her native Tapachula.

Women who work as sex workers generally do so in a location far from family and friends, which provides them with a degree of anonymity that most workers feel is necessary in order to perform such highly stigmatized labor. Juanita's choice to prostitute was in part precipitated by her move from her home city to Tuxtla, a town where she knew few people and could work in the Galáctica without the fear of encountering a relative or acquaintance. During my time in the zone, I met not one woman who was a native of Tuxtla.

As in Juanita's story, many women enter the ambiente after a second party introduces them to it. This individual is sometimes a padrote or *madrote* (female pimp, or madam), a person who gains financially from a woman's entry into sex work. Other times, the person is simply a relative or acquaintance associated with the ambiente who provides entry into a world of commercial sex that initially seems, for most outsiders, unknown, frightening, and dangerous.

When writing about sex work, *choice* is a pivotal and sometimes contentious word. While radical feminist theorists who oppose sex work in any form argue that there is always some degree of force or coercion present, others have argued that many women enter sex work through a rational, and often economic, decision, and that it is indeed a choice.[8] Women arrive at the zone in a variety of ways for a variety of reasons. For some, the choice is a last resort. Others, like Lorena, more freely choose sex work. Speaking of her previous jobs, Lorena says:

> Oh, I have had a thousand uses. I worked in fishing, I worked sowing melon in the countryside, I worked harvesting, cutting melon, lime, mango. I worked packing, carrying, shipping, picking, and [was a] personnel manager. My strength has always been brute force. Before, I had a good job in a PEMEX [Petroleos Mexicanos, the national oil industry] store in D.F. [Distrito Federal, Federal District of Mexico City]. I was a security guard. I was a bodyguard. My value was in carrying heavy things, before I had my son. The moment they gave me the caesarean, I lost half my life. I couldn't lift the same way, keep up the same rhythm that I had previously. I was practically left, as they say here, an invalid.

Thirty-one years old and gay, Lorena was born and raised in Chiapas. She is different from most zone workers; Lorena has completed high school, along with secretarial studies and three years of university, where she studied psychology. She says her studies were not about earning money but rather a way for her to understand both herself and others, to "give respect to others and see your own value too." But for work, Lorena, a large, imposing woman, has always used her body.

For many lesbian women with female partners, relying on a male lover for economic support is neither a desire nor a possibility. Lesbian sex workers in the Galáctica, while not dependent on or seeking a male partner for economic support, enter into another kind of dependence on men in the form of a client–sex worker relationship. (Of course, this statement is true for all sex workers, both gay and straight.) There are a handful of lesbian women currently working in the zone. Though the work demands sexual intercourse with men, for most workers this act is linked neither to sexual desire nor sexual orientation, though some straight workers did speak to me of their preference for clients they considered handsome. Lorena became a sex worker in 1994, following the complicated birth of her son, which left her weakened, and during a difficult period with her girlfriend, who had been working in the sex industry for more than a decade.

For Lorena, entering sex work was an attempt to resolve problems in her personal life. She had been working in the home, caring for her own child and the two children of her partner. But relying on her lover for financial support was difficult for the independent Lorena, and it made her feel, she says, like a *padrotito* (little pimp). Furthermore, rumors had reached Lorena that her partner was romantically involved with another zone woman; her girlfriend would often arrive home drunk and belligerent. Lorena decided to take control of her crumbling home life and feelings of dependency by becoming a sex worker herself: "So, I said to her, 'Know what? From here on in, I'm no longer going to be the fool. You stay home and I'll go to work. I'll show you what it is to work.' And so, she returned to the house, and I began to work in this."

When describing their entry into the ambiente, sex workers often speak of their immediate and individual circumstances of emotional desperation and/or economic need. Rarely do they reflect on the broader structural constraints faced by poor women throughout the region and their own place within this population. Forty-two-year-old Mónica is a pretty woman, tall, with a movie star smile (thanks in part to the Galáctica's former head doctor–dentist) and short brown hair. Dressed in dark leggings and a loose T-shirt, she looks like a middle-class suburban American housewife. She entered the ambiente a few years after her husband shot and killed himself, leaving twenty-two-year-old Mónica alone with their young daughter. They had been together since Mónica was fourteen. Her in-laws tried to find Mónica work in law enforcement, where her husband had been employed, but could not because she had only a second-grade education. Speaking of her entry into sex work, she says, "Nobody put a knife to me, but always a person is a little bit influenced by bad friendships." She attributes her entry into sex work primarily to another woman who led her into it, along with what she describes as her own "insecurity and lack of education."

While some sex workers, like Mónica, describe those who introduced them to the ambiente in negative terms, others like Alejandra express gratitude. Born in Guatemala, Alejandra left school at a young age, unable to attend classes because of a debilitating respiratory illness. Had she been healthy, she probably still would not have attended school; her father was absent and her mother struggled to feed the family. When Alejandra recovered from her illness, instead of returning to school she began to work. It was not chronic poverty that provoked her initial foray into prostitution but rather an acute financial crisis: Alejandra's mother became gravely ill and was hospitalized; there were no funds to pay for medical care. Desperate, one day Alejandra simply sat down in the street and cried. She was approached by a "very well-dressed" woman who gave her one hundred pesos (US$11.75), told her to pay the hospital and buy herself some food. Stunned by the woman's generosity, Alejandra neglected to ask the woman her name or address so she could repay her. Days later, she began to look for her. She found the woman, who invited her to eat in a restaurant, though shame kept Alejandra from ordering more than a cup of coffee. "It was she who got me into this ambiente," says Alejandra, "She had a noble heart."

Not all persons who recruit or introduce women to the ambiente have such noble intents. Many women speak of deception and trickery when they recall their entry into prostitution. The degree of deception ranges from misleading a woman about the nature of the work or her potential earnings, to the use of physical force. Twenty-year-old Bonita was brought to the Galáctica from El Salvador by an aunt, who also worked there. During her first months, her aunt practically pimped out Bonita, taking much of her money and spending it on herself, until Bonita was able to hide some of it and move out of her aunt's house. It is not unusual for women to enter the ambiente following a relative's entry. Women in the Galáctica are not social isolates without family, as prostitutes are often portrayed; many have a cousin, aunt, or sister who also works in the ambiente.

Magda says her entry, too, into the ambiente involved a degree of deception. Magda used to work in a restaurant near the bus station in the port city of Coatzacoalcos, Veracruz (the same city where Mónica entered the ambiente). Separated from the father of her son, she sent the child to live with his paternal grandmother while Magda worked long shifts waiting tables. Each parent contributed to the maintenance of the child: the father gave money for food (which is fairly inexpensive), while Magda provided funds for more costly items such as clothing.

Though the father of her son had left her, while waiting tables Magda found a new man to support her. He was the captain of a ship based in Isla Mujeres; he treated her respectfully and left generous tips. The two fell in love, and though the captain was married and had two children, he also gave economic support to Magda, whom he convinced to leave her job. "He took me out of work. Bought me everything: a fan, a bed, everything. He gave me my quincena [the formal pay given an employee every fifteen days, and a term also used to refer to the payment that a man gives to his partner] and opened a bank account for me in my own name. When I would go to visit my little son, he would buy me things for him. Very responsible."

Suddenly, without warning, the love letters, telegrams, and money wires stopped arriving. Some twenty years later, the pain is still fresh. Sitting in her room in the Galáctica, Magda begins to cry softly and says,

"By the way, here I still have the telegrams and letters, hidden away as a beautiful memory."

After six months of desperate waiting and hoping, a depressed Magda returned to work at the restaurant, a job she liked and felt she was well-suited for because of what she refers to as her "affectionate disposition." One day she met a female customer who would change her life: "So, this lady came to eat. 'What is there to eat?' she asked. I told her, 'Mi amor, there's some of this and that.' I offered her the best we had. 'Look,' I said, 'this is still warm. It just came out of the kitchen, mi reina [my queen].' I liked to treat people this way, because I knew that, even if it were only twenty or fifty cents, they would leave me a tip."

Like many service workers, Magda knew that by fully and pleasantly fulfilling her role as server, she could earn greater income. The woman asked Magda how much she earned and told her, "Look, where I work, you can earn a lot. And with that friendliness you have, you'll make good money." The woman told her she would be working in a restaurant in Huimanguillo, Tabasco. "I was ignorant and innocent," recalls Magda.

Magda arrived in Tabasco surprised to find that the restaurant was actually a cantina, a men's bar. "I said to the woman, 'Señora, where is the kitchen?' and I looked around for it because she told me the place was a restaurant. I said, 'Ay, ay, Dios. It's a cervecería (beer joint)!' And there I was, carrying my little box of clothing, innocent with my little long-sleeved dress and little collar up to here [she gestures to the middle of her neck]. My clothes, well, they were the clothes of a decent woman, no?" Magda worked that very day as a fichera (a woman paid to serve and drink with clients, who may also have sex with them for money), serving beer to clients who would comment on her appearance and try to touch her. "I would say to them, 'Listen mister, don't you disrespect me!' I didn't know. I didn't know that I was working in the ambiente, and that this was how it was."

Though Magda says that she initially thought the cantina was a horrible place, the promises of financial gain were too good to leave behind; she began waitressing and socializing with the clients, receiving one peso for each beer the clients bought for her. Magda never describes how she made the transition from waitressing to prostituting and never uses the word *prostitution*. When she speaks about her work, she emphasizes the economic rationality of her choice. The owner of the bar provided her with a bed and birth control pills, and the clients paid fifty pesos (US$5.90) for sex.[9] She worked Fridays, Saturdays, and Sundays and would return to Coatzacoalcos during the week. Through sex work, Magda earned in three days what she had earned at the restaurant in a month of fourteen-hour shifts. Though Magda did not ever intend to enter the ambiente, she says, "That's how I came to like the money, and I said to myself, 'Well, I'll stay.' That is how I came to like the ambiente."

While the majority of the approximately 140 women who work in the Galáctica do so independently, nearly a dozen women are *obligadas*, women coerced into prostitution by one of two pimps active in the zone. Women generally become obligadas through deception or physical and verbal abuse by men they presume to be their boyfriends, or by women who promise them employment. The padrote or madrote often takes the woman away from her home and familiar surroundings to a place where she has no social relationships or other support, thereby increasing her vulnerability and their control.

Ramona is a twenty-five-year-old Chiapaneca who has worked in the ambiente for two years. She is a shy and modest woman, petite, with straight brown hair that grazes her shoulders. Ramona grew up in rural Chiapas, where her family had a small farm. She left school in the third grade to help her father and sisters tend the plots of corn and beans they grew both for sale and for subsistence. Reflecting on her childhood, she feels little nostalgia: "I worked hard." She attributes her dark skin to the many years spent working under the hot sun: "This is why I am so dark, because I spent so much time in the fields." It is more likely that Ramona's skin coloring comes from indigenous descent than from a childhood spent toiling under the sun. But in a society and a sexual marketplace that privileges those with lighter skin, her attitude is not surprising.[10]

At fifteen, Ramona left home for Tuxtla. This decision was precipitated in part by a desire to escape her difficult life in rural Chiapas. She got a job as an employee at a small lunch counter, where she worked for eight years earning "good money," until she met and fell in love with Damian. Soon afterward, the two moved to Puebla, where Ramona says they lived "like man and wife," until the day they came to live as pimp and prostitute. While she expected to work in Puebla, she could never have guessed that the man she loved would demand that she work in prostitution. Yet soon after their arrival in Puebla, Damian insisted that Ramona engage in sex work to support them. "I began to understand then that what he wanted was money; before, I didn't know what his intentions were." Ramona refused, thinking of her family—"What would they say?"—and of the physical dangers: "That cannot be, that kind of work is horrible; a person runs the risk of infection." Damian did not accept her refusal: "And he told me I couldn't say no, and that was when he came at me and started to hit me. 'You have to work, you have to do it,' he said. And that's how he did it, hitting me until I said yes."

Pimping is not a purely male phenomenon. As Sonia's story illustrates, women too are involved in the recruitment and exploitation of other women in prostitution. Sonia first came to Chiapas in the late 1980s with her infant son at the invitation of a woman she had met in her home country of El Salvador. The woman told Sonia that she had many businesses in Mexico: stores, clothing boutiques, a restaurant. Then eighteen years old, Sonia was eager to leave urban El Salvador, where she lived in a single room with her son and the father of her child, with whom she sometimes had violent arguments concerning his suspected infidelity. When the woman offered her well-paid work in Mexico, Sonia packed a bit of clothing, some milk and sugar, and soon found herself crossing borders with five other girls, some as young as fourteen. She left not only because of the father of her child but also "because of the poverty I was living in. I wanted to have my own things, so that I would be able to say, 'This is mine.' But when I left my house, I thought there were jobs that paid well here [in Mexico]."

Arriving at Mexico's southern border, the group was surprised to come upon a manned migration checkpoint. Those transporting the girls told them to get out of the vehicle and run. Unable to move quickly with her baby in her arms, Sonia hid herself in the bushes, covering the child's mouth with her hand so his cries would not give them away. When she felt it was safe, she began to walk, crossing the border into Chiapas. Sonia's story—living in poverty, fleeing with her child, hiding from those who might harm them, covering her child's mouth so his cries would not reveal their location—is not unique. Writing of his fieldwork experience in Sonia's home country of El Salvador during the violence of the early 1980s, Philippe Bourgois tells a similar story. While traveling with Salvadoran refugees from Honduras back to El Salvador, the U.S.-supported Salvadoran military began a "search and destroy" operation in the region against civilians and suspected guerillas alike. Amid the explosion of grenades and machine-gun fire, he remembers "at one point being crouched near a woman under cover of some bushes when her baby began to cry. She waved at me with her hand and whispered to me to run away as fast as possible before the government soldiers heard the noise. I obeyed, and sprinting forward I heard machine gun bullets and shrieks all around me. Mothers and infants made up the bulk of the casualties that night."[11] While the organized and widespread state-sponsored political violence in Central America of the 1980s has ended, for poor migrants like Sonia life can be something like war.

Sonia settled in southeastern Chiapas, where she found work as a servant. During this time she encountered the woman who had arranged her journey from El Salvador. The woman claimed that Sonia still owed her for the transportation, and forced her to work in a club in Tapachula by separating her from her son. Of this time, Sonia said, "I had only had one man in my entire life. How was I going to go with others? But that señora said to me, 'If you don't want to come out of your room, girl, you'll lose your son. I'll give him away to who knows who, because you don't want to work for him.' And so I went to work. They put makeup on me. Never before had I worn makeup."

While in the bar, Sonia met a man who saw she was upset. She told him her story and the man, an official with the National Migration Institute (Instituto Nacional de Migración, INM), demanded that the woman let Sonia and her son go, threatening to report her to the police for involvement in human trafficking. Sonia left the bar with her son and returned to work as a servant, until one day, while in the market, she happened upon a girl with whom she had made the journey from El Salvador, and who also had escaped from the señora. The girl said to her, "Listen Sonia, why are you working here as a servant? What you earn here in a month you can earn in a day." And so, Sonia took her son and went to Tuxtla to work in El Cocal and later in the Galáctica.

Workers' stories of becoming prostitutes reveal not only the diversity of this experience but also general underlying structures involved in the process. Women who enter prostitution rarely have the financial support of a male partner. More frequently they have been in unhappy relationships and also bear the economic burden of caring for children who are the products of those relationships. For some women, such as Gabriela, sex work provided a path to freedom from a physically and verbally abusive husband. Gabriela acknowledges that the work is difficult, and because of its stigmatized nature she struggles to maintain her self-esteem, but she also says, "You should have seen me when I first arrived here [in the zone]." Free of her husband, she was transformed from a quiet, deeply depressed person to a sometimes outspoken, confident, and much happier woman. For other women, like Ramona, it was physical and verbal abuse by a partner that forced them into prostitution under circumstances very different from Gabriela's. While Gabriela found some degree of liberation in sex work, Ramona, while working for a pimp, experienced only degradation and exploitation. Through an ethnographic exploration of prostitution, it becomes clear that highly polarized sex-work debates, which pit women's exploitation against women's liberation, simply cannot capture any fundamental truth about the nature of prostitution.

"LOVELY" MEXICANS AND "FILTHY" FOREIGNERS

A small group was gathered in Lorena's room when I arrived. Lorena leaned over, kissed my cheek and asked, "Did you hear there is a United Nations meeting happening today?" Confused, I told her I had not. She began to laugh and said, "Yeah, right here: El Salvador, Mexico, the United States, Guatemala," referring to the national origins of those of us in her room. Happily impressed with her own wit, she continued laughing, disappearing behind the curtain that led to her bathroom.

In the zone, a worker's identity as a Mexican or an *extranjera* (foreigner) is relevant for a number of reasons. First, though not paramount, a foreign woman must take certain precautions in order to keep from being deported. Second, because of their precarious migrant status, this population is more vulnerable to abuses by police, INM officials, landlords, clients, and zone staff. Third, one's identity as a Mexican or foreigner can influence work patterns, habits, and consumption. Finally, one's citizenship becomes an important issue in the economic and quasi-moral competition in which many zone workers find themselves embroiled.

As zone workers are a floating population, it is impossible to cite fixed statistics, but at any given time, anywhere from 30 to 60 percent of the worker population may be foreign born—specifically Central American. The Reglamento de la Zona de Tolerancia (Regulations of the Tolerance Zone) and Mexican law state that registered prostitutes working in regulated zones must be Mexican citizens. However, the law is only sporadically enforced, depending on location, practices of corruption, and current public opinion regarding undocumented migrants.

While Chiapas is one of Mexico's poorest states, many Central Americans find that its urban centers are places where they can settle and sometimes achieve a degree of relative economic stability, or are places to stop and earn money for their trip north to the United States. Immigrant zone workers come primarily from Guatemala, El Salvador, and Honduras, countries with histories of civil war, extreme poverty exacerbated by neoliberal restructuring, and in the case of Honduras, natural disasters such as Hurricane Mitch, which devastated much of the country and hit the poor the hardest.

Immigrant workers, and Guatemalans in particular, have a lengthy history in Chiapas. They have long been employed as workers in large state-funded construction projects and as braceros (rural day laborers) on ranches and coffee plantations. Between 1936 and 1942, when many large ranches in Chiapas began to feel the effects of agrarian reform, Guatemalan laborers became attractive to employers since, as immigrants, they could make no claims on ejidal lands.[12] Furthermore, it was believed that, as undocumented and therefore more vulnerable workers, they would be easier to control and less likely to unionize.[13] Like their Mexican counterparts in the United States, Mexico's immigrant laborers are often subject to exploitation at the hands of employers—they are paid even less than the poorly paid Chiapanecos and often live in miserable conditions. In any given year, there may be up to one hundred thousand undocumented migrants working in agriculture in Mexico.[14] In Tuxtla, much of the labor required by the state-sponsored urban growth that occurred in the early 1980s was performed by Guatemalan workers, many of whom were fleeing not only poverty but also the terror and abuses by a military government that routinely murdered and tortured thousands of its own citizens.

Today, Chiapas continues to be a main crossing point into Mexico for immigrants from Central America and South America, and from as far away as India and China.[15] Today, throughout Mexico, and in particular in Chiapas, undocumented migrants, both those who have settled in Mexico and transmigrants who aspire to reach the United States, are detained and deported. The United States Immigration and Naturalization Service works in conjunction with Mexican authorities to halt prospective migrants to the United States while they are still in Mexico, long before they have reached the northern border.[16] In Chiapas, authorities have initiated plans such as the Seal the Southern Border Program in order to quell this migration. Furthermore, they have increased the presence of INM officials along the southern border. Undocumented migrants are targeted by both the migration authorities and the state criminal justice system, which often intercepts migrants as part of its new Zero Tolerance against Delinquency Program.

Migrating Central Americans are seen as both a source of crime and victims of delinquency in Chiapas, particularly in the southeastern border regions. Newspapers are replete with stories of Central Americans carrying drugs; robbing citizens; and contributing to vice, in particular prostitution; and even contributing to the spread of AIDS. According to newspaper accounts, citizens have asked for increased controls on immigrants, who "have come to take up prostitution and gang activity," "begin to commit crime," "perform dances known as 'table dances,'" and "prostitute in order to save money and then continue their journey to the United States." So synonymous have delinquency and illegal migration become in public discourse that the two are sometimes paired together in newspaper articles. For example, two unrelated incidents were described in a single article in two separate newspapers: "The PGF Intercepts Illegals in Ciudad Hidalgo—Also Secured 970 Grams of Cocaine in Tonalá" and "In Two Separate Police Raids: They Seize Drugs and Detain 12 Illegals." Such discourse demonizes migrants while masking the harsh economic realities that drive them from their home communities.

This same population is also subject to abuses by INM authorities, the polleros who transport them, and those who prey on vulnerable immigrants. In December 2005, the nation's National Human Rights Commission declared that Central American migrants are the victims of persecution and abuse by both the police and the military.[17] While many immigrants suffer rape, robbery, and abuse during their stay in Mexico, other aspiring migrants never complete the journey. They drown crossing the river that separates Guatemala and Chiapas. They fall off the cargo trains they hope will take them north.[18] In one instance, two small boats carrying undocumented migrants crashed off the coast near the Chiapas-Oaxaca border, killing more than thirty people. The Salvadoran Central American Resource Center estimates that between 1998 (following Hurricane Mitch) and 2002, twenty-five thousand Central Americans have disappeared during their migration to the United States.[19] Though there is strong anti-immigrant sentiment in some parts of Chiapas, government authorities such as the Beta Sur Group for the Protection of Immigrants, along with faith-based nongovernmental organizations, have organized to offer support to undocumented Central Americans in Mexico.

That Central American women work in the Galactic Zone is known by the municipal government, and these workers experience minimal intervention by the INM. According to workers, the landlords pay *mordidas* (bribes) to immigration officials who allow the foreign women to work there. This arrangement was briefly in jeopardy during the spring of 1999, when migration agents sought to increase the mordida. During this time there was fearful talk in the zone of a possible visit by migration agents, who ordinarily come only if they are searching for someone in particular or have been ordered there by supervisors. Eventually, owners and agents reached a compromise. During my year in the field, I never saw an INM official in the zone. As Antonio, part of the zone staff, said of the foreign workers, "Migration lets them work without any problems."

Yet bribery offers only partial protection to foreign workers: during the first months of 1999, it was not unusual to see a red Chevy Suburban belonging to the INM parked at the crossroads of the Pan-American Highway and the major road south. Authorities often stopped vehicles entering Tuxtla, intercepting "illegals." Before 1999, this checkpoint would have been of little consequence to zone workers, as it was located about one-quarter mile east of, and past, the zone entrance, in the opposite direction from the city center. But the state government constructed a highway divider replete with struggling palm trees and wilting flowers that made it impossible for anyone to exit the zone, turn left, and head west, directly back to the city center. The divider not only "beautified" the gateway to Tuxtla but also effectively controlled zone traffic, diverting departing traffic toward the busy intersection where the INM's Suburban was parked. Yet zone workers found a way to outwit the migration agents: during the height of immigration worries in the zone, they simply exited the car at the Pan-American Highway, walked across the road and over the divider, and waited on the other side for the driver to return after he had passed the migration checkpoint with an empty taxi. I participated in this subterfuge several times.[20]

Encounters with the red Suburban illustrate both the unevenness of law enforcement in Mexico and the sense of national pride found among many zone workers. When Flor was "caught" by migration, for example, she refused to lie about her origins or her employment; she expresses scorn for those who do. She told the agents, "I am Honduran and I work in the Zona Galáctica." She did lie though when the officer, hoping to exact a payment, asked her how much she earned. She told him, "Oh, I make maybe a hundred pesos a day, enough to pay the rent and food." The officer let her go. Lydia, a Guatemalan worker of Belizean descent, has not had any encounters with migration in Tuxtla but laments that she is unable to make a trip home to visit her family as other women do; because she is black, she is extremely visible. Of the INM she says, "They'd grab me. And with this skin, they'd know immediately."

Foreign-born workers are also vulnerable to exploitation or betrayal by Mexican co-workers and others in the zone who may use their precarious status as undocumented migrants against them. Angry with Roberto, the janitor, following a vicious argument that almost came to blows, Mónica threatened to report him to the INM. Some clients, police, landlords, and co-workers see the "foreigners," as they are called, as individuals easy to exploit or, at the very least, easier to control. But foreign workers are also, as evident in the strike of 1996, more assertive and politically informed than many Mexican zone workers. Despite the difficulties faced by foreign workers, Central American women will continue to cross both physical and moral borders in order to work in the zone, as long as global economic inequalities mean there is less opportunity in their home countries.

There are various reasons why, besides bribery, immigrant women are allowed to work in the zone relatively undisturbed by migration authorities. First, as Tuxtla is in the western half of the state, far from the southeastern border and coastal regions where many immigrants first arrive, there is less of the hostile discourse regarding Central Americans that one finds in border cities like Tapachula. Furthermore, because of the workers' location outside the city and in a regulated zone, municipal and migration agents receive no complaints from city residents, as is common in border cities and towns. The Central American prostitute population in Tuxtla remains for the most part invisible. In addition, as prostitution is a culturally embedded phenomenon viewed by many, including sex workers themselves, as a necessary social service, women working invisibly in the regulated zone, Mexican or not, are subject to less harassment by government authorities than visible street workers.

Pepe, who runs the food stand just inside the zone entrance, has a different view on the matter: Central American zone workers used to suffer more harassment from migration officials, but now, with "free trade," as he put it, they are allowed to work undisturbed. To illustrate his point, he said, "Before, you couldn't even bring an orange into the country, and now, with free trade, you can!"

Some Central American women express longing for their homes and return regularly, often during Holy Week and during the rainy season in August, when business in the zone is slow. Sonia worries aloud about dying in Mexico, far from her family and her native El Salvador. Others have become accustomed to Mexico and the economic benefits it offers. Both Esperanza and Sonia, when traveling to Central America, cross the Suchiate River on small rafts at the border in order to avoid migration agents manning the bridge, who sometimes charge as much as eight hundred pesos (US$94) to let people pass through. While many zone workers are stable, having settled in Tuxtla and having remained in the zone for many years, others view it as a temporary workplace where they can earn money to fund their trip to the United States. Sonia dreams of moving to the United States. She has a cousin in Los Angeles and a brother in Virginia, though she calls the latter a hypocrite. She says her brother, who recently became a Jehovah's Witness, has become self-righteous and selfish. She complains that he continues to neglect their mother in El Salvador and has abandoned a woman pregnant with his child. Olga, from Lima, Peru, is a recent arrival in the zone and intends to make it to the United States, where she has a brother in New Jersey. Juanita has only recently returned to the zone from New York City, where she was visiting a sister. She returned to Mexico, she says, because of the extreme cold and her inability to speak English.

Much of the discussion surrounding possible travels to the United States is positive. Workers tell stories of women who simply perform striptease (without sexual contact) and earn in an hour what they themselves earn in a week. Another worker, under the spell of movies and television programs from the United States that are ubiquitous in Mexico, suggests that everyone in the United States is thin and pretty. Despite my insistence that there really are many overweight and unattractive people in the United States, she will not be dissuaded. The United States represents a promised land to many zone workers, though few actually have the initiative or ability to make the journey.

Other workers have no aspirations to leave Mexico. Elena, a friend of Mónica's, is an argumentative and caustic woman who works in a private brothel in a neighboring town. The mother of two teenage girls, she is a chubby woman with large almond-shaped eyes, full lips, a round nose, pale skin, and a headful of orange curls. Her incessant complaining is somehow endearing. On my birthday a small group of us gathered at

Cahuaré, a local balneario (swimming pool with an outdoor restaurant and music) situated alongside the Grijalva River. Looking at the glasses of water the waiter brought, Elena found a chip in one. "*That,* that to me is an insult." Of the waiter, she exclaimed, "He should be standing right here, ready to serve us. At Quinta Los Robles [a similar establishment just up the road], the service is much better and the food too!" When conversation turned to the subject of the United States, Mónica said she would consider going if she could speak English. Elena, on the other hand, claimed she had no interest in going and spat bitterly, "The American dream. Ha!" punctuating her sentence by contemptuously raising her middle finger toward the blue sky.

A worker's status as Mexican or immigrant influences how she may work and, more important, the ways others perceive her. The presence of Central American workers and what they represent is sometimes hotly contested in the zone. Among many Mexican workers, there is a decidedly anti-immigrant sentiment, fueled in part by a competitive work environment. As workers compete against each other for clients, both Mexican and Central American workers use the banner of national identity in a variety of ways. Gabriela sums up the situation rather well:

> And they [the foreigners] say to us Mexicans, "Ay, those Mexicans. They are foolish, stupid, because they don't know how to get ahead." Because they do services that sometimes we Mexicans don't do. So, they will do it, and for a low price—and that's the worst thing, because, for example, I as a Mexican could do it, but say, for instance, that they charge the minimum. I could charge more, but if all were in agreement on the price, well, there wouldn't be a problem. But if she charges less, it's logical that she is going to win out, even if she just earns the smallest amount, but she does it so that the client doesn't leave. And this is what they do, and that is why there is a great difference between us and them.

Such attitudes toward migrant workers are, of course, not unique to Mexico. As global capitalism causes widespread social and economic dislocation in poor populations, immigrants are increasingly forced to leave their home countries in eastern Europe, Africa, Asia, and Latin America to find work. The pattern of ethnic or racial hatred—engendered by the structural vulnerability of native workers and competition (real or per-ceived) between them and new immigrants—found in the zone repeats itself again and again the world over. Mexicans against Central Ameri-cans in Mexico, Puerto Ricans against newly arrived Mexicans in Spanish Harlem, native Parisians against Polish workers in France—new stories of an old pattern of ethnic resentment and economic competition are being enacted throughout the globe.[21]

Some immigrant workers in the zone work longer hours, charge less money (like many immigrant workers worldwide), and sometimes per-form "special services." Few workers speak in detail of the services they provide to clients, particularly if those services include anal or oral sex, acts that are highly stigmatized. Sometimes, however, workers are able to discern what services are sold by co-workers. If a client arrives at one's door requesting oral sex, is refused, and then enters into negotiations with a neighboring worker and enters her room, it is likely that that worker has agreed to perform special services. Other clues to how a woman works include the sounds of pornography emanating from her room and the nature of her clientele—some regular clients are known for their sexual proclivities, and it is obvious to most zone workers which women they frequent. Yet it is not only the immigrant workers who per-form special services. Furthermore, many immigrant workers will not perform special services. Sonia, from El Salvador, groans with disgust at the thought of engaging in sexual acts other than vaginal intercourse. Such a perspective on sexuality is not uncommon in Central America. In Nicaragua, Roger Lancaster found that many of his informants also expressed revulsion at, and at times ignorance of, certain sexual activi-ties, oral sex in particular. He attributes this revulsion to cultural beliefs regarding the mouth as "a primary route of contamination" and sex as *sucio* (dirty).[22]

The intersection of nationalism, sexuality, and morality within the realm of prostitution is not a new phenomenon. In her study of prosti-tution in Mexico City, Katherine Bliss describes a letter written in 1927 by Mexican prostitutes to President Plutarco Elías Calles, in which they decry, among other things, the foreign prostitutes who provide "inde-cent" services to their clients.[23] Despite the likelihood that special services are performed by some Mexican and foreign workers alike, many Mexican workers, particular older women, denounce what they perceive as the changing nature of sex work and attribute these changes to the presence of foreign workers. According to fifty-year-old Magda, "It's the foreigners that are very, very depraved. They make a disaster of things and are too flamboyant. Like the Paquita La del Barrio [Paquita, the one from the barrio] song says, they do it all, the foreigners. They use pornography. Things that a Mexican woman wouldn't dare do, much less speak of. And they won't just tell you about it. They'll do it with you, and that's the problem of the filthy foreigners and the lovely Mexicanas."[24] Here the Central American prostitute is the "other," not simply a foreigner, but a foreigner who constitutes an immoral, disreputable being who has created a new division of sexual labor in prostitution and whose "immorality" is viewed as unfairly increasing economic competition in the zone.

Nationalist discourse describes Central American workers as both foreign and deviant. One worker even suggests that it is not Central American women who are responsible for demands for special services by clients, but rather gringas, North American and other Western women who come to Mexico and engage in noncommercial sexual relations with Mexican men. Though sex workers may rebuke and refuse clients who ask for special services, these clients generally are not blamed by sex workers for their desire for anal and oral sex. As men, their sexual desires are less circumscribed by cultural beliefs, which stigmatize women for engaging in the very sex acts that men (and women too) may desire.

A few women, like Lorena, a Chiapaneca, reject this constructed division between Mexicans and Central Americans. She asserts it is "foolishness" to refer to the latter as "foreigners." "Before anything else," she says, "they are human beings." Likening the situation of the Central American women in the zone to that of Mexican immigrants in the United States, she says, "It's like a Mexican that leaves for the United States. She automatically knows that, if she screws around, she won't get anywhere. If she goes to the United States, it's because she has the drive to earn money. It's the same with those from Guatemala that come here. They come, but they don't just come to spend the day or whatever. No, they come for the money. Because if they venture to come here, with the risks and the danger and everything, it's for money."

In a comment that echoes Benedict Anderson's notion of imagined communities,[25] Lorena rejects the notion of the nation itself, acknowledging the socially constructed nature of borders and national identities: "I am Guatemalan. Do you know why I am Guatemalan? Because if many of us were familiar with our real history, they would know why I say I am Guatemalan. I am Guatemalan because of the simple fact that, before, the state of Chiapas was part of Guatemala. And not that long ago. A hundred years ago. I don't know. It belonged to Guatemala. So, I carry Guatemalan blood. All Chiapanecos, we are all of Guatemalan blood. So why do we act so innocent?"

Lorena's informed perspective on Central American zone workers is not the norm. More often, they are looked upon as depraved women, unfair competition, and troublemakers. Some Mexican women in the zone view Central American workers as complainers who create undesirable turmoil with both the staff and clients. Indeed, Central American sex workers in the zone are often more politically engaged, likely a product of the recent tumultuous political histories of their home countries. When a representative from a prostitutes' organization in Mexico City came to speak to zone workers about organizing and later invited them to participate in a conference in Mexico City, the only workers who expressed interest, with the exception of Lorena, were immigrant workers. These workers were unable to participate because of their undocumented status.

For their part, many foreign workers view themselves as diligent and goal-oriented, believing their Mexican counterparts to be not only lazy but also weak women unable to assert themselves. Various conversations with workers highlight these beliefs. Flor, from Honduras, says she sometimes thinks of going to the United States; she believes that, as a Honduran, she would be welcomed, because it is well known that Central Americans work hard, while Mexicans, in contrast, do not. Salvadorans also take pride in their work ethic; as Cecilia Menjívar notes, they are sometimes referred to as "the Germans" or "the Japanese" of Central America.[26] Mexican women are perceived both as lacking a strong work ethic and as more willing to tolerate abuse from others, including romantic partners whom they may maintain financially.

Flor has been living for more than a year with Jacobo, the municipal employee who works as a health inspector rounding up street prostitutes. One day, Flor sat at Doña Paula's food stand, sipping soda and looking very sad; she had heard some gossip that Jacobo had been *bajando*, literally "going down," visiting another zone woman in her room and engaging in romantic or sexual relations with her. Some weeks later, she appeared much more animated, saying she had yelled at and hit Jacobo, and their relationship was now much better. "He is being very affectionate," she said, and he had even raised her quincena from six hundred to nine hundred pesos (US$70 to US$106). Her unwillingness to tolerate Jacobo's infidelity and mistreatment, according to Flor, stems from her national origins: "He can't treat me like that; I'm Hondureña." For Desirée, the main difference between foreign and Mexican women is that the former receive money from their romantic partners, while the latter give money. In the zone, a woman is identified and judged by the relationship between her money and her lover.

OBLIGADAS, MANTENIDOS, AND INDEPENDIENTES

In Puebla, Ramona's life with her partner-turned-pimp had grown increasingly difficult. She was working the streets steadily, seeing clients in hotels. She gave all her earnings to Damian, who threatened and hit her but occasionally used the money she earned for him to buy her clothing and new shoes. In those days, Ramona worked without a condom and received no medical care. Following a local social services organization's outreach to sex workers, Ramona told Damian she wanted to see a doctor. His response was, "Ay, what for? Here's your doctor right here. I can examine you whenever you want." On one occasion, when she became infected with a sore on her genitals, Damian applied a liquid to it that burned terribly, and "like that he sent me out to work." Since that time, Ramona says, she has tried to always use a condom. "I said to myself, 'It's my life.' It's not his life. He does nothing more than ask for the cash, but it is my life that is at risk."

Frequent physical abuse by Damian spurred Ramona to demand that he take her back to Chiapas, where she could be closer to her family, who did not know that she had become a sex worker. Reluctant to lose a source of income, Damian brought Ramona to Tuxtla to work in the Galáctica. During this period the pair did not live together, and Ramona began to suspect that he was seeing another woman. What she soon found out was that Damian had four other women working as obligadas for him in the zone.

Ramona recalls the "very painful day" that her relationship with Damian ended. He arrived at Ramona's apartment and accused her of infidelity, an act that would threaten his physical, emotional, and financial control over Ramona. He beat her and tried to strangle her. "He would have preferred I were dead before I left him, he told me. 'Oh God,' I was saying. 'Oh God, protect me,' because before I had believed in God. *Bueno*, I still do, but one quickly forgets when one begins to do this kind of work."

Ramona escaped with her life. Damian retained control of her apartment and took her belongings. Following this event, she moved to the southeastern city of Comitán, where she worked the zone there for a few months, waiting for the air to clear, serving mostly soldiers brought from northern Mexico to participate in the ongoing Zapatista conflict. Ramona eventually returned to the Galáctica, but to work for herself. She says she has little contact with Damian and has told him she will go to the police if he bothers her. For the moment, the four other women who continue to work for him leave her alone, but their anger is clear: "You can see it in their faces. Before, I would come and they would greet me, 'Hi. How are you? How good that you have come.' Very happy. But now they just turn their faces away and that's it. They see that I'm no longer giving [money to Damian], and that's what really gets to them—that I am working and earning my own money, my own money that is mine. That's what bothers them."

In contrast to obligadas, the *independiente* (independent worker) works for herself and may use her earnings to support her children or extended family. Located between these two types of workers are women who have entered the ambiente on their own or by the persuasion of a partner, who is then totally or partially financially maintained by his girlfriend and does not give her a quincena. Such a man is called a *mantenido*, a somewhat disparaging term that refers to a man who, in defiance of cultural expectations, is supported by his female partner.

These categories though, are blurred, subject to change and contestation, and not mutually exclusive. As Ramona's case illustrates, an obligada may become an independent agent. Furthermore, the distinction between a man who is a pimp and a man who simply accepts money from his partner is sometimes unclear. Alicia lives in small home made of concrete blocks located just off the main highway on the road that leads to the zone. Sometimes while riding to the zone in a pirata, we would see her or her boyfriend sitting outside the house. Some workers gossip that her spouse is a mantenido, implying both that he is not fulfilling his duties as a man and that she is foolish. One worker says he is a pimp. Alicia herself would likely deny both accusations. A woman who does have a pimp nearly always refers to him as her boyfriend or spouse (*esposo*). In addition, most workers, whether they are free agents, working to maintain a lover, or more rarely, pimped, experience some aspect of exploitation in work; it is often simply a question of degree and nature.

A woman's status as an obligada affects the way she works and socializes in the zone. Generally, these women must earn a certain amount each day that they will they give to their padrote. Unmet quotas may provoke physical or verbal abuse. In order to avoid these repercussions, an obligada may employ a number of strategies: she may work cheaply to attract many clients or, conversely, negotiate the highest price possible with a client; she may work without a condom, which may attract both those clients who refuse to use them and those clients willing to pay more for this service; she may work long hours; and finally, she may perform special services.

Though it is foreign women who are often suspected of performing special services, women who work obligada are generally of Mexican origin and may at times perform these same acts, thus challenging the division between the "filthy" foreigners and "lovely" Mexicans. Again, we see that this discourse is less about facts and more about an ethnocentric morality fueled by divisive economic competition among working-class women.

Obligadas tend to engage less in social interaction with independent zone workers and may go to great lengths to protect their padrote and his economic well-being.[27] They are often seen in one another's company, which allows the women to effectively police one another for the benefit of their padrote. When the independent workers Gabriela and Flor counseled one obligada to leave her pimp, they were threatened by the other women working for him, who said they would inform the padrote that they had been "advising" her. Gabriela's boyfriend, Miguel, a municipal police officer who used to work at the zone's front gate, recalled with dismay how, after he had arrested a padrote for beating one of his workers, the same worker had shown up to bail him out of jail, proclaiming her love for her padrote and her anger at Miguel. The situation, he said, made him feel helpless: "I felt about as small as an ant." Women who leave their padrote are often met with scorn by other obligadas, as in Ramona's case. These workers may have to earn more in order to cover the lost earnings or bear the brunt of the padrote's foul mood and increasingly violent efforts to maintain control following the loss of a worker.

In Mexico, the pimp is generally considered a nefarious character. This characterization is reflected in the Mexican legal system. There is no federal law against prostitution and, in Chiapas, no state law prohibiting such activity when it is regulated, but the state legal code devotes an entire chapter to the crime of pimping (lenoncinio). According to the state penal code, a pimp (padrote or *lenon*) is one who "exploits the body of another in sexual commerce and is maintained or obtains some profit from this commerce, who manages or sustains places destined to exercise prostitution." Also considered a pimp by state law is someone who facilitates another's entry into prostitution or who opens or manages a brothel or any other place where prostitution occurs. The punishment for pimping is four to eight years in prison and a fine; this punishment is increased by four years if the pimp is working in collaboration with law enforcement. Yet despite this perception of pimping, padrotes in the zone and the street continue to operate freely, reflecting the male domination embedded in both the execution of the law and the practice of culture. Discourses about the dangers of the padrote are common both inside and outside the zone. Before moving to Tuxtla from the small town of Soyalá, Ana María was warned by her mother not to fall prey to a pimp; she explained to her daughter how they might look and the ways in which they take advantage of young women. Ana María laughs at the irony of her mother's warnings—she now works in a brothel, but as a secretary, and says, "And I have yet to see a pimp!" On a number of occasions, Bárbara repeated a cautionary tale about an obligada from El Cocal. The woman was older, tall, and pretty with "an incredible body." According to Bárbara, the woman earned a good deal of money for her pimp, but "she got sick with cancer, of the uterus, I think. And do you think he was there to help her? When she died, she was left in her room for three days and there wasn't even money for a coffin. The dogs wanted to eat her! The women [in El Cocal] had to chip in and buy the casket." The obligadas, Bárbara says, "are squeezed like oranges, and when there is no juice left, they are thrown out."

Dominant cultural values continue to assert that men are to support women economically, rather than exploiting them for profit. Often the moral character of men who fail to adhere to these norms, even within an economic crisis that makes achieving this difficult, is questioned. The pimp is someone who not only rejects societal norms but also turns them on their head. Yet the pimp also *embodies* cultural values that assert that female sexuality must be controlled and male sexual "needs" must be met. By facilitating and controlling the sale of female sexuality while ensuring that other men receive the sexual activity due them as men, the padrote (much like the prostitute), though maligned for the role he plays, also reinforces certain gendered and sexual norms.

Some independent workers express empathy for women who work as obligadas, but many workers disdain the padrotes and others who unfairly benefit from the women's work. Bárbara says that, if she were able to leave the ambiente, she would never return to work as a madam or as a zone landlady. Other workers express similar sentiments. One afternoon in Gabriela's kitchen, she, Miguel, and I were eating *mixiotes,* a dish of chicken and chiles wrapped in little foil packages. We sat under the watchful eye of Alfonso, a green parrot with glaring orange eyes, who was perched outside the window in the decaying courtyard where residents wash clothes, bathe, and use the common toilet. Gabriela and Miguel speak of the padrotes, how they show up with nice, new cars, "Topaz, Jetta, all the latest models." They both express disgust as they describe how the padrotes abuse their workers and threaten to tell their families that they are working as prostitutes. Former obligadas such as Evita and Ramona express contempt for the men who forced them into prostitution.

When Sonia left the Galáctica to work in an alley in an unregulated part of the state of Morelos, she found she was the only worker there without a padrote. She said to one co-worker. about the woman's pimp, "You pay a lot to sleep with him!" to which her colleague responded, laughing, "Shut up, damn China!"[28] Sonia's astute comment reveals the complexity of the obligada's relationship with her pimp: she is both a prostitute and an employee but also in a sense a client, giving money to a man in return for intimacy, or the illusion of it.

The obligadas often find themselves in the unusual situation of having intercourse with strangers for money in order to have intercourse with their partners, again for money. Of former obligada Evita, Viviana says, "She is pretty but not very bright," adding, "nobody forced me to do what I am doing." Mónica refers to the obligadas as "poor things," and says that she entered the ambiente on her own, that "nobody put a knife to my throat." The obligadas represent an extreme form of prostitution in which women are forced to sell sexual services; their presence in the zone allows independent workers to mask the social and economic circumstances that brought them into the ambiente, replacing them with a discourse of free will.

six Sellers and Buyers

Edith and I watch clients come and go as we sit looking out the window of the Anti-Venereal Medical Service, where she distributes condoms to workers. Sex work, according to Edith (a single woman with a child) and many Tuxtlecos, is "the easy life"—"an easy way to make money." I tell her I think it seems like pretty hard work. We sit for a moment in silence and watch as a shabbily dressed, disheveled looking man with one arm, the other an oddly shaped stub with a pointed end, heads up the stairs to the exit. Edith finally speaks, saying it is awful to ride the bus back to the city center with clients, especially when they are "disrespectful." She pauses for a moment, looking pensive, and then says, "You're making me think, Patty. The women have to put up with a lot. What I said before about this being the easy life, well, maybe it's not so easy. They have to put up with a lot."

A common perception among many Tuxtlecos is that prostitute women are looking for "the easy life," a quick and simple way to make money. Inside the zone, workers tell another story. Riding in the pirate taxi one morning, Gabriela tells me of clients who claim the work is easy: "I tell them, 'You think this work is easy? You think this is easy? This is *not* easy!' The work is hard, going with man after man. Some think it's easy. Others think that we are women without hearts; that we don't feel." Bonita too despairs about the ways in which society "goes around criticizing," saying, "They call it the easy life, but it's not."

Performing sexual labor is far from simple. Complex dynamics of negotiation, refusal, and submission occur in the sex worker–client encounter. Workers must learn to exact the highest price possible for their services and develop the skills to "read" clients for their potential for danger and adjust their own behaviors accordingly.

SEX AS SERVICE

They need us and we need them.

Ramona

The thousand men who walk through the gates of the zone each day come in search of a woman who will provide them with the services they are looking for at a price they are willing to pay. The 140 women who wait in their rooms or doorways are looking for a client who will pay their asking price for the services they are willing to provide. The process of negotiating a sale is riddled with multiple, overlapping, and some-times surprising power relations: class, gender, age, appearance, experience, and ethnicity of both worker and client may come into play during negotiations. Negotiations can be difficult, since rarely are the desires of the seller and the buyer the same. Sitting in Pepe's food stand one day, Bárbara writes down the conflict in my notebook: "The clients prefer those that charge less—give all—don't use a condom, and the women prefer giving normal services, charge what is fair, and put on a condom."

A typical encounter may go something like this: the client enters the front gate, purchases his three-peso (US$0.35) entry ticket, is briefly searched by municipal police manning the entry, and heads down the pathway between the food stands of Pepe and Doña Paula, past the SMAV, to the rooms. He moves from courtyard to courtyard, room to room, peering through doorways at the workers, who are lying on their beds, watching television, reading comics, or talking with co-workers. When he finds a woman he likes, he asks, "How much?" and might also inquire about any special services he would like. If the pair come to an agreement, the client will enter. If not, he will continue his search. Regular clients who come to the zone to see particular workers can forego this selection and negotiation process, instead heading directly to the rooms of their favored workers, knowing in advance what services they can have and how much they will pay. As a client chooses a prostitute, so may the prostitute choose or reject a client. It is not unusual for a client to have a door slammed in his face, be yelled at, be ignored, or in one memorable incident, have a bucket of water thrown at him.

As the service-sector economy, prostitution included, expands globally, workers are increasingly expected to perform labor that meets both the material desires and emotional wants of the consumer. This growth in the service sector stems from recent economic changes that have led to decreasing options for other forms of employment as a result of neoliberal privatization, foreign competition, and technological advances that leave human workers behind. Furthermore, the feminization of the workforce has led to what Cameron Lynne MacDonald and Carmen Sirianni call "a self-fulfilling cycle in which the entrance of more women in the workforce has led to increased demand for those domestic services once provided gratis by housewives (cooking, cleaning, child care, etc.), which in turn has produced more service jobs that are predominantly filled by women."[1]

Yet the zone is one place where the worker, even though she is in the service industry, retains some degree of freedom from the expectations about service. Many workers resist the notion of service, as well as clients' perspectives that a "whore" should and will do anything, if paid. As Bárbara said, "They [the clients] think that we are here just to serve them, but that's not how it is." Furthermore, the workers often refuse to interpret clients' resistance to paying them what they ask as an indicator of their own self-worth, instead asserting that the client unwilling to pay a good price is "miserable" and "cheap."[2]

Many workers prefer their regular clients to *extraños* (strangers): they feel comfortable and safe with them, having developed a relationship that has some basis in trust. The worker knows she will be well paid and will sometimes even receive a tip for the services she is willing to provide in a safe, predictable situation. Some workers, like Bárbara, are very discriminating, typically refusing to serve many unknown clients, preferring to wait for the arrival of their regular customers. Bárbara has five regular clients who arrive twice a week and others who may arrive once or twice a month. Of her regular clients, Desirée says, "I have many clients that I can say are good. They come a few times a week and treat me with respect, with tenderness." But sometimes the intimacy of a regular client can cause problems as well—as Bonita notes, they may become difficult and expect more because of their status as a well-paying, regular client.

As with most service-sector jobs, the sex worker must often contend with a demanding and sometimes hostile public. Clients may verbally or even physically abuse a worker, they are often unwilling to part with their money, and they may even steal from a worker. They may smell bad or be physically repulsive. Some workers choose the more desirable clients (well paying, undemanding, and relatively good-looking), while others do not or cannot afford to discriminate. Client appearances are important to some workers; sitting outside her room on a hot day, Sonia sighed, "There is not one good-looking man here today." Others, like Lorena, place no importance on appearance: "I couldn't care less what they look like." Cleanliness, however, is a quality that most workers hope for, but do not always find, in a client.

If she wishes to earn money, a worker often has to ignore her aversion to certain types of clients, instead feigning politeness and even interest. In *The Managed Heart*, Arlie Hochschild comments on the dangers of personality control and the lack of freedom of emotion linked with service-sector employment. Such disciplining of emotion, she suggests, may lead to estrangement from self and problems of identity. Service workers must contend with weighty issues, asking, "What is my work role and what is 'me'? How do I do deep acting without 'feeling phony' and losing self-esteem? How can I redefine the job as 'illusion making' without becoming cynical?'"[3] Many zone workers complain of a lack of self-esteem, the difficulty of emotional detachment, and the problems of redefining sex as work.

Some workers have few repeat customers. Sonia tells me she is unwilling to falsify emotions or feign interest in her clients; of them she says, "They come once or twice and then they never return." Other workers cannot afford to behave in such a way or be so discriminating and may service any client who agrees to their price, and even some who do not.

While there are workers like Lorena who seek only a consumer who is willing to pay, others may cater to a specific clientele or prefer clients of a certain age or appearance. Bárbara says she prefers middle-aged men to the young boys from the high school, who she says are "demanding" and so cheap that "they won't even buy you a Coke." Indeed, many of the high school and even junior high school students who frequent the zone lack the maturity and experience to view their visits to the zone as part of a socially constructed sexual and commercial experience in which clients are expected to fulfill particular roles.

NEGOTIATING SERVICES: FROM THE MARRIAGE BED
TO SPECIAL SERVICES

I am sitting with a friend, a panista who works in Tuxtla's Department of Public Health, beneath the tall thatch roof in Los Explosivos, a popular palapa [thatched-roof] bar. We order drinks, wait for his girlfriend to arrive and for the show, a transvestite cabaret, to begin. When Graciela finally arrives, she is angry. Her taxicab driver mistook her, a woman traveling alone to a bar, for a prostitute; she got out of his cab and hailed another. Francis, a tall, thin, blond male in drag, soon takes the stage. She tells one joke after another and cuentos colorados (off-color stories). She excitedly launches into a story about three old friends who reunite over dinner after many years apart. One woman has become a nun. Another is a housewife. The third confesses that she has become a prostitute. They eat and talk, and when the waiter arrives to offer dessert, each woman orders a banana. Francis goes on to describe and imitate each woman eating the banana. The nun, she says, holds it delicately, caresses it with wonder, makes the sign of the cross, and eats it gently while looking up toward the heavens. The prostitute peels it roughly, and goes right at it, all business. And the housewife puts her hand on the back of her head and forces it down quickly and roughly over the banana. The audience bursts into laughter.

Though beliefs and activities surrounding sexuality in Mexico are diverse, some sex acts are disparaged in certain sectors of society, relegated to those operating beyond sociosexual norms, as the previous excerpt from my field notes shows. While clients (and men in general) are occasionally discussed by workers in terms of their "perversions," it is more frequently sex workers (and women) who are stigmatized for performing sexual acts beyond the realm of what is considered "normal."

In the zone it is an unusually hot day, nearing one hundred degrees. Bárbara and I sit at Pepe's, watching the few clients pass us by. An exiting client catches my eye: he is light skinned with glasses, his long hair is pulled back in a ponytail, and he is dressed in black chinos and a long-sleeved, black, button-down shirt. I comment on his unusual choice of wardrobe on such a hot day, and Bárbara tells me that the fellow "wants it all." I press for more information, and she says, "Tocho morocho. Ask Pepe what it means." I look to Pepe, who is standing behind the counter, dishrag in hand. As I repeat the words tocho morocho, Pepe is overcome by a fit a giggles as he repeatedly makes the sign of the cross. Seeing Pepe's inability to speak, Bárbara gives a bored sigh and tells me, "It means everything, all sexual services, referring more than anything to different positions."

In the Galáctica, there are prostitutes who work "normally," those who will "do it all," and those in between. To work normally is to engage only in vaginal intercourse, and more often, though not always, in the missionary position. "Special services" may consist of oral or anal sex, or other varieties of sexual activity. These services are sometimes referred to as "chico, mamey, and papaya." *Chico* refers to the fruit *chico zapote* and is a euphemism for anal sex; *mamey,* another fruit, sounds much like the verb *mamar*, meaning to suck, and refers to fellatio; and finally, *papaya*, a fruit that has a vaginal appearance when sliced in half, refers to cunnilingus.

In addition to these services, some women who have VCRs in their rooms may provide pornographic movies for clients. The decision to use pornography, though condemned by some workers as depraved, is less a moral decision than a common economic strategy among prostitutes. Lydia often has pornographic videos playing in her room. The loud moaning and grunting, accompanied by a bad 1970s soundtrack, ensures there is always a small group of men lingering around Lydia's open door. For some, it is their first exposure to pornography. When her door is closed and the client enters, the visual stimulation often brings the client to orgasm faster, allowing her to earn money more quickly.

While the decision about whether to provide special services is ultimately an economic one, it is often linked to conceptions of morality, deviance, sexual norms, and even the sense of fair play among competing co-workers. Because there is competition for clients in the zone, tension sometimes arises between those workers who provide, or who are believed to provide, special services and those who say they do not. Workers who say they work "normal" pass judgment on both special services and the women who provide them. Magda is extremely opinionated regarding what she refers to as "depravity": "I'm not a maniac. I'm not depraved. And I don't do things outside of what would normally happen in marriage. Like I say to the client, 'What happens with me, you should realize, that you are with your wife, *mi'jito*. You are not with a woman of the street.' I am a woman of the street, but with dignity, with shame."

Magda's viewpoint may be related in part to her age (she is fifty) and the number of years she has been working in the ambiente. She says that "depravities" occur because "the women let them happen," in particular the foreigners. In the zone in Villahermosa, where she once worked, men who even suggested such depravities were not tolerated. Though surely there have probably always been workers willing to perform special services in the ambiente, recent changes in Mexican sexual culture and consumption practices (increasing availability of pornography; increasing options for commercial sex; changing media presentations of sex, often influenced by the United States; and of course, the Internet) have likely led to an increasing demand for such services.

While women who work "normal" often refuse to perform other services, even at a higher price, women who do provide special services see them as an economic opportunity. Former obligada Evita recently refused a Western man who wanted to pay her for oral and anal sex. The man, the workers said, was handsome, recently divorced, and on his way to Cuba (very likely to take advantage of the flourishing sex tourism industry there). Lydia, on the other hand, speaks in detail, and in a detached manner, of the services she provides. She describes services involving oral and anal sex and, in one instance, a carrot. One recent client gave her four hundred pesos (US$47)—a hefty sum for the zone or the street. Both clients and workers take time into account when negotiating price, and considering the large sum, one would assume the client was with her for an hour if not more. When I asked, she replied, "No, [it took] only a few minutes. Let me show you why." She reached over and turned on the television mounted on the wall over the bed and popped into the VCR a hardcore lesbian pornography video, with Spanish subtitles. For Lydia, showing clients pornography has little to do with morality, rather it is simply another strategy to maximize her income and minimize her effort. Unlike Magda, Lydia doesn't feel the need to mitigate the stigma associated with her work by laying claim to a sense of shame.

While there is a certain sexual freedom and relaxation of sexual norms in the zone, negotiating services is not completely unmarked by dominant cultural and moral beliefs. Clients who come seeking special services often have to learn how to ask for what they want. Because many men who respect their wives or girlfriends are unlikely to ask them for anal or oral sex, customers often arrive at the zone unable to articulate their desires, lacking the proper and acceptable vocabulary.

Uneducated sexually, and often in other ways, many clients arrive unprepared to negotiate services. Some negotiations, even when they do not result in an exchange, are smooth and professional. When a client arrived at Gabriela's door and asked, "How much?" and then "How much for oral sex?" she replied that she didn't do that. He told her,

"That's cool," and moved on. According to Gabriela, some of her neighbors do not handle such inquiries professionally, instead yelling obscenities at the clients. The interaction is worsened when clients do not know the proper terminology. A man wanting oral sex should ask for oral sex. A man asking, "Will you suck me?" is more likely to have a door slammed in his face, at the very least.

Sex in the zone, then, is not a straightforward uncontested activity. Nor is it quite the romanticized and fantasy-laden sex often portrayed in books and film. As much as the Galáctica is another space, free from dominant norms regarding gender and sexuality, where men and women both may learn and experience alternative sexualities, it is also a place where cultural codes are reinforced. And, it is a public marketplace where the Mexican tradition of haggling (distinctively premodern) is very much alive.

NEGOTIATING PRICES IN THE CHEAPEST BROTHEL IN THE MEXICAN REPUBLIC

> One could say that the tolerance zone is one of
> the cheapest places there could be in the Mexican
> Republic. Yes, Tuxtla Gutiérrez and its tolerance
> zone is one of the cheapest places there is. Not
> Oaxaca. Not Mexico City. Minimum, minimum,
> minimum, a woman who works a normal service,
> fifty, eighty pesos minimum. And here, twenty.
> Fifteen sometimes. A woman who is elderly will
> charge you ten.
>
> Lorena

The women of the Zona Galáctica are reputed to offer the least expensive sexual services in Chiapas and southern Mexico. A woman providing normal services in the Galáctica may earn anywhere from ten to forty pesos (US$1.20 to $4.70), though the average price is somewhere around thirty or thirty-five pesos (US$3.50 to $4.10). Sonia left the zone to work in Morelos, where she earned sixty to seventy pesos (US$7.05 to $8.25) per client for normal services. In Comitán, workers serving a largely military clientele, who have pesos to spend, often earn seventy pesos (US$8.25) for each encounter. Street workers generally charge more than zone workers and in some cases may earn as much as two hundred pesos (US$23.50) per client.[4]

Located at the intersection of elite fears about working-class sexuality, urban growth, and desires for modernity, order, and hygiene, the zone is by design and necessity a place where sexual services can be purchased cheaply. The competitive market puts a ceiling on what a worker can charge for her services. A lack of organizing among workers (due partially to competition and the resulting individualism) helps ensure that sex workers will not come to any agreement about charging a set price. Furthermore, if the women were to find a way to collectively charge more, it is unlikely that a price increase would be tolerated by city officials, as many of the clients would then be unable to pay for services in the zone, thus undermining the state's goal of managing the "dangerous" sexuality of the lower classes.

The consumption of sexual services in Tuxtla varies according class. Katherine Bliss, describing early twentieth-century Mexico City, notes that working-class men are associated with "low-rent" prostitutes.[5] In the zone, the state provides these prostitutes. Just as a moneyed consumer will buy his clothing at Fábricas de Francia, the upscale department store in western Tuxtla, and his sexual services from a pretty college student working for an elite hostess agency, so will the working-class consumer purchase his clothing at one of the small, inexpensive markets in downtown Tuxtla and his sex at the Galáctica. Furthermore, state sponsorship of the zone also detracts from its status. In the neoliberal era, the "private" is highly valued: private clubs, schools, and even communities have an allure that attracts those who can afford to buy. That which is public loses status: public schools, publicly run businesses, or in this case, a public brothel. In the neoliberal era, the increasing acceptance of exclusivity and privilege lessens the attractiveness and even the "sexiness" of publicly run enterprises.

Competition in the zone can be fierce. Business has slowed since the days of clients and workers drinking together at the rowdy Galactic

Chicken and later during the early months of the Zapatista conflict, when the zone was so saturated with military men it "was a green zone, as if they were plants." Though the upper price range in the zone is subtly institutionalized, price ranges are influenced by a number of overlapping factors briefly noted earlier: a worker's age and appearance; services provided; a worker's economic need, which may vary; a client's status as a regular or stranger; the number of potential clients arriving; the amount of money clients are willing to spend; and the prices charged by other workers performing similar work.

A woman's value is determined partly by her age and appearance. According to municipal statistics, zone workers are from nineteen to fifty-five-years old. In reality, the range is surely somewhat greater. Women may lie about their age for a number of reasons: to enter the world of regulated prostitution, to attract more clients, or to avoid the shame that accompanies being a middle-aged or older prostitute. Young Central American women who arrive seeking employment in the zone often lack the documents to prove they are eighteen, the legal minimum age for practicing prostitution. Marta, for example, arrived from Guatemala, claiming to be eighteen but unable to prove it. She was subject to a dubious dental exam by the SMAV staff and, based on the appearance of her molars, was deemed to be of the proper age. Desirée alternately claims that she is eighteen or nineteen, when she is in fact twenty-four; such misrepresentations of truth serve various purposes. Younger workers may receive a greater price for their services; they may also be perceived as more "innocent" and thus may be treated more sympathetically by clients and staff.

Women in their forties and fifties who have made a career of prostitution are considered by staff to be beyond "rehabilitation." Older prostitutes transgress a cultural boundary that defines older women as nonsexual creatures. They may also suffer greater stigmatization because they no longer have small children to maintain and are perceived as less economically needy than younger workers. While some researchers have suggested that the lives of women in most cultures appear to improve with the onset of middle-age—as they experience fewer restrictions on their behavior, and as their authority in decision making becomes more socially accepted[6]—there are few benefits for the mature zone worker. In fact, as a woman ages in the ambiente, she suffers increased stigmatization: she is transformed from a young worker there *por necesidad* (because of need) into one who is there *por gusto* (for pleasure).

While advanced age does not prevent a sex worker from receiving clients, it does determine a worker's value, her clientele, and in many cases, her own sense of self-worth. A younger woman may set her average price at forty-five or fifty pesos (US$5.30 or $5.90), while a woman in her fifties may accept as little as eight or ten pesos (US$0.95 or $1.15). Though I never formally met her, I repeatedly heard stories of the *señora* nearing sixty who worked for anything from five to ten pesos (this figure was subject to change, depending on the storyteller). Nearing the end of her career and no longer considered attractive, she was said to have huge breasts, which she would show by wearing very low-cut blouses (this I knew to be true, as I had seen her and her notorious cleavage on a number of occasions). Her clientele consisted mainly of teenagers from the local high school who had little disposable income to spend on sexual services. She had found her niche market and, according to one observer, told the young men "she will teach them, treat them like a son." As a woman ages in the ambiente, concessions like those made by the *señora* must be made if a worker hopes to receive clients.

At forty-two, Mónica is extremely conscious of her age and how it determines her value in the zone. In her youth, Mónica was stunningly beautiful. One day as we sat in her room, she pulled out old photos. One showed her and her young husband who had killed himself. Another was a photo of Mónica soon after she entered the ambiente. She sat on the hood of a car, dressed in shorts and a flowing, indigo, hippie-style shirt, looking like a young Sophia Loren. On her head she wore the bright yellow hardhat of an oil worker, brown curls flowing over her tanned shoulders as she stared into the camera confidently, smiling. Nowadays she complains that clients call her "old lady," and she speaks of retiring from the ambiente because, as she puts it, "I'm getting old." Sitting at Pepe's on a slow, hot day, Mónica and I watch Desirée leaving early in the afternoon. Mónica turns to me and says, "And she is young," meaning that even the younger and therefore more desirable workers are not finding clients on this slow afternoon.

Physical appearance is of great concern to zone workers, and fashion in particular offers insights into how workers identify themselves and relate to their work. Women arriving from the *campo* (countryside) often lack the attire of urban women and must learn from others how to dress.[7] Many workers come to the zone in their street clothes: jeans and tank tops, sweatpants and T-shirts, skirts and blouses. The change some women make from street clothing to work clothing is extreme: Gabriela arrives wearing pants and a loose T-shirt and changes into a blue negligee with black lace and high heels. For others the change is less drastic and more symbolic, marking a shift from home role to work role: Rafaela changes from a black miniskirt and tank top to a multicolored miniskirt and tank top. Still others do not change their attire. For some, this signifies their complete immersion in the ambiente; for Mónica, who lives in the zone and has worked in the ambiente for nearly fifteen years, the leggings and T-shirts she wears serve her both in the zone and during her outings to downtown Tuxtla. For the young Bárbara, who normally wears a long, full skirt and modest blouse, her refusal to change her attire represents a resistance to identifying herself as a prostitute or to dressing according to the dictates of the ambiente (even though there is a wide variety of dress): "From the beginning, since I came, well, many [women] change. They come from other places, dress in long skirts, very discreet. And when they stay: thongs, miniskirts; they catch on. But not me. Even though I am in the ambiente, I keep dressing the same. I arrived with a long skirt. And know what they would tell me? That I looked like a crazy old woman. But I couldn't care less and I have never stopped [dressing this way]."

Others remark on the changes they have made in order to attract clients. The first time Sonia ever wore makeup was when she was forced to work in a bar in Tapachula. Bonita notes the difference between her work and home personae:

> They have said to me, "You don't look like you work in this place." Because they see me like a normal person. And when I leave here, I don't make myself up like I do here. I change everything. I dress more casually, sporty, and only put on a little makeup. On the other hand, here I put on blush, eyeliner, red lipstick, everything. I'm not the

same. Even my behavior is different. Here, I try to walk so that my
butt stands out. When I'm in the *centro*, I tie back my hair. and here I
leave it loose.

At the time of this conversation, Bonita had been working in the ambiente for only a short time. Despite her own description of the changes she
made to her appearance in the zone, Bonita looked very much like a
sporty, middle-class young woman when I first met her. When I returned
to the zone the following year, I was shocked by the dramatic change in
her appearance: she had put on a great deal of weight, had begun to wear
the specially made revealing dresses that some workers prefer, and had
heavily increased her use of makeup, all signs of further embeddedness
in the ambiente.

Workers' concern with weight reflects recent shifts in Mexican cultural
standards of beauty. Slender women, once widely considered less than
womanly in Mexico, are now popular with many clients, as are women
with fair skin and hair. One need only turn on the television and watch a
telenovela (soap opera) to see who currently embodies female beauty:
most actresses are young, fair, and of course, thin. But despite the empha-
sis on thinness, much of a worker's social life revolves around eating.
Women may gather at one of the four food stands to share gossip, relax,
or escape the confines and boredom of their small, dimly lit rooms. As the
zone lacks facilities for the women to do their own cooking, and making
the trip to the city center to eat would be time-consuming and costly,
workers largely depend on vendors like Pepe and Doña Paula for their
daily meals.[8] In the morning, many workers pass by their favored vendor, asking, "What did you bring?" Some women, like Flor, complain of
their weight and claim the gain has come with their entry into the zone.
Mónica complains of the zone's "T" diet: taco, tortilla, *torta* (sandwich);
she is convinced these foods make a person fat.

Younger and more attractive women receive more clients than other
workers. These women often use up the allotted amount of free condoms
(one hundred every two weeks) and need more, a situation that has created an underground condom economy. Workers who do not use all their
condoms sell them, at a price lower than in the city center, to workers

who serve more clients. This situation annoyed the zone administration, which was spending municipal dollars to provide the women with condoms. Moreover, the rise of a condom black market directly countered (and ironically, was a product of) the city's effort to decrease such informal economic activity by regulating prostitution. It also caused resentment among the women who were buying the condoms when they felt the SMAV should be providing them to ensure that every sex act was a "safe" one. On his first day as new director of the SMAV, Dr. Ruiz met with a small group of workers who aired complaints about the situation, hoping to convince him to provide more condoms to the women, free of charge. The doctor refused, replying, "The truth is that only a few women, I'm sorry to say, those that are younger and prettier," needed more than the allotted amount, since they received more clients.

A woman's asking price is also influenced by the services she is willing to provide to a client whom she is willing to serve (though a woman may accept a client she would not ordinarily serve if business is slow). For example, Flor receives thirty pesos (US$3.50) for vaginal intercourse in the missionary position; this fee is increased to fifty (US$5.90) if the client requests *de perrito* (dog style). Many women do not work completely nude and charge extra when they do.[9] Though a worker may have her ideal asking price and way of working, these ideals and the bargaining power of workers are subject to change because of temporal shifts in economic need—a woman behind on the rent or under other acute economic pressures may work without a condom or perform an act not ordinarily in her repertoire in order to not lose a client. On a slow day when a woman has not yet earned enough to pay her daily rent and food costs, she may be willing to expand her repertoire of services without raising her asking price.

Shifts in the Mexican economy and local political activity also affect a worker's asking price. During the summer of 1998, heavy rains and storms destroyed harvests in much of the state. Men who earned their living from the land had less disposable income to spend on sexual services. As competition for clients increased, some workers lowered their prices. Others suffered financially because they refused to do so. During the conflict with the ejidatarios of Francisco I. Madero, many clients believed that the zone was closed, or they stayed away for fear of becoming embroiled in a violent land dispute. Again, workers were forced to lower their prices in order to compete for the few arriving clients. Bárbara says she sometimes accepts a client "just for the damn fact that I have to pay the rent." Though she has her set price, which she tries to stick to (a strategy for maintaining dignity and a sense of self-worth), she says, "Sometimes dignity only goes so far." At other times, especially on the days following the quincena (bimonthly payday), the zone may be busy enough that workers will receive their asking price.

Sexual activity has long been considered a necessity for soldiers, and militarization throughout the globe is often accompanied by prostitution.[10] But it is important to remember, as Cynthia Enloe reminds us, that the link between militarization and prostitution must be not naturalized. Rather, its existence requires a particular cultural construction of "militarized, masculinized sexual desire" along with "rural poverty, male entrepreneurship, urban commercialized demand, police protection, and overlapping government interests."[11] Militarization of the state following the EZLN uprising in 1994 brought an increase in prostitution in Chiapas, particularly in the conflict regions in the eastern half of the state. But local political manifestations not of a military nature also affect activity in the zone. During a statewide teacher's strike, in which educators from throughout Chiapas came to participate in a protest and work stoppage, the zone was overflowing with educators, who formed a long line at the front gate before the Galáctica had even opened.

Some workers may ignore variables such as services, age, and condom use, and may, because of the lack of solidarity or organizing in the zone, undercut their competitors by charging a low price. Such was the case with Sandra, a new, young worker who was considered to be very beautiful. During her early days in the Galáctica, she charged as little as fifteen pesos (US$1.75) and at times had a line of clients waiting outside her door, much to the dismay of her co-workers. Likely because of pressure from co-workers, this situation did not last long.

Workers can also earn money for activities other than sexual services. Some clients come only to talk and be heard. Esperanza fondly recalls one client who wanted only to caress her. Bárbara charges a client if he wishes to use her bathroom or shower. Sonia sells clients photocopies of the textbook we used together in English class. Sometimes a man will be charged simply for entering a woman's room. If the door has been shut behind him, he has begun to use a worker's time and may have even prevented her from seeing another client. If upon disrobing, a client is found to have some kind of infection (many workers learn to look for signs of sexually transmitted diseases), the worker will normally not serve him and may even offer medical advice, but she will also charge him for the time he has used. This can lead to an argument and even violence between client and worker.

Clients, for their part, often draw on a variety of methods in order to pay as little as possible. Some, according to Bárbara, will try to use their social standing as a way to receive free services, asking the worker, "Don't you know who I am?" Bárbara's typical response is, "I don't care who you are." Of course, few men of public importance arrive at the zone; they go to more discreet and costly places such as hotels and private "hostess" services.

Though women in the zone transgress hegemonic moral codes by selling sex and are sometimes portrayed as (and indeed are) women who live by an alternative system of gendered belief and practice, many workers, as noted earlier, adhere to cultural norms that claim a woman should be supported by a man. While they may in some ways be financially and emotionally independent, zone workers are also vulnerable to clients who make romantic and economic promises in an attempt to get inexpensive or even free services. Clients may put on a romantic act, pay compliments, and promise a continuing emotional and financial relationship. Such was the case with Vicente, an older man and new client of Mónica's who paid for her services, flirted with her, and told her he would lend her one thousand pesos (US$118) so she could leave the ambiente and set up a taco stand. He returned to the Galáctica four times afterward, romanced Mónica with compliments and promises of money, received services without paying, and even stole a music cassette from her nightstand. He never returned. Telling me the story, Mónica is hurt, saying she had begun to fall in love with the man. In vain, she had angrily gone to the city center to look for him.

Other clients use less subtle methods. Some will steal their money back on their way out the door if it has been left on a bedside table. Others will claim they paid when they did not and sometimes risk leaving it to the municipal police to sort out the situation. Some will haggle down to the last peso; according to Bárbara there are clients who moan, "But it's for my chewing gum, it's for the bus fare." As Desirée describes it, a client will come and ask, "How much?" Once the worker gives her price, a client will say, "How come so expensive? How about cheaper? Twenty." If the worker refuses, the client may continue his efforts, "Twenty. That's a lot to be giving you." These sorts of encounters rarely happen with regular customers; as Bárbara notes, "It's not so easy to separate the extraños from their money."

Not all clients are *codo, tacaño, miserable* (cheap, miserly, miserable), as Sonia describes them. And while relationships between workers and clients are defined by physical and economic exchange, they are not always free from emotional exchange. On February fourteenth, Día de Amor y Amistad (Day of Love and Friendship), some workers left the zone with candy, stuffed animals, and other gifts they had received from regular clients. On hot days, a client may buy a soda for a worker, and in some instances may even take a woman out for dinner or a night on the town, as did the client who brought the serenade to my home after a night out with a group from the zone. Furthermore, both regular clients and strangers may tip above and beyond a woman's asking price.

Women's perceptions of a client's ability to pay well are influenced by his appearance and ethnic identity. According to Sonia and Rita, during the daytime hours many of the men who arrive are campesinos, peasants who are viewed as ugly and cheap and referred to as Chamulitos (a racist euphemism for Mayan men from the indigenous village of Chamula, applied to all people of indigenous descent). Handsome men are believed to have more money to spend, and while no worker ever admitted to me that she enjoyed the sex she had with a client, some did allude to the fact that they preferred to give their services to men they considered handsome. In her book about the Mustang Ranch, formerly one of Nevada's legal brothels, Alexa Albert found the matter of a worker enjoying sex with a client quite controversial. Some workers asserted that they never enjoyed the sex, and that it would be wrong to do so, but others disagreed. As one worker told her, "With as much sex as we have, how could a woman not enjoy it occasionally?"[12] But at the Mustang Ranch, a woman who enjoyed sex with a client did not speak about it for fear of being stigmatized by other workers. In the Galactic Zone, a woman who said she enjoyed sex with a client would also be stigmatized, as any claim to being in the zone not por gusto but por necesidad would be invalidated. No worker ever spoke to me of being in the zone por gusto, but it was not unusual for a worker to be pleasantly surprised by a client's appearance or to find a boyfriend in a client.

CONDOMS

The Galáctica's program of condom distribution is uncommon in Mexico and provides an incentive for some sex workers from other parts of Mexico, like Magda, to transfer their business there. Co-workers in Tabasco who had worked in the Galáctica told Magda of its condom distribution. Of her decision to leave Tabasco in order to work in the Galáctica, Magda says:

> I came to try it out and, more than anything, for the condoms. I came for my box of condoms, because there [in Tabasco] they are bought. One has to buy them in the pharmacy; they don't give them out. It's very expensive. The cheapest are 3.50 pesos [roughly thirty-five cents a condom]. But I would buy them, because I didn't like to lose a client because of a [lack of a] condom. And I didn't like to tell the client that I would charge him 30 pesos plus a condom: "Oye, give me 5 pesos more," and there goes the client. So, it's better that I would have it, and I would buy it with my own money, and that I would already have a set price, including the condom, whether they want one or not.

While there are clients who request the use of a condom, others do not, and some refuse to use one. Some workers, like Alejandra, work "only with a condom." This phrase—sólo con condón—has worked its way into prostitute discourse, in part because of outreach efforts by the Comitán Center for Health Research. A large handwritten sign on Alejandra's wall next to the bed states her terms clearly: "35 pesos (US$4.10). Only with a condom." This frees her from the sometimes troublesome process of trying to convince clients to use a condom. Yet for each worker who always uses a condom, there is another who will work without one in order to keep a client. Other workers use condoms sporadically or, as they say, "Ninety-nine percent of the time." Desirée says of her condom use, "I use it with all the clients, except with my partner and clients who only see me." Sometimes clients insinuate that, if a worker wishes to use a condom, it is because *she* carries a sexually transmitted disease.

Like workers who do special services, women who don't use condoms are reputed to "work more," in that they can serve both clients who want to use a condom as well as those who refuse. Women who insist on condoms often have to labor to get their clients to use them. According to Bárbara, "You have to convince them. Sometimes I tell them the important reasons, the risks, the benefits. I tell them, 'Look if you do it with a condom, you can enjoy it more. And if you do it without a condom? Infections. You can be calmer [with a condom] and do it without regrets. With safety and confidence. For your family. You don't have to worry about your well-being.'"

Gabriela says that about half her clients "know what can happen, know the risk of not putting it on." She has her own way of telling clients about her strict use of condoms:

> For example, they say to me, "How much do you charge?" and I tell them, "This much." "Good." And then, if I tell them before they enter the room [that they must use a condom], before the door is shut, I see they sometimes go. So, once they are inside, I tell them, "You know, it's with a condom." "No, it's that I don't like it like that," they say. And I tell them, "Look, I'm going to help you. I'll put it on you and I'll take it off you." And so in order to motivate them and convince them, I put it on them. "It doesn't feel the same." "We'll try to make it feel the same." And I will convince them. But there are some that say, "No. No, I don't want to use it." And then one must battle to convince him, and some even say, "Know what, I'm not going to stay. It's better that I go." And I tell him, "But this is lost time." And he says, "Give me back my money." And I tell them, "Time is time, and you know in this place one runs the risk of an illness." "No," he says, "you all protect yourselves." *Bueno,* I protect myself, Patty, but *them?*

Within a cultural system of male privilege and dominance, one that is bolstered by the expected subservience of workers found in the exploitative global service economy, the male clients of prostitutes, though sometimes seen as symbols of disorder, are rarely viewed as purveyors of disease. Anne Stoler writes that not all bodies are viewed as equally susceptible to disease;[13] furthermore, some individuals, because of their class, gender, or ethnicity, are constructed as "victims" of disease, while others are seen as those who transmit it. In the brothels of Belize, British soldiers stationed in the former colony were encouraged to provide authorities with the names of prostitutes whom they suspected of having exposed them to a sexually transmitted disease); the prostitutes were then punished or fired.[14] In Tuxtla, government officials and the media do not speak of the consumers of sexual services as men who transmit illness. Only sex workers and a few vocal feminist leaders speak of such a thing, though wives, other female sexual partners, and women who work as prostitutes (all of whom are socially and physically more vulnerable to contracting HIV than their male counterparts) continue to be infected with STDs by male partners. In a listing of the number of reported cases of HIV/AIDS among Mexican women by occupation, housewives, who have little power to negotiate condom use with their husbands, ranked third, while sex workers occupied sixteenth place.[15]

Workers use other methods besides talking about risk to encourage condom use. MEXFAM (Fundación Mexicana para la Planificación Familiar, Mexican Foundation for Family Planning) and other organizations taught the women how to put a condom on using their mouths— though I never had a worker tell me she used this method. They also taught them to place a drop of lubricant inside the condom to help it feel more "natural." Bárbara has used this latter method, but says that, because of a lack of trust between workers and clients, and a dearth of sexual knowledge on the part of the client, some men fear the worker has put something inside the condom that will harm them. Such male anxiety may be described as a part of a broader pattern of gender antagonism present wherever extreme forms of gender inequality exist. Men, fearful of losing their dominant role, may harbor fears about the changing social order and women's increased power. The brothel, then, is not only a site where certain patterns of male dominance are enforced but also a location of struggle where gender identities and male dominance (particularly in the arena of knowledge about sexuality and health) may be subject to question, causing some clients to view the prostitute both with desire and with suspicion and fear.

SEX AND COMMITMENT

Listening to the radio one morning, I hear an ad for a local hardware store. The deep-voiced announcer offers construction-related items for "all your building needs for your *casa grande* and your *casa chica.*"[16] At the advertisement's end a female voice asks sweetly, "Is the *casa chica* for my mama, *amor?*" and a male voice, presumably her husband's, answers haltingly, "Uhhhh . . . yes, *mi vida.*" The *casa chica* (little house) is an enduring Mexican institution, in which a married man provides a home and financial assistance for his mistress. This radio advertisement, intended to be humorous, demonstrates the cultural embeddedness of rightful male infidelity and presumed female naïveté or denial.

The ability of men to provide a casa chica for *la otra* (the other woman) is subject to changing economic conditions. Sarah LeVine notes in her study of gender roles in Cuernavaca that the economic crisis of the early 1980s forced many men to give up or refrain from building their casas chicas.[17] For men who cannot afford to romance a woman and provide her with financial assistance, or for those who simply desire a mere dalliance without commitment, there is the prostitute.

I asked Tuxtla's director of public health why he thought men frequented the zone. He responded thoughtfully, "I think that for these people, well, it is the easiest and simplest way to be able to have sex, because the other [having sex with a romantic partner] would imply many other things. Having a girlfriend and talking with her. Probably trying to convince her in order to be able to have sexual relations. Many of these people have a girlfriend, but one could say, in quotes, 'They respect them,' and they look for an easier way, without a commitment."

Though one would assume that clients arrive at the Galáctica for one obvious reason, motivations for visiting a prostitute are complex, bound

up with cultural attitudes toward gender and morality.[18] Some clients
come because they are seeking sex specifically without an emotional
commitment. Having sexual relations with a girlfriend, as the director of
public health suggests, often implies a moral obligation of some kind, a
commitment that many young men are not willing to make. Others may
come *because* of emotion, seeking conversation and comfort. Some clients
seek a variety of partners, and others a variety of activities. Though there
are certainly couples who engage in all forms of sexual activity, some
Mexicans believe there are sexual acts a man performs with his wife and
other sexual acts that he does not (such as the special services performed
in the zone). A wife may reject certain sexual desires, or she may share a
desire but refuse the act because it is considered inappropriate for a
woman of her status, as wife and mother and, therefore, as a "decent"
woman. While a man's desire is generally circumscribed only by his
choice of partner (wife, lover, or prostitute) or the role he plays (active),
certain activities and desires are taboo for all "respectable" women and
ultimately determine, to some degree, whether a woman is a "whore."

It is a Saturday afternoon in the Galáctica, and there are nearly a
dozen clients seated at Pepe's food stand. Rarely does Pepe see such business, but today he has a way to attract clients: he has brought in a small
black-and-white television that sits on the counter showing a soccer
game, Mexico versus Japan. Though generally working class, the crowd
is in other ways diverse: seated at a table sipping a Coke is fifty-three-
year-old Fernando, a gas company employee and zone regular. At
another table sits a thin, dark-skinned man wearing fancy black cowboy
boots with intricate stitching. At his feet is a boy of no more than twelve,
shining his boots. The man stares intently at his boots. The boy's hands
move quickly and deftly, almost hypnotically, cleaning and shining.
There are a few high school boys and a handful of middle-aged men, all
sipping Sprites and Cokes. Some men are noticeably better dressed than
the others. Standing at the edge of Pepe's booth is an elderly campesino
wearing a cowboy hat and a yellowed button-down shirt that was probably once white, his crusty feet enclosed in sandals. He does not enter the
food stand or buy a Coke, but simply stares at the television from a
distance.

In the days when alcohol was permitted in the zone, clients would sometimes spend an entire day or an evening in the Galáctica, drinking, watching sporting events, eating, and buying sex. Some men, referred to as *mirones* (men who look but do not buy) could spend hours in the zone without ever actually buying services. Today, clients rarely spend an entire day in the zone, because there are not enough activities beyond sex to keep them there. Mirones, though, still frequent the zone, incurring the wrath of workers who gripe, "They come here just to look as if this were a zoo!"

The Galáctica is primarily a local and regional phenomenon. Most clients are Tuxtlecos, or they come from neighboring towns such as Berriozabal or Chiapa de Corzo. But the Galáctica is also well known throughout southern Mexico, and clients sometimes come in from other parts of Chiapas, such as San Cristóbal de las Casas, Ocosingo, and Las Margaritas, as well as from other southern states, such as Yucatán, Tabasco, and Oaxaca.

Few foreigners and tourists find their way to the Galactic Zone, and when they do, word spreads quickly. Within hours of his visit, most people inside the zone had heard about the divorced gringo who wanted to purchase sex from Evita, who refused him because of the special services he requested. During my year in the zone, I heard of three foreign clients, two of whom I met. One happened to be from my hometown on Long Island. This client was older, a doctor, and coincidentally, had the same name as my mother's husband. I sat behind him on the bus on the way back to town and struck up a conversation with him in Spanish. He assumed that I was Mexican or, at the very least, not from the United States, and thus felt that his anonymity as a client was protected. When I suddenly and purposefully (and admittedly somewhat cruelly) switched to English, the fellow was shocked and dismayed. We went to lunch together and discussed his "bad luck" of being "caught" in a brothel by someone from his hometown. I completely destroyed for him the desired sense of anonymity that sex tourists often seek when in a foreign country.

Despite the global trends that have brought Central American women to the zone, and despite the workers' occasional use of imported pornographic movies and magazines, the prostitution that occurs in the

Galáctica, though deeply influenced by global political-economic trends, is unlike the sex tourism industry that has developed in places like the Dominican Republic or Southeast Asia. Rather, it is a local-regional industry whose labor force has been prompted to work there by a confluence of personal histories and complicated regional, national, and global political-economic events.

The majority of clients are working men: truckers (a group favored by workers for their generosity), taxi drivers, manual laborers, security guards, campesinos, police officers, and service workers. The teenage boys from the local high schools are an exception—as noted earlier, many of them come from middle- and upper-class families, but the boys may have little disposable income to spend on such diversions. Clients are generally ladino—few indigenous men frequent the zone. The poorest men cannot afford the Galáctica.

Despite the continuing Zapatista conflict, the deep relationship between prostitution and militarization, and the large military presence throughout Chiapas, soldiers are not a particularly strong presence in the Galáctica. Military men do make occasional appearances, but since uniformed military men and police officers are not allowed in the zone (or in establishments that serve alcohol), it is difficult to distinguish military clients from those in law enforcement. One can guess, however, that a client belongs to one of these groups by his crew-cut hairstyle. White-collar workers such as teachers, engineers, and, rarely, low-level local government bureaucrats also frequent the zone.

According to regulations, a client is supposed to be over fourteen years old in order to enter. But some young clients appear younger, snapping their chewing gum and boisterously pushing and shoving each other as they enter. The majority of clients are men in their twenties and thirties, though some are far older. In response to my questioning, one client proudly boasted, "I am eighty-five years old!"

In the zone, men teach one another what it is to be a man. Through their group visits they are practicing culture, reinforcing normative beliefs about gender and sexuality that need constant maintenance, especially in a rapidly changing Mexico. As Enloe writes, "Sexual practice is one of the sites of masculinity's—and femininity's—daily construction."[19] Cultural beliefs are not merely static givens but are subject to contestation and are shaped by human action. The zone, despite its modern reputation, is also a place where more traditional codes of gender are practiced and reinforced. A little more than half the clients arrive alone. These men tend to be older, that is, middle-aged, and accustomed to the routine of commercial sex. Regular clients tend to arrive alone more often than the others. They too already know their role and do not need the support or guidance of other men. But for many, especially younger men and boys, prostitution is a diversion that is to be shared with friends, and that sometimes requires the social support of a peer group. A boss may arrive with his employees in an act of gender solidarity. High school students tend to arrive in pairs or in larger groups. Sometimes packs of uniformed students from the nearby high school can be seen wandering the zone together.

LEARNING DESIRE AND PRIVILEGE

Young men come or are brought to the zone to learn cultural norms regarding sexuality, their roles as men, and desire. Just as there is little that is "natural" about sex and gender roles, desire too is a construct, shaped by history, culture, and power.[20] The brothel is a place not only where desire is regulated and expressed but also where desire is shaped and learned.

Standing at the zone entry, I see a young boy walking toward the rooms, accompanied by an older man. The boy is just that, a boy; he looks no older than thirteen. I ask the cashier who mans the main gate about the pair and he tells me, "For his development." Though I am not suggesting it is the norm, it is not unusual for a young boy to have his first sexual experience with a prostitute. For middle- and upper-class boys, a female servant is another alternative for sexual initiation. Fathers and uncles and brothers take them to the zone in order to initiate them into the world of sexual relations and desire.

The boys from the *prepa* occupy a liminal space between childhood and manhood. I'd often sit among them on the bus, amazed at how young they seemed, despite their manly consumption of commercial sex. I listened to them joke and laugh, watched them dig into their red, blue, and orange flavored ices with a spoon, burying their heads in their Dragonball comic books.

In his study of machismo in Mexico City, Matthew Gutmann refutes the common belief that "many or most Latin American men have their first sexual escapades with prostitutes."[21] He also writes that, with the exception of one man, all his informants told him they had never been with a prostitute. He further states that, while it could be possible they were not telling the truth, it was more likely that it was not common for men in that area of Mexico City to pay for sexual services.[22] Gutmann suggests that paying for sex may be more of a tradition among middle- and upper-class young men than among his working-class informants. It *is* doubtful that *most* Latin American men have their first sexual encounter with a sex worker, but the one thousand working-class men who enter the gates of the Galactic Zone each day are not an aberration or an isolated local phenomenon. Rather, they are a testament to the institutional status of paid sex in Mexico.[23]

Though family and friends might be enthusiastic, often the boy is not an eager participant in his own sexual initiation, experiencing both trauma and disappointment.[24] In the Galáctica, young boys who don't desire commercial sex can learn such desire. Dr. Otero, who works weekends in the SMAV, says he has seen young boys being brought to the zone on their birthdays. According to the doctor, the degree of coercion was visible, as elders dragged boys by their arms. He felt sorry for them, he said.

Sometimes boys are initiated not at the behest of older men but at the insistence of their friends who pressure them into a visit with a sex worker. One day while waiting outside the gate for transport back to downtown Tuxtla, I struck up a conversation with three teenage boys who were also waiting. Two of the boys were brothers, a fourteen- and a fifteen-year-old who had been to the Galactic Zone on previous occasions, brought there by a family member. The other boy, fourteen, was a friend the brothers brought to the zone for the first time. The brothers told me they thought prostitution was a fine thing and seemed quite happy about their visit, but the other boy looked somewhat shaken. When I asked him what he thought of his experience, he said he didn't like it, that prostitution wasn't "good." Clearly, boys' initiation into the world of sexual relations with prostitutes is not all fun and games. It's a complex matter.

FIDELITY

It is the wife who marries.

Mexican saying

Though the consumers of commercial sex may be single, married, divorced, widowed, or living with a partner, many clients, when asked, claim to be single. One morning, I conducted a survey with clients as they purchased their entry tickets. Two-thirds of the 162 men interviewed claimed they were single. Some paused before answering, looking me over, clearly uncertain about how much information to give me, a young woman of ambiguous ethnicity and nationality. One man began to say he was married before abruptly changing his answer to single. Certainly, my status had something to do with the men's answers—perhaps they were reluctant to admit to a seemingly "decent" woman that they were not single.

Fidelity and extramarital sexual relations are contested and complex topics of discussion in Tuxtla and throughout Mexico. A man who has sexual relations with more than one woman (that is, with women who are not sex workers) is a *mujeriego,* or womanizer. This behavior is generally accepted, encouraged, and even valorized by other men. Non-prostitute women who engage in similar behavior must do so discreetly, because as one female friend noted, "we have much more to lose" than a man does: "A woman who has lovers, well, people think there is no difference between her and the women in the Zona Galáctica."

Prevailing cultural norms surrounding gender and fidelity are beautifully illustrated by the live musical performance of the song "Valiente" (Brave). A popular afternoon ritual in Tuxtla among both middle- and working-class Tuxtlecos is a visit to a palapa bar, a huge, thatched-roof building where male and female patrons drink alcohol, eat *botanas* (appetizers of pickled vegetables, cheeses, and grilled meats), and watch live performances. The lineup generally includes a salsa band, a comedian, and a variety of singers, including the omnipresent Juan Gabriel impersonator (a singer of love ballads). The shows are entertaining but can also be somewhat heart-wrenching and make a Westerner feel like she's stumbled into the saddest, cheapest casino in all of Reno, Nevada. The palapa bar opens for business at two o'clock in the afternoon, and patrons generally stay for three to six hours, until they are too drunk and too full to consume any more, they have to return to work, and/or the palapa is closing.

The performance of "Valiente" is often the biggest crowd-pleaser. Performed by a man and one or two women, the song details the infidelity of a man and the angry reaction of his female partner. She sings at him, "You'll never again touch these lips, this body" and he feigns indifference, shrugging off her threats. She tells him, "Go with her!" and stomps about the stage alternately weeping and bitterly laughing as she struggles to retain some dignity. She hits him repeatedly, turning to the crowd before each blow and asking the women in the audience, "Should I do it, girls?" The women shout out encouragement. He grabs her by the hair. The audience goes wild. It *is* very exciting. Male audience members yell, advising him to smack her. Female audience members jeer the man and cheer on the woman. Sometimes "the other woman" will march onto the stage and a physical fight will begin between her and the "rightful" female partner. He croons to her, "You want me to cheat on you" and "You know that I changed who I am for you!" and then places his hands around her throat and strangles her a bit. He throws a chair across the stage. She grabs his crotch. He stands behind her and grabs her ass with both hands and then squeezes her breasts. She swings around and smacks him hard. We watch, entranced.

This performance resonates with audience members for many reasons: It is a performance of culture, of male infidelity, female sexuality, and female-female competition for men. But it is more than that. The performance is also a group activity in which audience members are encouraged to take part in reinforcing cultural beliefs, and it is a chance for women, some of whom perhaps have unfaithful husbands themselves, to express their discontent in a channeled and controlled manner while men plead their case.

According to both workers and clients, engaging in sexual relations with a prostitute does not constitute infidelity. A prostitute is not *la otra*. A man is unfaithful not simply by having sexual relations with another woman but by having a *compromiso*, or "commitment," to another woman. As Bárbara told me, "No, [visiting a prostitute] is not infidelity, because there is no sentimental commitment. Infidelity is when I have a wife and a lover—a romantic relationship. It is different." One client remarked that coming to the zone is not a "definite relationship" but simply "a coming and going, . . . a moment of satisfaction." He added, "My wife may have a fever, a cold, her period, or she may not want to. She may be busy with the children or thinking of other things. So, I come here, but she doesn't know." Though it is a common belief that a wife should indulge her husband when he wants to have sexual relations, clearly culture is not actually practiced in this way; a wife has many methods of and reasons for declining sexual activity with her spouse. Furthermore, women are perceived as not having the same sexual appetites as men. Finally, though prostitution is not considered infidelity by clients and workers, the fact that clients do not tell their spouses reveals that it is certainly not acceptable to wives.

What kind of sex is this, then, that does not constitute infidelity but still must be hidden by men from female romantic partners? Although the question of whether visiting a prostitute is an emotional or romantic betrayal may be argued, visiting a prostitute in a culture where men are expected to provide for their female partners is an economic betrayal, as well as a potentially physical betrayal that could endanger a spouse's well-being if her husband does not use a condom. The way men spend money on luxury items instead of household needs is a source of domestic conflict common to many Mexican households, especially working-class households.[25] Though a client would have to be very poor (or very virile) in order to cause the economic collapse of a household by purchasing services at the zone (it is the cheapest in the state, and now that alcohol is no longer served, a client would be hard pressed to spend more than sixty pesos [US$7.00] during a visit), money spent at the zone is money that could be spent on the family.

For some clients, visiting a prostitute is a form of male rebellion against female domination within certain arenas of the household realm. A man who is dominated by his wife is called a *mandilón* (from the noun *mandil* [apron]; it implies that the man has assumed a wife's role).[26] A defiant mandilón may arrive at the zone on a Saturday afternoon with a sack full of tomatoes and garlic that his wife sent him out to buy. Having sex with a prostitute is a way of enacting one's masculinity while also passively resisting the label *mandilón*.

CLIENT PERCEPTIONS OF SAFE SEX

Since many clients mistakenly believe that sex in the zone is risk-free as a result of the health examinations workers receive, they may be even less likely to use a condom, thereby undermining one of the ostensible aims of the regulationist system—to protect public health. This perception among clients, combined with the low prices that may induce some sex workers to have sex without a condom, makes the zone perhaps less "safe" than authorities would care to admit. As the researchers from the Comitán Center for Health Research suggest, "The Zona Galáctica implies fantasies of security against sexually transmitted diseases. The zone 'guarantees' control over health. The men are unfamiliar with the exact mechanism under which the women are tested and what types of examinations are done. They simply know that there is medical attention, which instills in them a fantasy of control and guarantees of health."[27]

Rafael is a young Tuxtleco who works in a bank. He says he comes to the zone because the sex workers receive medical examinations and thus it is safer to buy commercial sex from them than from street workers. Félix came to the zone after propositioning a teenage worker in downtown Tuxtla whom he found, upon closer inspection, to be covered with "bumps, pimples, and stains, and was dirty." He told himself, "Better I go to the zone." Clients generally believe that the zone is a "safe" place to buy commercial sex—"safe" in that it is a secure environment manned by police, where clients are unlikely to be robbed or abused; "safe" from public view; and "safe" from exposure to sexually transmitted diseases.

While it is true that clients are less likely to be robbed there or seen by a spouse as they enter, the physical examinations that workers are required to undergo do not ensure that a client (or a prostitute for that matter, though this is not the primary concern of the SMAV) is safe from contracting a sexually transmitted illness. This situation raises serious questions about the purpose of this modern brothel and the regulation of commercial sex in Tuxtla Gutiérrez.

SEVEN

The Secrets We Keep

SEX, WORK, STIGMA

Or which is more to be blamed—
though both have cause for chagrin:
the woman who sins for money
or the man who pays money to sin?

Sor Juana Inés de la Cruz,
seventeenth-century Mexican nun and poet

Flor and I are having lunch in the small, sparsely furnished home she shares with her health inspector boyfriend, Jacobo. We are eating shrimp with garlic and a salad of cabbage, radish, tomato, jalapeño, cilantro, and lime, when a teenage girl from the neighborhood arrives carrying plastic sunflowers that Flor will bring with her to a baptism she has to attend later in the day. Though she is young, the girl's breasts are very large and her face has a haggard, aged quality about it. After the girl leaves, Flor confides to me in hushed tones, "She is not a *señorita* [literally, "young woman," but figuratively, "virgin"], and she is fifteen years old. She gives herself away." Flor clearly finds the girl's situation unsettling, as did the girl's mother, who kicked her out of the house. She now lives near Flor with an aunt. Flor has befriended her and sometimes gives her small sums of money to run errands.

Though there exists a continuum between sex work and sexual relationships that take place within free unions and formal marriage, there are important distinctions between sex within marriage or a formal relationship (unión libre), sex that is "given away" (regalada), and sex purchased in the zone. Bárbara speaks of women who look for lovers, who "give it away" without receiving anything in return. "People see women that sell it as bad, bad because of the simple fact that they charge." But she recognizes that women who have many lovers and do not charge are also viewed negatively by society. For Bárbara, and for many Tuxtlecas, implicit in every sexual relationship is an expectation of material exchange. A client pays directly; a romantic partner provides financial assistance and gifts.

Yet despite the common thread of men's payment (direct or indirect) for sexual relations, sex workers say that relationships with clients and with partners are nothing alike (though these boundaries may sometimes blur, as was the case with Mónica and Vicente). Many workers have had hundreds of clients; many of these same women have had few boyfriends. Bárbara herself estimates that she has served more than two thousand clients, but of romantic partners she says she has had five. Of her last partner, she says, "He broke my heart." After eight months together, she found that he had another girlfriend. He gave the other woman money so she could support a child she had conceived with another man, while he rarely gave Bárbara anything. Sex with a client, says Bárbara, is "totally different" from sex with a partner, as there is an emotional bond and commitment between the pair.

Sex workers delineate or mark this boundary between romantic sex and sex as work in a number of ways: clients will receive certain sexual services, while other acts, such as kissing or even the fondling of breasts, will be reserved only for partners. In this way workers are able to redefine sex as work, dividing sexual activity into acts that take place in the arena of work and acts that are for romance. Other strategies that create a distinct work identity include the following: workers put on a "uniform" at work, which consists not only of makeup, dress, and a change of name but sometimes of attitude as well. They also often leave on some article of clothing, such as a bra, during sex with clients rather than disrobing entirely; in this way they are literally and figuratively not entirely exposing themselves to clients as they may to a partner. Some women, like Lydia, say they immediately wash after sex with a client, while they do not with their partners.

Prostitution is distinct from other kinds of sex in that it is labeled an economic transaction that, though it has its own norms and rites, is ideally unmarked by the intricacies and complexities of a committed relationship. The Galáctica is a place where modern principles of efficiency, order, and hygiene are purportedly practiced, where an effort is made to streamline sexual relations. It is a place where poor women's sexual services are transformed into commodities, and they themselves become consumers. Working-class men too become consumers in the service economy while also enacting traditional notions of masculinity in a confined place in order not to pollute the city center. The Zona Galáctica provides a way of maintaining (and sometimes contesting) traditional and "deviant" gender roles in a controlled environment.

TIES THAT BIND

As noted earlier, women work as prostitutes primarily because of economic need. The opportunity to earn, on a good day, up to ten times the daily minimum wage in Chiapas (which is twenty-seven pesos, or US$3.15) is the greatest benefit of sex work. In a country where women with little education or resources have few options, prostitution offers a viable alternative to a life of material deprivation.

Sex work can give women economic freedom and self-sufficiency. It gave Bárbara the opportunity to escape an unhappy home life, and it gave Gabriela, who realized she could support herself and her two daughters through prostitution, the incentive to leave her violent husband. As Gabriela says, "I could have worked as a servant, but what I would have earned wouldn't have been enough to pay the rent, to send my daughters to school, and to feed them. I wouldn't let my daughters eat nothing more than beans or some simple little thing, or [accept the fact] that they didn't have milk, or that they walked around without shoes or were in the street begging."

Another option for economic survival is to rely on a male romantic partner for money and housing. But single women with children discover that finding a partner willing and able to support children can be difficult. For many women, the work they do in the zone, though viewed by the culture as the antithesis of the behavior of a "decent" mother, enables them to provide their children with the necessities of daily life.

Deeply rooted cultural beliefs that tie daughters to their families of origin motivate many women who work in prostitution to provide financial support for parents, siblings, and even cousins in some cases.[1] Even as economic changes and migration strain traditional family bonds and alter the family roles of men, women, and children, the cult of family remains strong in Latin America. Many sex workers migrate from rural areas or depressed cities, leaving behind dependent families that they must still support. Prostitute women employed in urban areas throughout the developing world send remittances to families; often these are a family's single most important source of income.[2]

Both immigrant and Mexican workers in the zone use their earnings to support their immediate as well as extended families. Esperanza, from Guatemala, worked in the ambiente for eight years to support her extended family back home; she recently left the ambiente. Her family had finally achieved some degree of economic stability, and she wanted to start her own family with her husband, an engineer employed by the state. A large portion of Sonia's earnings are sent to El Salvador to support her mother, brother, and teenage son. Of her family, she says, "Economically speaking, they depend on me." Sonia moved to Morelos from the zone to earn better money so she could raise funds for cancer surgery for her mother. Her life has long been characterized by sacrifice for family. She has worked to help support them since she was a child, picking cotton and planting coffee in El Salvador. Of the work, she says, "It was in order to help my mother, because we didn't have any place to live, nothing." During her youth, she received only one year of schooling. She never met her father, or the eight siblings who came before her and died of curable illnesses, and she speaks little of El Salvador's long guerrilla struggle, saying only that there was war and poverty. Sonia's story is not unusual; many poor, uneducated women bear the burden of economic responsibility for entire families.

The combination of cultural norms, obligation, need, guilt, and familial love that compels many women to work for their families can be a volatile mixture. Ironically, many workers, though they support entire families, gain little status from their role as breadwinner. In yet another manifestation of the contradiction that sex workers must live with, they, as family breadwinners, receive little compensation themselves in terms of social standing in their families or communities. This is, in part, because of the stigmatized nature of their work and also because of their position within a patriarchal gender system that expects women to unselfishly serve their families as daughters, mothers, and spouses, without reward.

Many families of sex workers are unaware of how the remittances they receive are earned; some families are grateful and supportive, while others are not. Magda's family lives rent-free in a small home on a piece of land she owns in the southern city of Tapachula. Though she has not yet constructed a well-built house made of wood on this land, which she laments, she does have many "good things," such as a refrigerator, armoires of cedar and mahogany, and a cedar dressing table. Magda has assisted her younger sisters for many years. The youngest, an unmarried mother, received a great deal of "help" from Magda, who also supported her nephew. She says, "I helped her with the little boy since kindergarten, buying uniforms, shoes, sneakers, school supplies, everything. I saw him as though he were my own son. I took care of him and I took care of the bills."

In 1997 Magda fell and badly broke her leg. To this day she walks slowly, with a noticeable limp. Unable to work or even walk well after the accident, she returned to Tapachula to recover. At this time she stopped giving her sister money for her nephew's care. According to Magda, her first week or two at home was wonderful. She was happy to be home, she had missed her family, and she felt as if she were "in heaven, . . . like I was Carlos Salinas de Gortari."[3] Tears well up in her eyes as Magda speaks of how, after a few weeks, her family began to "behave badly." It is something she says she rarely speaks of to anybody; she is ashamed and does not want anyone in the zone to know.

My sister would arrive home from the market and give the best fruit to her daughters and to me, she would give maybe two or three little fruits. . . . One time we were eating, and my sister said to me, "Do you want the stew that is in the refrigerator? It's three days old, but in the refrigerator [it is still edible]." I told her it was a shame to waste it and to leave it for me, and that I would eat it. And my unmarried sister said, "Ay, what a pig. She's like a swine that eats rotten food."

Magda's nieces would sweep but leave the area around her bed dirty. They did not help her make her bed or bring her clean sheets. These are things Magda says she will never forget, "not even in my coffin under twenty tons of dirt, will I forget!" The mistreatment Magda suffered at the hands of her family might be explained by her work as a prostitute. Though she claims they do not know what she does for work, it is likely that, after nearly three decades in the ambiente, her family has somehow surmised what it is she does for work and treats her accordingly. Or perhaps their mistreatment of Magda stemmed from her inability to give them money during her recuperation.

Whether within a romantic or paid sexual encounter, in relationships with family members, or in relationships with co-workers, the notion of reciprocity plays a central role in the lives of zone women. Because of her family's lack of reciprocity, Magda now says she feels alone, that she has no family. She uses the phrase "one hand washes the other" to explain the nature of reciprocal relationships within the zone. As we are sitting in her room, a co-worker comes by with a sweet roll for Magda. She says, "See how just now that girl gave me some bread, and now I give her a little coffee, and like my mother said, may she rest in peace, 'One hand washes the other.' And look, that is why what my family did hurts me so much."

Bonita sends remittances to El Salvador to support her parents, her son, and two younger siblings. She clearly remembers the difficulties her family experienced during the political violence of the 1980s. "It was an ugly time. We would hear bombs dropping and bullets, and all of us would hide under the bed. We didn't have anything to eat and didn't want to go outside for fear of a stray bullet." The conflict in El Salvador has ended, but the poverty that spurred it has not, and Bonita's father, a former soldier who now works as a musician, cannot support the family. "There a tomato costs a peso. Everything is expensive. And the price of meat is sky-high—twenty pesos (US$2.35) for half a kilo! Everything costs so much." Though she understands her parents' need, she feels that they expect and often demand too much: "They want to wring the last drop out of me. If I had a hundred pesos in my hand [to give them], it would be gone in an hour."

CONSUMING DESIRES

Aside from allowing women to provide for themselves and their families, earnings from sex work have another important consequence: they allow poor women entry into a modern consumer economy. As Sonia lamented of her time in the zone, "Here, one becomes much more materialistic." When poor women suddenly find themselves able not only to survive but also to purchase consumer goods, they experience shifts in desire: new "wants" are created and transformed into "needs." In addition to work-related goods (clothing, shoes, and makeup), some workers also begin to purchase items such as inexpensive jewelry, clothing, electronic goods, and cell phones for themselves, as well as toys, clothing, and other items for their children.[4] This transformation from poor women with little disposable income into less-poor women who are consumers is particularly drastic for rural women, who are new to the urban environment—in which they are bombarded with messages about consumption via radio, television, and billboards—and the embeddedness of spending in everyday urban life.

Along with such shifts in spending habits come shifts in beliefs about identity, happiness, and self-worth. Magda's words reveal that sex work transformed her from a poor child to a "self-made" woman and proud consumer: "I grew up in a very humble house. We ate sitting on a mat on the floor, *tortillita* with salt and lime. And since I have been a woman who has suffered, today I am the happiest woman in the world. I have what I have from nothing. I made myself from nothing. Never did I think I would have a cassette player, or an air conditioner of two horsepower, or three pieces of property, thanks to God. I never imagined this, and three, four electric fans."

The situation that Magda describes makes it difficult for women to leave the ambiente, as there is no other job for which they are qualified that would allow them to earn and purchase as they do when working in prostitution. Though their work causes women to lose the worth ascribed to "respectable" women, by ascending the economic ladder they experience a new kind of worth associated not with gender but with class. This is yet another of the contradictions prostitute women must cope with: they earn more than many of their clients, but cultural beliefs regarding gender and morality still marginalize them. Becoming consumers allows the women to partially mitigate the stigma associated with selling sex.

Leaving the ambiente often means giving up the ability to earn and spend as one did when employed in prostitution. Desire to find other employment is further hampered by the demands of supporting families who have a vested interest in the continued prostitution of their daughter, sister, or cousin. While many workers speak of leaving the ambiente, few do. It is a difficult choice to make. Gabriela, like most other workers, had spoken frequently of leaving the ambiente in order to open up a little shop. When I returned to Mexico a year after I had left, I found her selling fish in a storefront not far from her home and the pirate taxi stand that serves the Galáctica. Gabriela sat on one side of a doorway inside a dark empty room on a wooden chair behind a metal table that held a pile of small *mojarras* (a common whitefish). A skinny white cat curled around the legs of the table. Gabriela's teenage daughter, Ximena, stood by, waving a rag over the fish to keep the dozens of flies from landing for more than a few seconds. On the other side of the doorway sat a woman with a large basket of plucked bright yellow chickens. Gabriela recounted how the other zone women had made fun of her for leaving the ambiente in order to become a fishmonger. While she admitted she made far less money selling fish than she did selling sexual services, Gabriela was happy to work outside the ambiente in a job she did not have to lie about, one that was close to home and in which her daughter could join her. It is important to note that Gabriela was able to leave the ambiente only because of the financial support she received from her partner, Miguel. In a subsequent visit, I found she had once again returned to the Galactic Zone.

As much as the zone provides illusion for clients, it also provides a fantasy of wellness and prosperity for workers. Though the work is difficult and stigmatized, the women work in nice clothing and makeup. The space is clean and fairly well maintained. One leaves work with cash in hand and is able to attain some of the respectability accorded persons with money to spend. This contrasts greatly with the reality of wearing an apron covered with fish blood while sitting in a dark, hot doorway, sprayed with silvery scales scraped off a pile of dead fish, only to earn a meager living.

Some workers who wish to leave the ambiente find they cannot. Roberto, the former sex worker from Guatemala, desperately wanted to leave, and though he did give up sex work, he continues to work in the ambiente as a janitor-gofer. Though no longer a sex worker, he still speaks of wanting to leave. When I asked why he didn't look for work elsewhere, he said, "Because of my lack of study and knowledge. . . . I've lived with people of the ambiente since I was a teenager." Roberto has been involved in the ambiente in some form since he was young, so he is reticent to leave an atmosphere he knows well, in which he feels relatively comfortable about fully expressing his sexuality, and where he has friends and acquaintances. Doña Paula, who runs a food stand across from Pepe's, used to work as a prostitute in the Galáctica. She eased her way out of it, running the food stand while still prostituting, before she finally was able to switch over to working her stand full-time and earn the respectable title of Doña, reserved for women who work in the ambiente in capacities other than sex worker.

STIGMA

Some feminist theorists argue that gender- and class-based exploitation constitutes the major reason why sex work is difficult for women. Though women come to sex work primarily for the money, I suggest it is the social construction of sexuality and gender—along with the resulting stigma, marginalization, silence, invisibility, and shame attached to selling sex—that many women find hardest to bear. Zone workers are stigmatized and disciplined as both women and workers for stepping beyond the boundaries of acceptable female behavior.

In his classic sociological work on the subject, Erving Goffman writes that, while stigma refers to "an attribute that is deeply discrediting," it is also about relationships—an attribute may not be inherently discrediting in itself but is sometimes constructed to define its possessor as discreditable in relation to another, who by lack of that attribute is confirmed as "normal."[5] The stigma that female sex workers suffer is what Goffman refers to as a "blemish of individual character": the stigmatized person is perceived as possessing weak will, unnatural passions, treacherous beliefs, and the like. Other groups who may bear such stigma of character include, according to Goffman, homosexuals, alcoholics, felons, the unemployed, political radicals, and the insane.[6]

For the women who work in prostitution, "passing" as an unstigmatized member of society is fraught with difficulties, as the following story illustrates. Mónica, Pepe, and I leave the zone together on a Thursday afternoon, heading by taxi to Los Explosivos, the popular palapa bar on Tuxtla's south side. We are going to attend a seventeenth-birthday party for Elena's teenage daughter, Larissa. Elena too is a sex worker, but currently she works in a private house in another town. I was surprised when Elena invited me. I didn't know her well and had never met her daughters. Pepe looks very put together and is particularly animated as we prepare to leave the zone. In his early sixties, he appears much younger. Short and thin, Pepe is beginning to go bald, and he wears his thin gray hair swept back off his angular face. He identifies as gay, but I have not known him to have a male partner. He is also more discreet than the other food vendors, who wear jewelry and feminine hairdos. Today Pepe has changed from his zone work clothes (a T-shirt, pants rolled up to the ankles, and plastic flip-flops) to a black-and-white button-down shirt, gray slacks, and shoes. Excited by the rare evening out, he speaks quickly, happily, loudly, explaining to nobody in particular why he brought such fine clothes to change into, "*Chinga tu madre* [Fuck your mother]. I'm not going to waste them [by working in them], get them all dirty."

I am surprised and saddened to find that the attendees of Larissa's party are largely affiliated with the zone: taxi drivers, sex workers, a food vendor, and me. The only other guests are Elena's younger daughter, Mari, and a sole friend of Larissa's. It seems a party more for us than for Larissa. We eat botanas, drink, and watch the stage show. I am impressed by Pepe's restraint—he is drinking what appears to be mineral water, and more impressed when I realize hours later that he has quietly been getting thoroughly tanked on vodka tonics. He begins to tell Mónica he loves her. Mónica, who had been attending a women's group organized by Alcoholics Anonymous, is drinking wine coolers. Pepe dances with Larissa. The normally brash and explosive Elena is unusually tranquil. Before we leave the bar to head back to Elena's house for cake, she approaches me in the bathroom, lowers her voice, and says of her daughters in a conspiratorial tone, "They don't know what I do." I reassure her that I will keep her secret. I have become an accomplished liar, skilled at keeping women's secrets and maintaining the lies they tell to the children and families whom I have come to know.

Back at the table, I lend Elena fifty pesos so she can pay the entire bill. We pile into one of the pirate taxis and head for Elena's apartment in the southern hills that overlook the city. The neighborhood is a poor one and home to other women from the Galáctica. The streets are not maintained, and some remain unpaved. Deep potholes resemble small canyons. The houses, though, are made of concrete and wood, unlike the poorer shanties in the southwestern hills where Lydia lives. Elena rents part of a large house—she has a kitchen, bedroom, bathroom and large rooftop porch. A green curtain is all that divides her section of the home from that of the other tenants.

We sit on the porch on rickety wooden chairs and continue to drink. Dolores and Lulu arrive from the zone. Lulu has dyed her hair from red to dark brown. Mónica admonishes her, "Why did you do that? You had it the perfect color. This doesn't suit you." Relationships in the zone are like this, complex, and they involve a great deal of lying and moments of brutal honesty. We all, Elena's daughters included, gather our chairs in a circle. Pepe sits in his chair, concentrating, it appears, on not falling out of it. He then begins to talk, as drunk people often do. His big, watery brown eyes look at me lovingly as he says to me in the little English he knows, "Come here. I done know. Yes, plis." We pull his chair over toward me, laughing, and he begins to hug me, saying loudly in Spanish now, "I love you. I love you more than anyone. I love you more than anyone in Mexico. I love you more than anyone in the Galactic Zone!" The last two words cut through the warm night air and everyone falls silent. It is a long and sobering silence. The words Zona Galáctica, rarely uttered outside the zone by workers, fall heavily onto every conversation on the porch, ending them like a giant period. Rather, we always refer to the zone as *allá*, or "there," as in "Are you going there?" or "I've just come from there." Finally Mónica's voice breaks the silence. "Pepe!" she hisses, scolding him. Even in his drunken state, he appears to know he has done something very, very wrong. We are supposed to keep each other's secrets. He stares down at the ground.

And as silent as it was only moments before, conversation suddenly erupts everywhere, as we attempt to cover up the awkward moment. We hope that Elena's daughters somehow missed the last few minutes, though surely they did not. Mónica firmly and quietly tells Pepe he should have more manners. I am sent off to the bedroom with Larissa and Mari, where we lie on the bed and I help them translate into Spanish the lyrics on an old Rod Stewart cassette. It is getting late and I decide to leave. Larissa and Mari tell me that the party will go on all night, and that they have to wake up for school at seven in the morning. "We are used to it," they say with resignation. I force Pepe into a cab with me, though he insists he is not ready to go home. I get dropped off first, but Pepe is too drunk to remember where he lives, so I dig out my address book and instruct the driver, praying that Pepe gets home safely without getting robbed or assaulted. Even on occasions like this, when Galáctica workers attempt to broaden their circle for celebrations, they remain isolated by stigma and fearful that their secret will be revealed.

The stigma of working as a full-time prostitute circumscribes one's social relations, causes fear and shame, and creates situations of inauthenticity in daily life. Unlike Tuxtla's street prostitutes, who work intermittently in order to supplement earnings from their day jobs, or work only a few hours late at night servicing perhaps only one or two clients, a woman who works as a prostitute full-time, particularly a registered zone worker, has made a greater commitment to sex work and so bears its stigma to a greater extent. The clandestine sex worker is clandestine in that she works at night in private locations, whereas the regulated prostitute often works during the day in the public Galáctica, where she is registered and on display.

As Elena's story illustrates, most workers attempt to keep their employment a secret, even from those closest to them. Keeping this secret requires a great deal of effort and can generate an enormous amount of anxiety and alienation. Erving Goffman tells us, "Close relationships that the individual had before he came to have something to conceal therefore become compromised, automatically deficient in shared information. Newly formed or 'post-stigma' relationships are very likely to carry the discreditable person past the point where he feels it has been honorable of him to withhold the facts. And, in some cases, even very fleeting relationships can constitute a danger, since the small talk suitable between strangers who have struck up a conversation can touch on secret failings."[7] Though workers employ various strategies to separate their work and home identities and conceal their "secret failings," this compartmentalization can never be fully complete. Workers often become known in town and may run across clients, zone staff, and co-workers in the city center. A sex worker must lie frequently and can rarely let her guard down, even in, or especially in, her own home. There are few occupations, aside from international spy, mobster, and police informant, that require so much subterfuge.

Women who work as prostitutes generally do so in places they are new to, where they have no family, so they do not risk the humiliation of being seen by a brother, cousin, or uncle. In this way, workers' worlds become divided spatially between places where the stigma they suffer is to be concealed or revealed. Yet with time, the anonymity sought by zone workers decreases as they become known by some of the hundreds of repeat customers who visit the Galáctica. As much as workers try to create borders between their lives outside the zone and their work in the ambiente, these borders are permeable. When zone and city center meet, it creates anxiety for workers. Adriana spoke of the horror she felt when she saw a man from her neighborhood in the Galáctica. She hid in her room for hours, working, but leaving her door open only a few inches. Workers may also find themselves approached by clients when in the city center. Gabriela remembers two such incidents:

> One time I was in the pharmacy with my boyfriend, when suddenly a man came up and grabbed me and hugged me and said to me, "Hi. You didn't go to the zone today?" Then the cashier stared at me and I just lowered my head. Another time I was going to the market with my daughter, and another man in the street said hello to me and wanted to hug me. I stepped to the side and said to him, "What is with you?" He asked me if I went to work today, and I felt bad because I was with my daughter.

These sorts of actions indicate to workers a lack of respect for the women. As Gabriela remarked to one client, "Look, inside here [the zone] I am whatever you want, but outside, respect me, because I too have a family."

Both being approached and being ignored reinforce a woman's role as a prostitute, something she tries to shed when she leaves the zone. Being ignored by those who staff the SMAV and administrative offices angers many women, who feel they are being snubbed. Sitting at Doña Paula's food stand one hot day, Flor expressed her anger with the "rudeness" of the zone staff. She had recently seen both the Accountant and the doctor while in town, and had been ignored by each of them. Even Olivia, a nurse whose husband is a pirate taxi driver and whose mother-in-law is Doña Mari, a zone landlady, ignores them, says Flor.

During my early days in the field, it was often difficult to know how to respond to workers outside the zone. One afternoon I stopped by the municipal government offices to speak with the mayor, and I soon found myself swept along into a parade that the city government was sponsoring. As I walked down the street with the mayor, his functionaries, and a few dozen people of Zoque descent in traditional dress, I looked up to see a woman who looked like Sonia standing nearby on the curb, smiling at me. I was unsure what to do. Would going over to say hello to her somehow give away her secret? I was new to the ambiente and didn't know. I smiled back and kept marching. In another instance, I was sitting in the plaza in San Cristóbal, immersed in conversation with a friend, when suddenly Viviana appeared in front of me with a few children in tow. We hugged and chatted for a while and made plans to get together for pizza that evening. Later she told me that when she had first seen me in the plaza that day she had waved, and that I had looked at her and gone back to talking with my friend. I had not seen her or her wave, but she said to herself, "Maybe Patty doesn't want to talk to me. Maybe she has changed." It took all her courage to approach me and possibly be rebuffed rather than simply walking off.

When Sonia entered the ambiente, she told her family in El Salvador that she was working as a clothing vendor who traveled from city to city. For someone who has never worked selling clothing, she is well informed about such businesses; she can easily discuss how to rent a location from the city, where to buy the clothing wholesale, how to price it, and travel. Of her knowledge, Sonia says, "It was a good idea for me to learn all that in case they (my family) ask me questions." Lying to her family was difficult at first, but she says, "After a while you start to believe it, until you think it is true."

While lying to family members who live in another city, state, or even country can be difficult, it is even more difficult to lie to one's children, who may live with sex workers. Many women find that as children grow older they become more curious and even suspicious. As Gabriela's children grew older, they often asked her what she did for work and even asked her to take them with her. She told them she worked as a waitress, a cook, and sometimes a maid—the sort of jobs she would probably be doing were she not in the Galactic Zone. But Gabriela chose to tell her children about her work when she felt they were old enough to understand. As she explains it, "I couldn't bear any longer what I carried inside from lying to them, and so when I saw that she [Ximena, her eldest daughter] was getting older and was already in her second year of secondary school, I told her I wanted to talk with her." Gabriela knew that her daughter probably already had some idea of what prostitution was from watching movies, soap operas, and dramatic television programs such as *Casos de la Vida Real*. (*Real Life Cases* is a television program that reenacts true and horrifying stories, along with delivering to viewers not so subtle social messages about the value of family. The one time I saw it, a very depressed teenage girl committed suicide by sticking her head in the oven. She was unhappy about her parents' divorce and the lack of attention from her mother.) Though fearful that her daughter would reject her, Gabriela could no longer lie:

> So, I said to her, "Listen, Ximena, I want to talk with you. What would you do if you were told that your mama is a woman of the street, or that your mama works in a place that is not decent, that is indecent?" She just sat there looking at me, and said to me, "Look Mami, if it is in order to help us move forward, I will defend you. Even if they were to say you are the worst of women, to me you are the best of mamas, because for me and my sister you are papa and mama at the same time." I told her, "Thank you," and felt like she didn't disappoint me, because I thought there are many children who reject their mamas when they find out they work in this. And I feel they shouldn't reject them, but on the contrary, they should support them and love them more because, even though, here we are, filled with sex with men, we don't do it with pleasure. It's because they are paying you a certain sum that you endure it.

Gabriela's story illustrates the complex interactions between stigma, morality, familial love, and responsibility. Many zone women work as prostitutes in order to support children and extended families, but do so at the risk of losing the emotional support and respect of those very people they financially support. While Gabriela's daughter defended her mother's choice to work as a prostitute, Mónica attributes her tempestuous relationship with her son, who lives in Veracruz, to his recent discovery of her employment after he overheard a phone conversation between the relatives he lives with and his mother. Bárbara suggests that, even if one's family members appear to accept a woman's work in the ambiente, "there is a wound, a certain feeling. On the outside they forgive you, but inside, no. I wouldn't be able to get along with my family. if they found out about this, because they wouldn't trust me and wouldn't treat me like their daughter. More like a stranger or something, and with a certain contempt. And I could not bear that."

Telling their friends the truth about their work is not a cause of concern for most women, as they have few friends outside the ambiente. Bonita says she has little contact with people outside the zone, such as neighbors: "I go home and I close the door." Gabriela explains her own approach to the problem: "For example, say I met you in the street and we became friends, and afterward you say to me, 'Hey Gabriela, where do you work?' 'Mmmmm, I work in a store,' I say. I'm not going to tell you, because if I tell you I work in the zone, you aren't going to talk to me." Working in the zone isolates women, cuts them off from the social relationships and support that other workers have outside the workplace, and makes it more difficult to leave the ambiente. Gabriela has few relationships with women outside the ambiente, because these women, she says, would reject her. They would fear she had a contagious illness or might make sexual advances toward their boyfriends.

As noted earlier, how a worker spends her earnings, and how she experiences the work, may mitigate the stigma associated with sex work. A prostitute who spends her earnings drinking, who neglects family members, and who appears to enjoy her work is considered less moral, or less "decent," even by other sex workers. Ideas about decent women, as opposed to "loose" or "immoral" women, are deeply ingrained, even in sex workers, who by their actions may appear to, and sometimes have been able to, free themselves from some oppressive cultural norms regarding gender and sex. One may work as a prostitute, but, as Magda says, a decent woman should do so "with shame."

Only the way a worker spends her earnings makes the work morally defensible. As Ximena told her mother, "Look Mami, *if it is in order to help us move forward, I will defend you.*" Gabriela's words, too, imply that sacrificing for one's family—doing the job not for pleasure but out of necessity—renders sex work less immoral. As Gabriela notes, "The bad thing is that people scorn us *without seeing the motives we have for doing this.*" There is a moral value attached to properly caring for one's children. Even other zone women look down on and sometimes gossip about the women they perceive as negligent in their responsibilities to their families. Obligadas, who give their earnings to pimps, are somewhat free from such moral judgments, as it is known that they haven't any choice as to how to spend their money (though they may be considered "stupid"). Most zone women accept a highly traditional view of motherhood, and it is their work as prostitutes that allows them to fulfill this idealized role.

One need not work as a prostitute to experience the shame that comes from being associated with the Galáctica. Roberto, though no longer a sex worker, was sitting in a worker's room one day when he was seen by a young man from the city center with whom he had a friendship. Roberto had been hoping this man was gay, like him, but had not told his friend of his homosexuality or his place of employment for fear of alienating him. When his friend asked Roberto what he was doing there, he lied, claiming he was just visiting a friend. This incident caused Roberto a great deal of worry: Did the man he was romantically interested in have sexual relations with the women in the zone? Did he know that Roberto worked in the zone? Did he now know that Roberto was gay?

This last cause of concern, having one's sexual orientation revealed simply by being a male worker in the Galáctica, may seem peculiar until one understands that it is generally well known by Tuxtlecos who have been to the zone, or who know somebody who has been there, that most men who do service work in the zone (all the male food vendors and Roberto, but not the police, administration, or handymen) are gay. Roberto's hopes about his friend's sexuality and his fears about being "outed" in front of his friend are, when seen in this light, entirely justifiable.

FREEDOM AND RESTRICTION

It is evening in the zone, and Carla has arrived for work. Carla looks like a boy: hair cropped close to her head, no makeup, an extra-large light-green polo shirt covering her thin torso, and skinny legs poking out of her short blue pants. She wears white sneakers and no socks. Carla is not a sex worker but a seamstress who sews strappy, revealing minidresses for the workers, the sort of dresses impossible to find in any store. She presents a tiny red Lycra dress to Ramona, who shyly goes behind the curtain to her bathroom to try it on. When she comes out, wearing the dress, Carla tells her the bodice is too loose, that she has nothing to fill it out. There is a brief discussion of breast size among the three of us that culminates with Carla lifting her shirt and pulling a breast out of a lacy black bra (a startling contrast to her boyish exterior) and complaining of her lack of "firmness."

Carla's willingness to expose her breast was surprising; in the zone, most workers, though they may sometimes dress in a revealing way, adhere to certain cultural notions of female modesty and propriety. Ramona would not change her clothes in front of us. My own social interactions with women outside the zone made visible the ways in which sex workers accept prevailing standards of female modesty, which often greatly contrasted my own norms. During at outing to Chicoasén for swimming, the sex workers would not let me wear my bikini in the river and loaned me loose shorts and a baggy top instead. It's not easy to swim fully clothed, but I wouldn't want to attract unwanted attention, they insisted. On another occasion, following a swim at a local pool, I returned from the bathroom in a knee-length skirt with my wet panties that I swam in (again under a long, shapeless T-shirt lent to me) in my hands. The women from the zone were shocked. Mónica worried aloud about what would happen were I to fall down and accidentally expose myself. I told her I didn't plan on falling down and exposing myself (and then began to worry about falling down). When a group of us entered a bar recommended by El Profe, the workers were dismayed to find it was a men's cantina and not a family-style bar. We stayed anyway, but not without a certain level of discomfort.

While some women may strut about the zone in revealing clothing and defiantly proclaim, "Soy puta" (I'm a whore), this demeanor often contrasts with the women's behavior outside of work. In the Galáctica, Flor is known for her consistent and loud use of profanity and sometimes refers to herself as a "whore." Yet she remains angry and unforgiving about the time Pepe called her a whore. At home, she speaks less loudly, curses infrequently, and hides her work from her neighbors and acquaintances. Lorena, the most educated and politically informed worker, defends the women's right to behave as they wish in the zone, including cursing and behaving in a raucous way. "After all," she says, "this is a whorehouse, not an office." But Lorena also compartmentalizes her life, separating her working self from her home self: "Here in the zone, I am Lorena, and in the street I am Lourdes."

The Galactic Zone is a space apart, where norms regarding gender and sexuality are enacted and subverted. Workers can find certain liberties in the zone. It is a place where women may leave behind the cultural restrictions on dress, speech, and behavior. More important, it is a place where women can live and work without the dependence on male spouses or family that Mexican culture prescribes. In her personal relationships, the independent worker is able to maintain a great deal control over both her finances and her sexuality—and the two are not unconnected.

In the zone, as noted earlier, individuals may also express their sexual orientation without fear. Homosexuality is generally tolerated and openly discussed among sex workers. Over dinner one evening, Viviana told me that her thirteen-year-old daughter had a *lesbianita* (little lesbian) in her class at school, and that she told her daughter to respect the girl. Another example involved Ofelia, who had recently returned to the zone soon after having a baby with her partner (she said that, since she was already having sex at home with her partner, she felt she might as well come back to work). One day a group of us sat in Lorena's room, where she was lying down on her side, and Ofelia sat leaning up against Lorena's stomach. Lorena began to jokingly moan with desire and grope around at Ofelia's large, postpregnancy breasts, accentuated by a tight halter top. Gaby and Ofelia began to tease Lorena, accusing her of getting excited, when Ofelia suddenly jumped off the bed and shouted at her, laughing, "You're wet!" Ofelia leaned over to look at Lorena's crotch for evidence of wetness that would indicate sexual excitement as Lorena lay on the bed laughing and hugging a pillow. She then went to open Lorena's sweatpants, as they were the style that button up the sides and may be opened up completely with a swift pull. Unfortunately, this pair had been sewn shut, and they ripped. "Oops," said Ofelia, apologizing. The room, Lorena included, erupted with laughter, and Ofelia revealed her own sexual history, saying, "It's been two years since I craved a woman, anyhow."

The zone, then, is simultaneously a place of confinement and restriction, a holding pen for populations defined as deviant, and also a space of freedom, where these populations can experience alternative expressions of sexuality, gender, speech, and dress. When I asked the director of public health why the majority of men employed in the zone as vendors are gay, he suggested they were there because of their own "perversions"—that they enjoyed watching the male clients come and go. Indeed, some of the vendors do enjoy looking at the clients; on slow days Pepe is prone to looking forlorn and sighing, "Not one handsome man here today." Of course, this behavior is not an expression of some deep-seated perversion but rather an open and rare expression of his sexual self that would be less acceptable in the city center. Yet the liberties found in the ambiente are diminished by the stigma of working there, which affects the women's home lives and effectively controls and separates the women, inhibiting them from engaging in collective activity as prostitutes outside the Galactic Zone.

EIGHT

Final Thoughts

UNDERSTANDING, IMAGINING

I believe that every human being is potentially
capable, within his "limits," of fully "realizing"
his potentialities; that this, his being cheated and
choked of it, is infinitely the ghastliest, commonest,
and most inclusive of all the crimes of which the
human world can accuse itself.

James Agee

People who have everything cannot imagine what
I have to do to earn money. Sometimes I don't
understand it either.

Sonia

Sitting in Pepe's food stand one morning, I watch workers arrive and head
toward the SMAV. Pepe is flitting about, in constant motion, wiping tables,
preparing tacos, doing a little waltz with a dingy gray dishrag that he
embraces like a lover, holding it up to the side of his face. Every now and
then he says a little rhyme out loud: *No quería María.* Maria didn't want to.
He sits down at a table, dishrag in hand, and sighs, finishing the rhyme: *No
quería María, pero sus piernas abría,* Maria didn't want to, but her legs opened.

Having sex with men for money can be difficult and demanding work.
Though all the workers experience commercial sex differently, it was not
the first job choice for any woman I spoke to. When I asked workers what
they would like to do were they not employed in the zone, nearly all

responded that they would like to set up a small shop or vending booth of some kind, be it a taco stand (Mónica), a clothing store (Bárbara), or a food stand (Gabriela). But Esperanza hopes to be a teacher one day, and the deeply religious Magda says that, when she retires from the ambiente, she plans to spend her time evangelizing. Workers' dreams for the future are pragmatic, shaped by the realities of the Mexican economy and their own educations and hard lives.

Still, as Sonia describes it, working in the zone is less difficult than working in other sectors of the ambiente, such as the cabaret. "There you have to dance, talk with them, drink with them. Here it is much easier. They come in [she makes a rocking motion with her hips], *suki, suki, suki,* and it's all over!" And while many zone workers are more likely to complain about issues such as working conditions, expenses, and stigma, they admit, during rare moments of openness when they are willing to express their vulnerability, that the actual work, intercourse with men who are strangers, can be emotionally challenging. Lorena says she closes her eyes when she is with a client so that "my eyes don't record it in my brain." Mónica agrees with Lorena and says that for many years she didn't even think about it, and drank heavily. It is not the actual physical act that is most challenging, though the number of acts performed in one day may be taxing, especially since they're performed on the zone's cheap mattresses sans box springs. It is the cultural attitudes toward gender, the meanings assigned to sexuality, the poverty in which the women live, and the social and economic context in which selling one's body occurs that make the work most challenging.

But, as Anne McClintock has written, such things "can and must be changed. Empowering sex workers empowers all women, for the whore stigma is used to discipline women in general; and encouraging society to respect sex workers encourages society to respect all women."[1]

UNDERSTANDING

In defiance of theorists on either side of the sex work–prostitution debates, in defiance of tendencies toward binary thinking and pat answers, in defiance of a craving for order and clarity, the lives of the women of the ambiente are filled with deep contradictions and, like Sonia says, are hard to understand. Sex work offers the women a decent living but is accompanied by great emotional and physical risk. They lie about their work to the people they love, whereas they fake intimacy with strangers. They redefine sex as an economic interaction and work, while retaining some conceptualization of it as part of romantic love. In prostitution, a social construction of gender that separates and ranks women is reinforced, demonizing some while sanctifying others, but sex workers are also freed from certain gendered cultural restrictions on behavior, speech, and dress. They simultaneously defy and enact sexual and gender norms. Society defines them as both essential and expendable. Through prostitution, women gain some degree of personal and financial independence but continue to live within a larger framework of dependency and inequality. Sex workers need not rely on male romantic partners and family members—and this gives them freedom from a cultural system that reinforces female dependency—but they must instead rely on male clients. They are entrepreneurs who make their own schedules, but their work lives are highly regulated by municipal authorities. They are service workers, but they resist notions of servitude, instead negotiating with and refusing clients, and even teaching them about sexual health. The stories of sex workers' lives illustrate that prostitution in the Galactic Zone is neither wholly oppressive nor liberating. Rather, the work, performed within a broader system of unequal power relations and burdened by stigma, contains within it a complex blend of exploitation and freedom. Entering sex work, women cross geographic and moral borders to do work that is, as Sonia says, beyond the imaginations of most people.

Women enter the Galactic Zone in a variety of ways for a variety of reasons. They come to escape abusive partners and, more rarely, they come because they are forced by abusive partners. They come for others and for themselves. Most of all, they come for the money. The work sometimes allows women a small degree of economic stability that, by virtue of their class, citizenship, gender, and their place in the global economic order, would normally be unavailable to them. In the Galactic

Zone, the women's services are consumed, and the women in turn learn to consume. As Magda told me, "I made myself from nothing. Never did I think I would have a cassette player, or an air conditioner of two horse-power, or three pieces of property, thanks to God. I never imagined this."

The turn toward prostitution by the women of the Zona Galáctica is also a testament to both an ongoing and lengthy history of economic inequality and injustice in Mexico and Central America and the tendency of neoliberalism to exacerbate rather than eradicate such inequality. The modernization of Chiapas offers little opportunity to poor ladinos, and still less to indigenous peoples, who struggle to enter into an increasingly global society on their own terms. The conflict over the ejido land on which the brothel was built was not just a battle for land but also a symbolic struggle between México profundo and modernity—between collective landholding and community, and growing consumerism and individualism. The selling and buying of sexual services in the Galáctica is part of a broader global trend toward increased commoditization and consumption of household activities, sex included. The women of the Galactic Zone are only a small sample of the burgeoning ranks of poorly paid women from the developing world, many of whom are the sole providers for their families, who sell domestic services such as cooking, child care, cleaning, and sex throughout the globe.

With fast food restaurants, big-box stores, and shopping malls transforming Chiapas's urban landscape, the Galactic Zone is yet another altar to a new, modern, and global political-economic order in which consumption is revered. Yet the zone is more than this. It is also a place where local authorities seek to streamline and reorganize the culturally institutionalized buying and selling of sex by the popular classes. This is not to say that they seek to end the stigmatization of women who sell sex. Far from it. The policies and regulations of the Galactic Zone all but ensure the continued stigmatization of sex workers. Rather, in the zone, authorities have tried to bring a new order to the sexual marketplace, to make commercial sex, which is potentially messy and even transgressive, clean and efficient and invisible. Governmental oversight of the zone teaches us that the state, under neoliberalism, is not reducing its role in public life.[2] State policy in Tuxtla encourages the free market, nurturing the growth of a low-wage, exploitative service-sector economy while eroding support for subsistence and community-oriented economic activities.

Rural poverty exacerbated by neoliberal reforms generates urban expansion as immiserated populations converge on cities seeking work. Farmers become service-sector or informal laborers. Women, often left responsible for financially supporting their families as men become economically marginalized, increasingly enter the market economy on terms that lay bare the inequalities of class, gender, and ethnicity. Tuxtla's skyrocketing population growth, due primarily to immigration, worries public officials, as armies of the poor descend on the city and threaten its hard-won modern reputation. Tuxtla is Chiapas, and Chiapas, as it has been said so many times since the Zapatista uprising, is Mexico.

Despite Tuxtla's relative prosperity, the Chiapas to which the Central American migrants and rural Mexicans come in search of economic well-being continues to advance a neoliberal policy that threatens to further impoverish women, children, and men throughout Mexico. And in Central America, the birthplace of half the women working in the Galáctica, things have taken a sharp turn for the worse. The Central American Free Trade Agreement (CAFTA), a comprehensive free trade treaty modeled on its cousin NAFTA, will soon be implemented in six nations. The agreement threatens to further quicken the pace of advanced capitalism in Central America, preparing the region for increased immersion in a global free market characterized by the exploitation of cheap labor and the degradation of environmental standards, labor rights, and rural life.[3] CAFTA, says Bishop Álvaro Ramazzini of Guatemala "not only fails to address the need of Central America's poor, sick, and vulnerable but may well make conditions here worse."[4]

Regulated prostitution in the zone, though it provides women with a work environment that is relatively free of the crime and violence that characterizes street prostitution, is of questionable value when it comes to diminishing the incidence of HIV in both sex workers and clients and among the population at large. In creating an inexpensive market for working-class consumers seeking commercial sex, the state attained, in part and temporarily, its goal of cleansing the streets of visible commercial sexualities. But focusing public health efforts on people who work as prostitutes does little to prevent the overall transmission of HIV and STDs; prostitutes themselves are not the primary or sole vector of HIV transmission in Chiapas. In addition, the zone, one of the "cheapest brothels in the Mexican Republic," may discourage condom use, since women who earn so little may be less likely to use a condom in order to earn enough to pay for meals and expensive daily room rents. Furthermore, clients, typically lacking solid information on sexual health, believe that regulated workers are free from disease simply because they work in a regulated zone where they receive medical examinations. But medical examinations do not in themselves prevent disease; and as McClintock points out, "it is not the exchange of cash that transmits disease—high-risk behaviors do."[5] Despite the workshops, health information, questionable medical testing, and condom distribution program, the Galactic Zone, while it may be a safe place to buy sex, is not necessarily a place for safe sex.

So, why regulate prostitution? Walking down the cobblestone streets of San Cristóbal's historic district, I pause to read on the wall of an old building some graffiti that, in part, answers the question. *Nos quieren domesticar.* They want to domesticate us.

IMAGINING

There are people who have, despite the odds, maintained their ability to imagine a reality different from the existing one. The Zapatistas, through their "uprising of hope," have dared to envision and create something different from and better than the inequality and despair that have for so long marked the lives of so many rural and indigenous Chiapanecos.[6] From Asia to Latin America to the United States, prostitutes too have organized, challenging existing social norms and inequalities that stigmatize and punish women who sell sexual services. Ten years ago, on that warm August afternoon when Desirée, Lorena, and the rest of the women took control of the brothel, the sex workers of the Galactic Zone too began to imagine and actively seek alternatives. Social change begins with the shared ability to imagine something different, something better.

Because prostitution is a varied and complex phenomenon, experienced differently by those who participate in it, and because it is marked by intricate, overlapping, and systemic power relations that reach beyond gender inequality, it is not easy to plot a straight path to the improvement of the lives of sex workers and the conditions under which they labor.[7] "There is not," McClintock writes, "a single, authoritative narrative of prostitution, nor is there a single, internationally correct blueprint for political organizing."[8]

The current social and political-economic context in which the prostitution of the women and men of Tuxtla Gutiérrez occurs makes their work and their lives far from easy. The stigmatization of women who work as prostitutes in the zone individualizes, shames, and silences female sex workers, many of whom lie to their families, demonize one another on moral grounds, and avoid engaging in collective action. Regulating sex workers, confining and disciplining them, and defining them as a threat disempowers women who engage in legalized prostitution. Criminalizing sex workers similarly disempowers and punishes. Why must sex workers be confined and highly supervised in order to receive the social benefits (education, relative freedom from violence, and access to condoms and health information) found in the Galactic Zone? Implicit in the regulationist system is both the disciplining and stigmatization of those who work legally and the criminalization of sex workers who do not work within the bounds of the regulationist system. While both groups are demonized, regulation further divides sex workers into those whose activities are state sanctioned and highly controlled, and those whose work is illegal and criminal and who are subject to arrest.

Loosening the controls and dismantling the regulationist system while decriminalizing the activities of all sex workers is a step toward reducing the stigmatization and empowering prostitute women and men. Stigmatization is a key factor in inhibiting sex workers from individually and collectively demanding and receiving the rights, respect, and remuneration they deserve. Ineffectual testing disguised as health care, exploitative landlords, impunity for violent clients and corrupt medical profes-

sionals, and insufficient access to condoms are issues that can be reme-
died by those truly concerned with the well-being of sex workers and
society. Yet any grand plan to ensure sex workers' health and human
rights must include sex workers' voices. They are the experts in their
field, and they have a right to participate in policy-making decisions that
will affect their work and well-being.

In thinking about how to improve the lives of sex workers, we would
do well to look beyond the Galactic Zone at the various approaches the
state takes in regulating, criminalizing, or decriminalizing prostitution.
In Tijuana, Baja California, city officials in 2005 revamped local prostitution laws, compelling sex workers to get tested for STDs at the municipal
clinic, fining brothel owners who do not adopt "more sanitary practices," and issuing high-tech credit-card-like ID cards to sex workers that
bear the woman's photograph and a magnetic strip that may be scanned
to instantly reveal a worker's medical status.[9] This modernization of regulation is, however, little more than the modernization of exploitation
and efforts by the state to control marginal populations. Taking a different approach, in 1998 Swedish government officials, guided by the belief
that prostitution is never voluntary, enacted reforms to criminalize prostitution under a measure titled "The Protection of Women." A 2004 report
released by the Swedish Ministry of Justice and the police assessing the
impact of the reforms found that, after the laws came into effect, prices
for sexual services dropped, clients were fewer but more often violent
and more often willing to pay more for sex without a condom, and sex
workers had less time to assess the mental state or violent potential of a
client because of the need to quickly make arrangements to serve the
client, for fear of getting caught.[10] Criminalizing prostitution criminalizes
prostitutes, impels them to work in unsafe situations, and increases violence against them.

New Zealand's 2003 Prostitution Reform Act is, to date, the most progressive and informed response to the complex issues surrounding commercial sex. The act, which decriminalizes prostitution, seeks to create a
legal and social framework that, in the words of the new law, "safe-
guards the human rights of sex workers and protects them from
exploitation, promotes the welfare and occupational health and safety of

sex workers, is conducive to public health, [and] prohibits the use in prostitution of persons under 18 years of age."[11] Under the act, sex workers are protected by the country's occupational health laws, are not required to undergo compulsory medical testing or provide health certificates, and have the right to refuse clients. Furthermore, clients, sex workers, and brothel owners alike bear equal responsibility for minimizing the risk of acquiring or transmitting sexually transmitted illness. Extending responsibility to clients and beyond the individual sex worker is more than just legal discourse. In 2005, a New Zealand district court convicted a client of violating the Prostitution Reform Act when, unbeknownst to the sex worker, he removed his condom during sex.[12] In addition, the reforms give workers a new voice in government decision-making that affects them. The eleven-member Prostitution Law Review Committee, created to review and assess the reforms, includes three members of the New Zealand Prostitutes Collective, a sex-worker advocacy organization. Though the outcome of the New Zealand reform remains to be seen (and the fact that it does not extend to immigrant workers is a major flaw), this sort of model for the decriminalization of prostitution offers the most protection for the health and rights of women and men who labor in the sex industry.

Still, I remain ambivalent about prostitution, a form of work that often separates self from body and sex from pleasure, but I can't say the exchange of sex for cash is wrong. The problem is not prostitution but what prostitution represents in this particular context: a global shift from subsistence to service; a detachment of people from the land base and from their ability to support themselves; a separation of people from their communities, their families, their bodies, their emotions. It is not necessarily sex work that cheats and chokes women. It is an unjust economic system paired with an unequal gender-sex system that cheats and chokes women. Ironically, within such a system, women can sometimes find in prostitution a life better than the one they might have had.

Derrick Jensen writes, "Fearing death, fearing life, fearing love, and fearing most of all the loss of control, we create social rules and institutions that mirror our fears and reinforce our destructive behaviors. Having surrounded ourselves with images of ourselves, and having silenced all others, we can now pretend that the false-front world we've created is instead the world we've been given."[13] The Galactic Zone, one small part of the acceleration of advanced global capitalism in Mexico, is Derrick Jensen's "false-front world," Bonfil Batalla's "imaginary Mexico," a place not natural, but a place created. This book offers a step toward understanding the Zona Galáctica and the time of which it is a part; toward understanding the lives of women workers made invisible as they are "cheated and choked" of their potential by an economic system that exploits, a construction of gender that oppresses, and a moral order that demonizes; and toward understanding the faith, defiance, and dignity that endure even in the midst of such extraordinarily constraining circumstances. And it is these things—faith, defiance, and dignity, along with the realization that we've created this place and time and so can change them—that encourage imaginings of something better.

Epilogue

I

The road between San Cristóbal and Tuxtla climbs high into the clouds, curving and winding all the way until it slowly descends through corn-fields into the central lowlands of Chiapas. This road has recently been modernized, replaced by a much straighter and far less beautiful high-way that has cut travel time between San Cristóbal and Tuxtla in half. Past the indigenous community of Navenchauk and its strange, still lake that comes and goes like the rains. Past Piedra Parada and its namesake giant rock, painted white now, jutting two stories skyward. It's a cool, foggy morning and I stare out the window of the collective taxi into the lush green and fog and mist, willing away the nausea that the hairpin turns bring. I've made this journey dozens of times over the past year, and this ride is one of my last—I've gotten a fellowship that will pay me to write up my dissertation back in New York City. This good news makes me sick. It is not easy to leave the ambiente. The driver mercifully pops a loud salsa cassette with an anxiously frenetic beat out of the tape player. He slides in another, ABBA. Soothing Scandinavian 1970s pop. We're nearing the highest point in the mountains now. Heavy rains have washed much of the road away this year; at points the two-lane road is reduced to three-quarters of a lane. Orange traffic cones appear out of the green, warning. Somebody, feeling playful, has filled the orange cones with wild purple flowers. I think of the women of the zone and all they've shared with me. I think of the wild purple flowers and whoever put them there. I'm grateful for the gesture.

I I

Back in New York City, Sonia and I are slowly climbing the stairs inside the Statue of Liberty, crowded in along with hundreds of other tourists on a warm summer day. When she told me she wanted to see the statue, I balked at first. I had just been there a few months before with my niece, and being trapped on a staircase for hours in a giant piece of metal on a hot July day didn't sound like a good time. But there was a certain tenderness in her desire that it aroused in me something. It was the first time I could clearly understand the kind of struggle that would make a person truly yearn to see the Statue of Liberty.

As we climb higher, the stairs narrow, becoming a small, single-file staircase that spirals up and up, seemingly endlessly, though I knew we'd eventually reach the crown and the tiny windows that offer a complete view of lower Manhattan. We move slowly through the strange vertical tunnel, just a step or two at a time. Though we are all there by choice, the other pilgrims around us moan and complain about the trek. An overweight white woman with a Midwestern feel about her huffs about the physical effort required of her. Others cast anxious looks at their watches, worrying aloud about missing the Broadway show for which they have tickets. A few give up shortly after beginning, squeezing their way back down the steps against the throngs pushing upward. One guidebook to New York City describes the 354 steps as "excruciating."

Amid the complaining crowds, who are beginning to challenge my sense of goodwill and fleeting national pride, Sonia recounts the story of how she came from the Galactic Zone to the United States to find work. Sonia and the hundreds of other migrants who set out from their homes for the United States each day are propelled northward by neoliberalism's failure to provide. She, along with nearly thirty others, had paid a pollero to help them cross Mexico's northern border. Of the journey, Sonia, who has experienced an undue amount of suffering in her thirty-one years, tells me, "Never, Patty, never have I suffered like that." The group, mostly Salvadorans like Sonia, walked without pause for two and a half days. The days were unbearably hot and the nights too cold. On the first day, she drank all the water she had brought. By the second, her dry lips began to crack open, spilling blood down her chin. Sonia's shoes were not made for such a journey; one by one her toenails began to separate from the tender pink skin beneath and fall off. She wanted to stop, but the others walking at her side urged her to keep going. She was the only woman among them.

In front of us on the stairs is a group of young men from Texas. One occasionally turns around to ogle Sonia, who is attractive and looks younger than her age. The men hoot and holler, as thrilled about the ascent as if they are overtaking Everest. The ogler tries to engage Sonia in conversation. Mistaking her giggling for coy flirtation, he doesn't pick up on the fact that she doesn't speak a word of English.

Climbing and occasional interruptions aside, Sonia continues her story. There on the border, in the desert that takes the lives of hundreds of would-be new Americans each year, Sonia prayed that the Immigration and Naturalization Service authorities would catch her and send her back to Mexico. Or even El Salvador. She was in pain and not sure she would survive. But they didn't catch her.

During her early days living in a Latino community in New Jersey, she worked in a bar where she danced (fully clothed) salsa with men, immigrants like her, seeking not sex but companionship for only as long as a song or two. She later worked in a Salvadoran restaurant and then

Figure 13. A client heads home. Photo by Patty Kelly.

in a Burger King. By the end of a few weeks' time, she had sent three hundred dollars to her mother and son in El Salvador. The last time I spoke with her, she told me she had stashed away thousands of dollars in her pillowcase.

I have returned to the Galactic Zone again and again over the years. Since the initial period of my fieldwork, there has been both change and continuity in the zone. The outcome of the ejido conflict gave new life to the phrase "Mexican standoff." For nearly a year, both the city government and the Ejido Commission continued their efforts to win the rights to the land beneath the Galactic Zone. Finally, a federal judge ruled in favor of the ejidatarios, but decided that they could not take control of the land until they paid the city of Tuxtla Gutiérrez for the eighteen modules constructed there to house sex workers. The ejidatarios, being poor people, cannot afford to pay the city, and the land beneath the Galactic Zone remains, for now, in municipal hands.

Many of the women I came to know in the Galactic Zone remain there, while others have moved on. Gabriela returned to the zone after her efforts at earning money as a food vendor in downtown Tuxtla did not bear fruit. Esperanza, who had stopped working in the zone but who continued to take the adult education classes offered there during the period of my fieldwork, graduated from a school where she received a certificate in early childhood education. She had been lucklessly searching for work for many months. Bonita became totally immersed in the ambiente. She gained the weight that many women do when living and eating in the Galactic Zone and began to wear the specially made revealing clothing and heavy makeup preferred by some workers. Flor and Jacobo, the health inspector, broke up. Having lost a good deal of weight, Flor is no longer the *gordita* she says she once was, and she continues to be depressed by Jacobo's departure.

Mónica, who had been intent on leaving the ambiente and opening up a taco stand in her home state of Veracruz, left the Galactic Zone with high hopes during my last month in the field. Little had been heard of her, and rumor had it that she was doing sex work somewhere on the northern border. When I returned to the zone on a subsequent visit, I found that Mónica too had returned. She seemed sad and perhaps even embarrassed by her return. The close confidence we had once shared was all but gone. I recently heard that Mónica has again left the zone and married an old friend. She returns from time to time to sell clothing to her former co-workers. It is not so easy to leave the ambiente. Pepe and Doña Paula still feed the women and the staff of the Galactic Zone. Pepe saved enough money to finally buy the small food stand he had been renting from a cousin for nearly a decade. Dr. Ramos, thankfully, has been replaced. Magda, it was said, returned to her home in Tapachula after nearly three decades in prostitution. Bárbara, too, left the zone, though no one is sure what became of her. The three women who tested HIV positive during my absence were immediately and permanently suspended from work. One of these women may have been Lydia, for whom this book is named, and who died of an AIDS-related illness last year. Flor tells me she had to beg the zone administration for money to buy her a coffin.

And a client stabbed Alicia to death in her room. I didn't know her well. She had a tattoo on her arm. She tended to pal around with Lorena and Verónica. Small details. She lived in a concrete home near the Pan-American Highway with her children and a man. Some said he was her husband. Others whispered that he was a *mantenido*. It's really not important. The newspaper said she was originally from Campeche. Small details. Bleeding from the neck, Alicia managed to alert her co-workers who sought help for her. Her killer, presumed by many to be a soldier, successfully fled the Galactic Zone nude, leaving his clothing behind in Alicia's room. Weeks later, authorities claimed that the body of a man found in the nearby Sabinal River was that of the man who killed Alicia, but people in the zone disagreed, arguing that the description of the corpse did not match that of the client, and that authorities were trying to close the case without finding Alicia's murderer. Pepe told me that she had been stabbed in the neck in such a way that there was little chance of survival, but others said Alicia bled to death because she didn't receive adequate medical attention from the staff of the Anti-Venereal Medical Service, who may have been reluctant to treat her for fear of HIV—though there was no evidence she was HIV positive.

Lorena left the zone to give birth to her second child. Desirée's sister Viviana also had a child with her husband but is now back at work. Esperanza, who had been trying desperately to get pregnant with her first child during my time in the Galactic Zone, finally did so. The last time I saw her, she was living with her husband in a new rental home, content with her rapidly growing belly. The women of the Galactic Zone are resilient; some succumb to the dangers of their work, but most continue on, living and creating new lives, sometimes singing rather than crying.

Notes

PREFACE

1. Mies 1986, 24–25.
2. Bliss 2001, 15.
3. Weitzer 2000, 13.
4. For a more detailed discussion of my experience in the field, see Kelly 2004.
5. Rabinow 1984, 197.
6. Stacey 1988, 21.
7. Unlike the term *gringa, güerita* may be considered flattering. The politics of ethnicity and skin color are alive and well in Mexico, where lighter-skinned, non-indigenous populations continue to dominate in most realms of society. My own experience in Chiapas also reveals the culturally relativistic nature of appearance: in the United States, I am an olive-skinned, dark-haired, petite woman, while in the Galactic Zone I was transformed into an average-sized, light-skinned, green-eyed woman.
8. Jensen 2000, 99.
9. I have changed the names of all the sex workers and staff of the Galactic Zone. The names of major public figures have not been changed.

INTRODUCTION

1. Brennan 2004; Kempadoo 1999; Lim 1998; Wilson 2004.

2. Harvey 2005, 2.

3. Fernández-Kelly 1983; Ong 1987; Safa 1994.

4. For a good introduction to maquiladoras and their role in neoliberal development in Nicaragua, see Witness for Peace, n.d.

5. A brief example of the ways in which free trade can affect small-scale Mexican farmers: Following the 1994 passage of NAFTA (the North American Free Trade Agreement), trade barriers to the importation of corn produced less expensively by U.S. agribusiness were dropped, resulting in the flow of cheap corn exports into Mexico. Mexican farmers could not effectively compete with such cheap imports—as Public Citizen reports, "The price paid to farmers in Mexico for corn fell by over 70% as huge amounts of U.S. yellow corn were dumped into the Mexican market" (Public Citizen, n.d.).

6. Harvey 2005, 103–4; for more on the emergence of the Latin American billionaire during the neoliberal era, see NACLA 1997.

7. White, Salas, and Gammage 2003, iii. For the complete article about Bill Gates's wish, see http://business.timesonline.co.uk/tol/business/markets/united_states/article713434.ece, accessed July 15, 2007.

8. White, Salas, and Gammage 2003, 20.

9. For more on the gendered elements of neoliberalism, see Adamache, Culos, and Otero 1993; Nash 1994; Nash and Fernández-Kelly 1983; Sparr 1994; White, Salas, and Gammage 2003.

10. White, Salas, and Gammage 2003, 19.

11. UNICEF 2005, 16.

12. Farmer 2005, 40.

13. Rubin 1984, 267.

14. Weeks 1985, 16.

15. See Suárez Findlay 1999.

16. Foucault 1990 [1977], 69.

17. In late-nineteenth-century England, the Contagious Disease Acts called for the mandatory medical inspection of suspected sex workers; these laws were repealed in 1886 following organized feminist campaigns against them (Walkowitz 1980). Social anxiety regarding the white slave trade was high during this period in many countries, including England, Argentina, and the United States (see Guy 1990; Meil Hobson 1987). Nineteenth-century Puerto Rican liberal elites, reeling from the 1873 abolition of slavery and other forms of forced labor, sought to reorganize society through moral reforms focused on combating interracial promiscuity and taming elite women's sexual passions through education (Suárez Findlay 1999).

18. French 1992, 529. It should be noted here that the liberal tradition in Mexico is different and, in some ways, in opposition to a U.S. understanding of the term *liberal*. In the Mexican context, Liberalism in general, and economic liberalism in particular, are associated with policies such as free trade, privatization, and social conservatism.

19. Bliss 2001. An updated 1898 Reglamento increased the minimum legal age to sixteen (ibid., 32).

20. Ibid., 29.

21. Ibid., 5.

22. Ibid.

23. Ibid., 214–15.

24. Bello 1994, 25.

25. Witness for Peace, n.d., 6.

26. Bello 1994, 31.

27. Harvey 2005, 99.

28. Bello 1994.

29. For a fuller discussion of this and other aspects of privatization in Mexico, see Teichman 1993.

30. Marichal 1997, 28.

31. Nash 2001, 8.

32. CIACH 1997, 23.

33. Russell 1994, 283.

34. Ibid.

35. See Collier 1999 [1994].

36. Unfortunately, the electoral ballots were destroyed in 1992, preventing anyone from finding the truth. See Castañeda 1994, 157.

37. The PAN would win Tuxtla again in 1998 with the election of Paco Rojas and in 2001 with the election of Vicky Rincón. In 2004, the city would be back under PRI control.

38. Though the EZLN uprising is the best-known, poor Chiapanecos have been building independent campesino movements in the state since the 1970s. For more on other movements, see Collier 1999 [1994]; Harvey 1994, 1998; and Nash 2001.

39. For more on the Zapatista's alternative development strategies, see Earle and Simonelli 2005.

40. Among these were the misleadingly named Paz y Justicia (Peace and Justice), a pro-PRI peasant organization responsible for forced evictions, violence, and numerous killings in northern Chiapas. For more on this topic, see Human Rights Watch 1997, 43–45.

41. See Collier 1999 [1994], 88–89, for a deeper discussion of NAFTA and the timing of the EZLN uprising.

42. General Command of the EZLN, "Declaration of War," in ¡Zapatistas! Documents of the New Mexican Revolution (Brooklyn, NY: Autonomedia, 1994), 51.

43. On June 28, 1995, police shot and killed seventeen members of the Campesino Organization of the Southern Sierra and wounded twenty-three more. Members of the group were known for their activism protesting the loss of agrarian lands to national and international timber corporations.

44. Senzek 1997.

45. Instituto Nacional de Estadística, Geografía e Informática, "Conteo de Población y Vivienda 2005," 2005, www.inegi.gob.mx/est/contenidos/espanol/rutinas/ept.asp?t=mlen22&c=4168&e=07, accessed September 8, 2007.

46. Womack 1999, 21.

47. Subcomandante Marcos 1994, 30.

48. See Womack 1999 for more on González Garrido's changes to the penal codes. Collier 1999 [1994], 127, also provides a detailed analysis of changes to the penal code and their effect on agrarian activists in Chiapas, many of whom were jailed for dissent.

49. Miguel González Alonso, "Mexico a un paso de la anarquía," Cuarto Poder July 25, 2005, B12–13.

50. Collier 1999 [1994], 140.

51. Subcomandante Marcos 1994, 226.

52. See Harvey 1994. June Nash provides an example of changing regional priorities and practices surrounding privatization with the case of the sugar mill in Pujiltic. The mill began operating in the 1960s as a private enterprise, was sold to the government in the 1970s, reprivatized during the presidency of Carlos Salinas, and later sold back to the government (2001, 103).

53. Rojas Wiesner and Tuñon Pablos 2001, 85.

54. González Garrido's interest in matters of sexuality were not strictly limited to prostitution. During his governorship, abortion was decriminalized in Chiapas in December 1990. The new legislation, which allowed for abortion as a means of family planning, had a life of only twenty-two days: following pressure from the Catholic Church, it was suspended. It would be unwise to mistake the decriminalization of abortion under González Garrido's governorship as a feminist action. In a 2005 interview with the newspaper Cuarto Poder, the former governor is quoted as saying, "The wife of a president has no function other than in the bed, the kitchen, or the DIF [the national social welfare agency]." Abortion is allowed in certain circumstances, such as when the pregnant woman is HIV positive. Abortion following rape is legal in all Mexican states but is often actively discouraged by government and medical authorities. For more on this topic, see Human Rights Watch 2006.

55. Untitled document on the Galactic Zone, 1989, Servicios Coordinados de

Salud Pública en el Estado de Chiapas, Archivo Municipal de Tuxtla Gutiérrez, Expediente Zona Galáctica.

56. The use of accusations of homosexuality against public figures in common in Mexico, as such activity shakes societal foundations and public standing in ways that opposite-sex infidelity does not.

57. Otero 1996; Teichman 1996.

58. For a further discussion of debates about the meanings and impact of globalization, see Held, McGrew, Goldblatt, and Perraton 1999.

59. Harvey 2005, 2.

60. For further discussion of the ways in which the neoliberal state has shifted its attention to issues of the gender-sex system and away from social welfare, see Lancaster 2003.

61. Otero 2004, 3.

62. See Scott 1998, 2.

63. See Human Rights Watch 2006.

64. Ibid.

65. In 2001, the Mexican Constitution was amended to prohibit discrimination, including sexual discrimination. In the same year, the federal government created INMUJERES, the National Women's Institute, whose sole purpose is to promulgate equality for women in Mexico. While these changes were made during the presidential administration of Vicente Fox, do not mistake him for a feminist. In a recent speech, Fox compared women to washing machines, stating that 75 percent of Mexican families now have such appliances and "and not with two legs and feet but metal washing machines" (See *Lawmakers Protest Remark, The Herald,* February 11, 2006, www.eluniversal.com.mx/miami/16951.html, accessed June 14, 2006).

66. Gutmann 1996, 251.

67. Alonso 1995, 74–75.

68. LeVine 1993, 54.

69. Instituto Nacional de Estadística, Geografía e Informática, "Estadísticas al Propósito del Día del Amor y La Amistad. Datos Nacionales," 2004, www.inegi.org.mx/inegi/contenidos/espanol/prensa/contenidos/estadisticas/2004/amistad04.pdf, accessed September 17, 2005.

70. Gay Mexico News and Reports. Neither female inequality nor the stigmatization of homosexuality is uniform or predictable. There exist regional and ethnic variations: among the indigenous and matrifocal Zapotec of southern Oaxaca, women play strong roles in the community; and homosexuality and male transvestism, according to Beverly Chiñas, are a relatively accepted part of daily life. There, the *muxe,* a biological male who maintains some culturally feminine characteristics, and who engages in transvestism and sometimes same-sex sexuality,

is viewed as a third gender, alongside male and female. Though her accounts of the muxe have been questioned, Chiñas writes that "Mestizos in El Centro may harass and even persecute *muxe* boys on occasion, but Zapotec parents (especially mothers and other women) are quick to defend them and their right to "be themselves" because, as they put it, "God made them that way" (Chiñas 1992 [1973], 109).

71. Carrillo 2002; LeVine 1993; Prieur 1998.

72. Lancaster 2003, 330.

73. Gutmann 1996.

74. Ibid., 251.

75. Ibid.

76. For Paz, ideal Mexican women are passive, pure, and modest. Confined to the domestic sphere, they are the embodiment of motherhood. Physically and figuratively, they are permeable and therefore vulnerable. They are the repositories of honor for their families and the maintainers of morality for society at large. Women who do not embody these virtues can be sources of shame to the family. They are dangerous and a threat to the social order. Men, in contrast, are machos, active and independent. They merit masculine honor and respect as long as they use their power in a manner considered appropriate and dignified, though their machismo may also be characterized by the unpredictable and destructive use of that power (Paz 1985).

77. Carrillo 2002; Gutmann 1996; Higgins and Coen 2000; Lavrín 1978.

78. Jelin 1990; Lavrín 1978.

79. Gutmann 1996, 32. For further discussions of the macho and machismo, see Gutmann 1996; and Mirandé 1997. Though I do not make much use of these terms in this study, I suggest we interrogate them but not dismiss them too readily, as they are still relevant for Mexican women and men, who experience them in some form daily.

80. Gutmann 1996, 221.

81. I thank Anne McClintock for this point.

82. Gill 1994; Gutmann 1996.

83. For a deeper look at women factory workers in Mexico, see Fernández-Kelly 1983; and Iglesias Prieto 1997. See Ong 1987 for the Malaysian experience.

84. Fernández-Kelly 1983, 135.

85. Barry 1979; Dworkin 1981; Overall 1992.

86. Assiter and Avedon 1993; Bell 1987; Church Gibson and Gibson 1993.

87. Shrage 1994.

88. For recent work that moves beyond the liberation/exploitation debates, see Kempadoo 1999; Kempadoo and Doezema 1998; Nencel 2001; Weitzer 2000.

89. It was Carol Leigh, an activist, performer, and author, also known as Scarlot Harlot, who coined the term *sex work* in 1978.

90. Other sectors of the sex industry have adopted English words to describe services. The Gitano, a nightclub in the tolerance zone, offers a Show Table Dance, Estilo Las Vegas (Las Vegas–Style Table Dance Show). Its advertisements say, in English, that there is "No Cover." Massage parlors that offer male customers hand manipulation of the genitals refer to this service in English as "relax."

91. "Unquestioned beliefs are the real authorities of a culture. Therefore, if an individual can express what is undeniably real to him without invoking any authority beyond his own experience, he is transcending the belief systems of his culture" (Combs 1978, 2, in Jensen 2006, 5).

92. Galeano 1991, 120.

93. Bradburd 1998.

94. Agee and Evans 1960 [1939], 12.

95. Scheper-Hughes 1992, 28.

96. Galeano 1991, 121.

ONE. MODERN SEX IN A MODERN CITY

Epigraph: Greene 1939, 194.

1. Writing in the 1980s, Robert Wasserstrom noted, "Perhaps more than any other social group in recent history, the native people of the central Highlands of Chiapas have been the subject of a prolonged and continuous scrutiny, of a rigorous examination of the most intimate details of their daily life" (1983, 11, translation mine). The Zapatista uprising also generated an abundance of information about Chiapas as international media coverage brought the rebellion to a global audience (see Nash 1997).

2. For exceptions to this trend, see Colby 1966; Siverts 1973; Rus 1997; and Wasserstrom 1983.

3. The quotation is from Cleaver 1994, 15.

4. Chiapas constituted the northernmost territory of Guatemala until September 14, 1824, when it was annexed by Mexico. The annexation was contested by many, including merchants living outside the Central Highlands in the cities of Comitán, Tapachula, and Tuxtla, who feared that union with Mexico would cut them off from Guatemalan markets while disproportionately favoring the economically powerful elites of San Cristóbal de las Casas. See Benjamin 1989, 8, 42.

5. Ibid., 45.

6. H. Ayuntamiento 1988, 109, translation mine.

7. Del Carpio Penagos 1995, 78.

8. The quotation is from Mérida Mancilla 1995, 123.

9. Ibid.

10. H. Ayuntamiento 1988, 116–17.

11. INEGI 1993, 60.

12. Ross 2005.

13. Despite resistance by groups such as the Civic Front to Defend the Teoti-huacán Valley, the store opened in late 2004, with the support of the National Institute of Anthropology and History, whose officials deemed the building site archaeologically insignificant.

14. INEGI 1993, 22. Chiapas is also home to nearly 15 percent of Mexico's indigenous people (CIACH 1997, 87).

15. Of the 2,403 municipalities in Mexico, Tuxtla ranks just 2,260th in terms of its level of marginality, making it one of the least impoverished of Mexican municipalities (CIACH 1997, 7). Indicators for marginality include infant moral-ity, employment, and access to electricity and running water.

16. Ibid., 18.

17. Ibid., 40.

18. Carrillo 2002, x.

19. It is worth mentioning here that the term *gay* (and sexual identity itself) is complex and contested. *Homosexual* is a term that may be applied to any man or women who is sexually attracted to his or her own sex; alternatively, it may also, as we will see in the following chapter, apply only to the man in a same-sex rela-tionship who plays the "feminine," passive, or receptive role during a sexual encounter. See Carrillo 2002, especially chapters 3 and 4. Also see Carrier 1995. For Nicaragua, see Lancaster 1992.

20. While it could be argued that the consumption of sexual services by clients has a negative impact on their families, a discussion of clients and prices in the following pages reveals that the low prices charged by zone workers can make their services accessible even to men of few means, though certainly such money could be spent on food or clothing or other household needs.

21. Curtis and Arreola 1991.

22. As noted earlier, the ejido is a form of communal landholding in Mexico. This system of landholding was protected by Article 27 of the Mexican Constitu-tion, which stated that communal lands could not be sold, bought, or rented. Car-los Salinas de Gortari reversed Article 27 in 1992 in order to prepare the ground-work for the 1994 North American Free Trade Agreement, opening up communal lands to private enterprise and agribusiness.

23. Untitled, undated document on the Galactic Zone, Archivo Municipal de Tuxtla Gutiérrez, Expediente Zona Galáctica.

24. Enloe 1989, 2.

25. Untitled, undated document on the Galactic Zone.

26. Today there is no waiting list at the Galáctica and always a few rooms available for incoming workers.

TWO. HIDDEN IN PLAIN SIGHT

1. Foucault 1990 [1977], 45.

2. See Lopez-Jones 1987.

3. See Kempadoo and Doezema 1998; and Delacoste and Alexander 1987, for more on organizing among sex workers.

4. Delany 2001.

5. Caldeira 2002 [1999].

6. Delany 2001.

7. Ironically, during my year among pimps, consumers of sexual services, and a wide assortment of undesirable men, I found that the doctor in charge of inspecting women to make sure they had not been assaulted in any way by authorities was among the least principled characters I had met.

8. Walkowitz 1980, 3.

9. Ibid., 71.

10. La Jornada, May 21, 2005, "Cero creación de empleo formal en el gobierno de Vicente Fox," www.jornada.unam.mx/2005/05/21/020n1eco.php, accessed July 27, 2007.

11. Douglas 1966.

12. Ibid., 35.

13. Ibid., 39–40.

14. See Curtis and Arreola 1991; Gilfoyle 1992; Marín Hernández 1994; Symanski 1981.

15. Guy 1988, 61.

16. Walkowitz 1980, 5.

17. What I present here is a very brief overview of a complex and contested system of identity and labeling. For more, see Buffington 1997; Carrier 1995; Carrillo 2002; Liguori and Aggleton 1999; Prieur 1998.

18. See Carrier 1995; Prieur 1998.

19. Liguori and Aggleton 1999.

20. See Carrillo 2002, 63.

21. Prieur 1998.

22. Higgins and Coen 2000, 115. For a similar situation in Brazil, see Don Kulick's wonderful ethnography Travesti (1998).

23. See Kulick 1998 for a similar situation in Brazil.

24. See Buffington 1997.

25. Carrillo 2002, 38.

26. See Carrier 1995; Carrillo 2002; for a similar discussion on Nicaragua, see Lancaster 1992. The phenomenon is not unique to Latin America; see Khan 1999 for an Indian example.

27. Ibid., 77.

28. Gay Mexico News and Reports, "Action Called against Tecate Council Discrimination," n.d., www.globalgayz.com/mexico-news00-03.html, accessed April 6, 2005.

29. *La Jornada*, July 2, 2004, "Vestidas en arresto domiciliario?" www.jornada .unam.mx/2002/julo2/020704/ls-tir.html, accessed May 22, 2005.

30. Amnesty International 1997, 15-16.

31. It should be noted here that sexual difference is not uniformly punished in Mexico or other parts of Latin America. Rather, there exists what Roger Lancaster calls a "tolerant intolerance," in which certain activities and behaviors are allowed and expressed in "certain tacitly agreed spaces" (2005, 263-64). The Galactic Zone may be viewed as one of these spaces.

32. Carolina Gomez Mena, "En nueva años hubo cerca de 900 asesinatos por homofobia: ONG," *La Jornada*, May 16, 2005, www.jornada.unam.mx/imprimir .php?fecha=20050516&nota=038nlsoc.php, accessed May 22, 2005.

33. Liguori and Aggleton 1999, 121. For a discussion of Brazilian travestis (who differ from Mexican travestis) as "not-men," see Kulick 1998.

34. The murders in Juárez were not immediately a matter of public and police attention; it took years of struggle by activists and the mothers of the slain young women for authorities to take the problem seriously.

35. See Reding 1998, 16-20.

36. Liguori and Aggleton 1999.

THREE. INSIDE THE GALACTIC ZONE

Epigraph: Foucault 1990 [1977], 36-37.

1. Ibid.

2. Ibid., 138.

3. Ibid.

4. In her study of women and social change in Cuernavaca, Sarah LeVine found that, while many older informants revealed that, lacking information, they had been shocked when their periods arrived and had believed they were ill, menstruation in Mexico today is more frequently discussed among daughters, female siblings, and mothers (LeVine 1993, 77). In the zone, some women, like Gabriela, speak openly about menstruation, and they share information about sexuality with their daughters. Sex workers who work while they are menstruating must pay a fee, known as a "menstruation quota." In their work on menstrual symbolism, Buckley and Gottlieb (1988) make clear that a universal menstrual taboo does not exist, and that there remains a need for ethnographic specificity when discussing menstrual meanings. I questioned various people in the zone

about the "menstruation quota," and none could tell me of its origins or reason for existence. It seems likely that the menstrual quota has some basis in cultural beliefs about the female body, about the "pollution" and potential power associated with menstrual blood, as well as in gender and class oppression.

5. Brussa 2003.

6. McClintock 1993.

7. Uribe et al. 1998, 184.

8. Bliss 2001, 204.

9. See McClintock 1993.

10. Rivera, Vicente-Ralde, and Lucero 1992; Uribe et al. 1998.

11. Rivera, Vicente-Ralde, and Lucero 1992; Uribe et al. 1998.

12. See Delacoste and Alexander 1987.

13. UNAIDS 2004.

14. Campbell 2005.

15. Uribe and Bronfman 1997.

16. Ibid.

17. Bautista, Dmytraczenko, Kombe, and Bertozzi 2003.

18. During my stay in the zone, MEXFAM, a local "family planning" organization, did once distribute information about HIV and STDs to clients at the main gate.

19. When I arrived, I suggested to the doctor in charge that perhaps I, along with the workers, could help make a newsletter for workers that would be a forum for discussion of zone issues and broader topics that workers felt were relevant. He told me it was not a good idea. It would just cause trouble because, after a group of human rights activists from Mexico City gave a talk on organizing sex workers some months before, the workers complained more and thought "everything" was an abuse of their rights.

20. This incident brought an end to any effort I made to stay neutral among conflicting parties in the Galactic Zone. Edith had crossed boundaries to tell me of the unwashed speculums and had asked me to go to the director of public health, knowing I was in close contact with him. I did this and brought him to the zone to have a private meeting with workers, where they could air their concerns directly to the municipal government. Though the meeting had little impact for zone workers, it did aid in the disintegration of my good relations with the staff of the SMAV. For more on the delicate balance of engagement and neutrality during my field experience, see Kelly 2004.

21. CIACH et al. 1997, 35–36.

22. Ibid., 36.

23. Rabinow 1984, 245.

24. Farthing 1995, 146.

25. Ibid.

26. Obligadas in the Galáctica generally arrive by way of Puebla, and so are sometimes called Poblanas (residents of Puebla), a word that, in the zone, has become synonymous with *pimped*.

27. Farthing 1995; Vilas 1993.

28. Vilas 1993, 41.

FOUR. CONVERGENCE

1. Bonfil Batalla 1996.

2. Ibid., 1.

3. George Collier (1999 [1994]) defines peasants as rural subsistence or small-scale agricultural producers who are often, but not always, indigenous.

4. Despite their integration into the urban economy, the ejidatarios still embody Bonfil Batalla's definition of México profundo, as they retain various Mesoamerican traits.

5. Archivo de Tuxtla Gutiérrez, Expediente Zona Galáctica, n.d.

6. Workers pay as much as US$125 per month to rent a small dark room in the Galáctica. For this same price, one could rent a two-bedroom house in an upper-middle-class neighborhood in western Tuxtla.

7. Cohen 1972; Goode and Ben-Yehuda 1994.

8. Weeks 1981, 256.

9. Guy 1990; Symanski 1981.

10. See Goode and Ben-Yehuda 1994, 28-29.

11. Though I focus here on the municipal effort to maintain control of the Galáctica, the campesinos also used the press to promote their cause, though to a lesser degree. During my first meeting with the Comisariado Ejidal (ruling body of the ejido), I met a journalist and friend of the campesinos who had just published a full-page article in a local daily paper about the dispute, detailing the injustices the ejidatarios had suffered.

12. See Bondi 1998; Albert 2001.

13. Brownmiller 1975, 391; see also Ward 1995. Yet while feminists' redefinition of rape as violence rather than as an act of sexual desire has been a necessary shift in the discourse, the ways in which the rape of women remains a great source of anxiety and fear for women and men across cultures is still problematic. As Vanessa Veselka says,

> The real problem is not that we treat rape as sex, but as theft. . . . You weren't just violated, we tell a raped woman. You were pillaged. Something of intrinsic value was stolen from you. The fervent belief that this is true is evident on all sides of the issue. From traditional cultures that treat a raped woman as bankrupt to progressive movements that speak in terms of "reclaiming" oneself and "owning" the experience, we tell a woman loudly and clearly that if she was sexually violated

she has been robbed, and that the objects stolen were her purity and innocence. . . . As long as we cling to the concept of rape or abuse as theft, we are ultimately led back to the belief that a woman's worth and sense of self lie in her sexual purity, and we can speak of her condition only in terms of ownership or loss. To imply that deep within every woman is something essential that can be seen or touched, a vessel containing the real her that can be stolen by someone else, is an absolute objectification of women. (2006, 58)

By suggesting that some intangible but essential resource, be it dignity, purity, or sense of self, can be stolen from a woman by a man through forced sex, by suggesting that rape, though awful, is *the worst* thing that can happen to any woman, we continue to reinforce sexist and homogenizing ideals about female worth and female experience and the belief that the vagina (or the female body in general) is the route through which we maintain or lose ourselves.

   14. Lim 1998, 1.

   15. CISC 1994, 8.

   16. Higgins and Coen 2000, 172.

   17. Palmer 1994, 218.

FIVE. "IT BEGAN INNOCENTLY"

There is no strict definition for the word *ambiente*. Taken generally, it means "milieu" or "scene." In much of Mexico, it is sometimes used to refer to the male gay scene. Higgins and Coen (2002) use the term when discussing the social world of gay male transvestite prostitutes in Oaxaca. Carrillo suggests it has been used since the early twentieth century as a euphemism for same-sex male desire (2002, 18). In describing female prostitution, the term *la vida* (the life) has long been in use (see Bliss 2001, 18), but in the Galáctica, sex workers refer to the world of commercial sex as the ambiente, as do sex workers in Peru (Nencel 2001, 152–55) and Costa Rica (Ortiz et al. 1998). This use of the term *ambiente* in the zone is perhaps related to Chiapas's history with and proximity to Central America, where the term is more common, along with the presence of Central American prostitutes in the zone.

   1. White 1990, 10.

   2. Barry 1979; Dworkin 1981; Farley and Kelly 2000; Overall 1992; Wynter 1987.

   3. Shrage 1994, 566; also see McClintock 1993.

   4. Chaney and Garcia Castro 1989, 3; Gill 1994.

   5. Chaney and Garcia Castro 1989.

   6. Fernández-Kelly 1983, 143.

   7. Gledhill 1995; Safa 1995.

8. Delacoste and Alexander 1987.

9. Sex workers' methods of birth control vary. From informal conversations, I learned that some workers relied on birth control injections like Depo-Provera and others used only condoms.

10. Though there is a preference among clients for lighter-skinned, nonindigenous prostitutes in the zone today, Katherine Bliss notes that, during the 1930s, a magazine reported that one Mexico City brothel procured young indigenous women from Chiapas and Oaxaca in order to please clients who had a particular penchant for such women (2001, 179).

11. Bourgois 1990, 49–50.

12. Wasserstrom 1976, 12.

13. Benjamin 1989, 205; Wasserstrom 1976, 12.

14. García 2006, 31.

15. Other southern border states are Tabasco, Campeche, and Quintana Roo.

16. According to local newspapers, as part of their efforts to combat illegal migration, the United States Immigration and Naturalization Service began to offer financial rewards for information leading to the detention of polleros, individuals who guide migrants across the border in exchange for money.

17. Ballinas 2005.

18. To learn more about the lives of migrants at the Mexican-Guatemalan border, see Kovic and Kelly 2005, 2006.

19. Najar 2003.

20. My fieldwork period was one of heightened political instability in Chiapas. As the PRI struggled to maintain control, researchers' areas of investigation were circumscribed. Deportations of foreign tourists (many participating in a phenomenon labeled Zapaturismo—Zapatista tourism), activists, and intellectuals alike were not uncommon. Even the Honduran reggae-rap band who performed at the Mother's Day fiesta was picked up by INM authorities, only to be bailed out by the municipal government, which felt responsible for their plight. As a researcher and foreigner working in an increasingly xenophobic region, I did my best to remain invisible to authorities of the INM, as the threat of deportation was very real.

After countless interviews and much paperwork, my research visa was approved six months after I made the initial request. Happening upon a caravan of Zapatistas in San Cristóbal for peace talks with the government, I returned home immediately; as I had learned through the experience of friends, accidental proximity alone could get a person deported. My efforts at invisibility were not always successful, though. Soon after the land conflict in the zone erupted, television news crews came to cover the event. I was urged by the staff of the SMAV to leave quickly through a side gate reserved for police and staff. I did this, but not soon enough. That evening both Pepe and I appeared on the evening news, eating tacos and sipping Cokes at his food stand.

21. In his study of Puerto Rican crack dealers in New York City's Spanish Harlem, Philippe Bourgois provides another illustration of the ways in which structural economic forces pit workers of different national origins (in this case Mexicans and Puerto Ricans) against one another. A Mexican man, prompted by Bourgois, told him why Bourgois's Puerto Rican informants cannot find well-paying jobs: "Okay, okay, I'll explain it to you in one word: Because the Puerto Ricans are stupid! Stupid!" Of Mexicans, the man said, "We come here to work and that's all." In contrast, a Puerto Rican man describes how he feels when he crosses paths with a Mexican: "Makes me feel like shit when I see them, 'cause I know they work for cheaper than me." Such feelings, Bourgois notes, often lead to violence against Mexican workers. See Bourgois 1995, 130–31.

22. Lancaster 1992, 241.

23. Bliss 2001, 2.

24. Paquita La del Barrio is a Mexican singer known for songs detailing the pain of love, with powerful titles such as "I Already Remodeled the House," "Like a Dog," "Human Scum," "Are You Listening to Me, Good for Nothing?" and "Two-Footed Rat."

25. Anderson 1983.

26. Menjívar 2000, 98.

27. Most of my ethnographic data regarding forced prostitution came from observations and formal and informal interviews with two women who had formerly worked as obligadas. Evidence suggested that a third women with whom I had frequent contact, Maura, a former college student from Puebla now working in the zone, was also an obligada. Maura refused to identify herself as an obligada, carefully referring to the man whom most zone workers and staff knew to be her pimp as her *pareja* (partner).

28. Because of her Asian features, Sonia is often referred to as "China" or "La Chinita," meaning "Little China girl."

SIX. SELLERS AND BUYERS

1. MacDonald and Sirianni 1996, 2.

2. See Foff Paules's 1991 discussion of "inverting the symbolism of the tip" for a similar strategy practiced by waitresses in a New Jersey restaurant.

3. Hochschild 1983, 181.

4. In the neighboring state of Oaxaca, Michael Higgins and Tanya Coen (2000) found that male transvestite prostitutes working the street in Oaxaca City charged between 80 and 150 pesos (US$9.40 and US$17.65) per client, while

older women (in their late thirties to fifties) working the streets charged between 40 and 60 pesos (US$4.70 and US$7.05), a price the authors refer to as "minimal."

   5. Bliss 2001, 154.

   6. Brown 1982.

   7. In her account of sex tourism in the Dominican Republic, Denise Brennan writes about rural women's unsuccessful efforts to use wardrobe to blend into the sex-work scene in Sosúa (2004, 143–44).

   8. On occasion a worker may have the opportunity to prepare her own food: one room in Doña Mari's module has been converted into a makeshift kitchen, where workers may sometimes prepare meals. Pepe sometimes lets a trusted woman prepare food in his stand, which will often be shared by a handful of workers

   9. For similar findings among male gay transvestite sex workers in Oaxaca, see Higgins and Coen 2000.

   10. See Enloe 1989; Pollock Sturdevant and Stoltzfus 1992.

   11. Enloe 1993, 147.

   12. Albert 2001, 136.

   13. Stoler 1995.

   14. Enloe 1993, 147.

   15. "La vulnerabilidad de las mujeres y el VIH/Sida," *La Jornada en Internet*, Letra S, March 2, 2000, www.salud.gob.mx/conasida/otraspub/letraese/ls2000/lsmaroo.htm, accessed July 26, 2007. For similar findings in Costa Rica, where housewives constitute 36 percent of the population of reported cases of HIV infection, while prostitutes make up 10 percent, see Ortiz et al. 1998, 262.

   16. See Gutmann 1996, 138–41, for a discussion of "urban polygamy" and the multiple meanings of the casa chica.

   17. LeVine 1993.

   18. Monto 2000.

   19. Enloe 1992, 25.

   20. Foucault 1985; Stoler 1995.

   21. Gutmann 1996, 132.

   22. Ibid., 133.

   23. The existence of the Galactic Zone's large client base, when compared with the men of Neza with whom Gutmann worked, also raises further questions about the nature of ethnographic data and self-presentation by both researcher and informants.

   24. See Carrillo 2002, 83, 106.

   25. Collier 1999 [1994]; LeVine 1993.

   26. Carrillo 2002, 99; also see Gutmann 1996, 232–33.

   27. CISC 1994, 13.

SEVEN. THE SECRETS WE KEEP

1. For similar processes in Southeast Asia, see Lim 1998; Phongpaichit 1982.
2. Carter 1987; Odzer 1994; Phongpaichit 1982.
3. Before the Zapatista uprising and the collapse of the peso, many Mexicans approved of Carlos Salinas. Today there are still some who think his presidency was a good one.
4. A cell phone is somewhat less extravagant than it may seem, when one considers that getting a telephone installed in one's living quarters can be costly and time-consuming, a process often involving many months of waiting.
5. Goffman 1963, 3.
6. Ibid., 4.
7. Ibid., 86–87.

EIGHT. FINAL THOUGHTS

Epigraph: Agee and Evans 1960 [1939], 279.
1. McClintock 1993, 3.
2. It must be observed that "the state" is composed of various sectors (local, state, federal) and different agencies that often have competing interests, and that are not always internally homogenous. Furthermore, the state is composed of human beings, some of them very likable.
3. For more on CAFTA, see the Washington Office on Latin America's testimony to the House Ways and Means Committee, www.wola.org/economic/cafta_ways_means_testimony.pdf, accessed April 27, 2007.
4. National Catholic Reporter Online 2005.
5. McClintock 1993, 5.
6. I borrow the phrase "uprising of hope" from the title of Duncan Earle and Jeanne Simonelli's 2005 ethnography about their work among the Zapatistas.
7. Furthermore, to borrow from Derrick Jensen, it's one thing to write about social change and "quite another thing to make it all happen" (2006, 384).
8. McClintock 1993, 9.
9. McKinley 2005.
10. Canadian HIV/AIDS Legal Network 2005.
11. "Prostitution Laws in New Zealand: Prostitution Reform Act 2003," Sex in New Zealand website, www.sexinnz.co.nz/news2.htm#commencment, accessed June 21, 2006.
12. Canadian HIV/AIDS Legal Network 2005.
13. Jensen 2000, 99.

Bibliography

ARCHIVAL SOURCES

Archivo de la Secretaría de Salud Pública de Tuxtla Gutiérrez
Archivo Municipal de Tuxtla Gutiérrez, Expediente Zona Galáctica

PERIODICALS

Cuarto Poder
Diario de Chiapas
El Sol de Chiapas
Este Sur
La Jornada
La Tribuna de Chiapas

SECONDARY SOURCES

Adam, Barry. 1995. *The Rise of a Gay and Lesbian Movement.* New York: Twayne Publishing.

Adamache, Robin, Claudia Culos, and Gerardo Otero. 1993. "NAFTA: Class and Gender Implications for Mexican Women." Paper presented at the Rocky Mountain Conference on Latin American Studies.

Agee, James, and Walker Evans. 1960 [1939]. *Let Us Now Praise Famous Men.* New York: Ballantine Books.

Aggleton, Peter, ed. 1999. *Men Who Sell Sex: International Perspectives on Male Prostitution and HIV/AIDS.* Philadelphia: Temple University Press.

Albert, Alexa. 2001. *Brothel: Mustang Ranch and Its Women.* New York: Random House.

Alonso, Ana María. 1995. *Thread of Blood: Colonialism, Revolution, and Gender on Mexico's Northern Frontier.* Tucson: University of Arizona.

Altman, Dennis. 2001. *Global Sex.* Chicago: University of Chicago Press.

Amnesty International. 1997. *Breaking the Silence: Human Rights Violations Based on Sexual Orientation.* London: Amnesty International.

Anderson, Benedict. 1983. *Imagined Communities: Reflections on the Origin and Spread of Nationalism.* London: Verso.

Assiter, Alison, and Carol Avedon. 1993. *Bad Girls and Dirty Pictures: The Challenge to Reclaim Feminism.* London: Pluto Press.

Balderston, Daniel, and Donna J. Guy, eds. 1997. *Sex and Sexuality in Latin America.* New York: New York University Press.

Ballinas, Victor. 2005. CNDH: Aquí se criminaliza a los ilegales. *La Jornada.* December 21, www.jornada.unam.mx/imprimir.php?fecha=20051221 &nota=003n2pol.php&seccion=nota. Accessed June 14, 2005.

Barry, Kathleen. 1979. *Female Sexual Slavery.* New York: Basic Books.

Bautista, Sergio Antonio, Tania Dmytraczenko, Gilbert Kombe, and Stefano M. Bertozzi. 2003. "Costing of HIV/AIDS Treatment in Mexico," www.phrplus .org/Pubs/Tech020_fin.pdf. Accessed June 27, 2005.

Bell, Laurie, ed. 1987. *Good Girls/Bad Girls: Sex Trade Workers and Feminists Face to Face.* Toronto: Women's Press.

Bello, Walden. 1994. *Dark Victory: The United States, Structural Adjustment, and Global Poverty.* London: Pluto Press and Food First.

Benería, Lourdes, ed. 1982. *Women and Development: The Sexual Division of Labor in Rural Societies.* New York: Praeger.

———. 1992. "The Mexican Debt Crisis: Restructuring the Economy and the Household." In *Unequal Burden: Economic Crises, Persistent Poverty, and Women's Work,* ed. Lourdes Benería and Shelley Feldman, 26–48. Boulder, CO: Westview Press.

Benería, Lourdes, and Shelley Feldman, eds. 1992. *Unequal Burden: Economic Crises, Persistent Poverty, and Women's Work.* Boulder, CO: Westview Press.

Benjamin, Thomas. 1989. *A Rich Land, a Poor People: Politics and Society in Modern Chiapas.* Albuquerque: University of New Mexico Press.

Bishop, Ryan, and Lillian S. Robinson. 1998. *Night Market: Sexual Cultures and the Thai Economic Miracle.* New York: Routledge.

Bliss, Katherine. 2001. *Compromised Positions: Prostitution, Public Health, and Gender Politics in Revolutionary Mexico City.* University Park, PA: Pennsylvania State University.

Bondi, Liz. 1998. "Sexing the City." In *Cities of Difference,* ed. Ruth Fincher and Jane M. Jacobs, 177–200. New York: Guilford Press.

Bonfil Batalla, Guillermo. 1996. *México Profundo: Reclaiming a Civilization.* Austin: University of Texas.

Bourgois, Philippe. 1988. "Conjugated Oppression: Class and Ethnicity among Guaymi and Kuna Banana Workers." *American Ethnologist* 15:328–48.

———. 1990. "Confronting Anthropological Ethics: Ethnographic Lessons from Central America." *Journal of Peace Research* 27(1): 43–54.

———. 1995. *In Search of Respect: Selling Crack in El Barrio.* Cambridge: Cambridge University Press.

Bradburd, Daniel. 1998. *Being There: The Necessity of Fieldwork.* Washington, DC: Smithsonian Books.

Brennan, Denise. 1998. "Everything Is for Sale Here: Sex Tourism in Sosúa, the Dominican Republic." PhD diss., Department of Anthropology, Yale University.

———. 2004. *What's Love Got to Do With It? Transnational Desires and Sex Tourism in the Dominican Republic.* Durham, NC: Duke University Press.

Bricker, Victoria. 1973. *Ritual Humor in Highland Chiapas.* Austin: University of Texas Press.

Brown, Judith K. 1982. "Cross-Cultural Perspectives on Middle-Aged Women." *Current Anthropology* 23(2):143–55.

Brownmiller, Susan. 1975. *Against Our Will: Men, Women, and Rape.* New York: Simon and Schuster.

Brussa, Licia. 2003. "Three Years of Dutch Legalization: Consequences for Legal and Undocumented Sex Workers." *Research for Sex Work* 6:14–16.

Buckley, Thomas, and Alma Gottlieb, eds. 1988. *Blood Magic: The Anthropology of Menstruation.* Berkeley: University of California.

Buffington, Rob. 1997. "Los Jotos: Contested Visions of Homosexuality in Modern Mexico." In *Sex and Sexuality in Latin America,* ed. Daniel Balderston and Donna J. Guy, 118–32. New York: New York University Press.

Bunster, Ximena, and Elsa Chaney. 1989. *Sellers and Servants.* Granby, MA: Bergin and Garvey.

Caldeira, Teresa. 2002 [1999]. "Fortified Enclaves: The New Urban Segregation." In *Theorizing the City: The New Urban Anthropology Reader,* ed. Setha Low, 83–110. New Brunswick, NJ: Rutgers University Press.

Campbell, Monica. 2005. "Mexico Tackles Discrimination to fight AIDS." *Chris-*

tian Science Monitor. June 9, www.csmonitor.com/2005/0609/p06s01-woam
.html. Accessed June 27, 2005.

Canadian HIV/AIDS Legal Network. 2005. "New Zealand and Sweden: Two Models for Reform." *Sex, Work, Rights: Reforming Canadian Criminal Laws on Prostitution,* Information Sheet No. 9.

Cancian, F. 1965. *Economics and Prestige in a Maya Community: The Religious Cargo System of Zinacantan.* Stanford: Stanford University Press.

————. 1992. *The Decline of Community in Zinacantan: The Economy, Public Life, and Social Stratification, 1950–1987.* Stanford: Stanford University Press.

Carrier, Joseph. 1995. *De Los Otros: Intimacy and Homosexuality among Mexican Men.* New York: Columbia University Press.

Carrier, Joseph, and J. Raúl Magaña. 1992. "Use of Ethnosexual Data on Men of Mexican Origin for HIV/AIDS Prevention Programs." In *The Time of AIDS,* ed. Gilbert Herdt and Shirley Lindenbaum, 243–58. Newbury Park, CA: Sage Publications.

Carrillo, Héctor. 2002. *The Night Is Young: Sexuality in Mexico in the Time of AIDS.* Chicago: University of Chicago Press.

Carter, Sunny. 1987. "A Most Useful Tool." In *Sex Work: Writings by Women in the Sex Industry,* ed. Frédérique Delacoste and Priscilla Alexander, 159–65. Pittsburgh: Cleiss.

Castañeda, Jorge. 1994. *Utopia Unarmed: The Latin American Left after the Cold War.* New York: Vintage.

Castells, Manuel. 1983. *The City and the Grassroots.* Berkeley: University of California Press.

Caulfield, Sueann. 2000. *In Defense of Honor: Sexual Morality, Modernity, and Nation in Early-Twentieth-Century Brazil.* Durham: Duke University Press.

Centro de Informacíon y Análysis de Chiapas (CIACH), Coordinación de Organismos No Gubermentales Por La Paz (CONPAZ), y Servicios Informativos Procesados. 1997. *Para entender Chiapas: Chiapas en cifras.* Mexico City: CIACH, CONPAZ, SIPRO.

Centro de Investigaciones en Salud de Comitán (CISC). 1994. "Resultados del analysis de la situation y propuesta para desarrollar una intervencion para aumentar la seguridad del sexo comercio, en Chiapas. Area de Tuxtla Gutiérrez." CISC Archives, Comitán, Chiapas, Mexico.

————. 1996. "Investigación/acción en salud reproductiva." *Boletín Informativo* 1(4).

Chaney, Elsa, and Mary Garcia Castro, eds. 1989. *Muchachas No More: Household Workers in Latin America and the Caribbean.* Philadelphia: Temple University.

Chiñas, Beverly. 1992 [1973]. *The Isthmus Zapotecs: A Matrifocal Culture of Mexico.* Fort Worth, TX: Harcourt Brace College Publishers.

Church Gibson, P., and R. Gibson, eds. 1993. *Dirty Looks: Women, Pornography, and Power*. London: BFI.

Cleaver, Harry. 1994. Introduction to *¡Zapatistas! Documents of the New Mexican Revolution*, ed. The Editorial Collective, 11–23. Brooklyn, NY: Autonomedia.

Clendinnen, Inga. 1991. *Aztecs: An Interpretation*. Cambridge: Cambridge University Press.

Cohen, Stanley. 1972. *Folk Devils and Moral Panics: The Creation of Mods and Rockers*. London: MacGibbon and Kee.

Colby, Benjamin. 1966. *Ethnic Relations in the Chiapas Highlands*. Santa Fe: Museum of New Mexico Press.

Collier, George. 1975. *Fields of the Tzotzil: The Ecological Bases of Tradition in Highland Chiapas*. Austin: University of Texas Press.

———. 1999 [1994]. *Basta! Land and the Zapatista Rebellion*. Oakland: Food First.

Collier, Jane. 1973. *Law and Social Change in Zinacantan*. Stanford: Stanford University Press.

Combs, Robert. 1978. *Vision of the Voyage: Hart Crane and the Psychology of Romanticism*. Memphis: Memphis State University.

Curtis, James, and D. Arreola. 1991. "Zonas de Tolerancia on the Northern Mexican Border." *Geographical Review* 81(3): 333–46.

Delacoste, Frédérique, and Priscilla Alexander, eds. 1987. *Sex Work: Writings by Women in the Sex Industry*. Pittsburgh: Cleiss.

Delany, Samuel. 2001. *Times Square Red, Times Square Blue*. New York: New York University Press.

del Carpio Penagos, Carlos. 1995. "Espacio y poder en Tuxtla Gutiérrez. Notas preliminarias." In *Cuadernos de arquitectura y urbanismo: Espacio y poder*, ed. Carlos Uriel del Carpio Penagos, 69–89. Tuxtla Gutiérrez: Universidad Autónoma de Chiapas.

Douglas, Mary. 1966. *Purity and Danger: An Analysis of Concepts of Pollution and Taboo*. New York: Praeger.

Dworkin, Andrea. 1981. *Pornography: Men Possessing Women*. New York: E. P. Dutton.

Earle, Duncan, and Jeanne Simonelli. 2005. *Uprising of Hope: Sharing the Zapatista Journey to Alternative Development*. Walnut Creek, CA: AltaMira Press.

Eber, Christine. 1995. *Women and Alcohol in a Highland Maya Town: Water of Hope, Water of Sorrow*. Austin: University of Texas Press.

Editorial Collective. 1994. *¡Zapatista!: Documents of the New Mexican Revolution*. Brooklyn, NY: Autonomedia.

Enloe, Cynthia. 1989. *Bananas, Beaches, and Bases: Making Feminist Sense of International Politics*. Berkeley: University of California Press.

———. 1992. "It Takes Two." In *Let the Good Times Roll: Prostitution and the U.S.*

Military in Asia, ed. S. Sturdevant and Brenda Stoltzfus, 22–27. New York: New Press.

———. 1993. *The Morning After: Sexual Politics at the End of the Cold War.* Berkeley: University of California Press.

Farley, Melissa, and Vanessa Kelly. 2000. "Prostitution: A Critical Review of the Medical and Social Sciences Literature." *Women and Criminal Justice* 11(4): 29–64.

Farmer, Paul. 2005. *Pathologies of Power: Health, Human Rights, and the New War on the Poor.* Berkeley: University of California Press.

Farthing, Linda. 1995. "Bolivia: The New Underground." In *Free Trade and Economic Restructuring in Latin America*, ed. Fred Rosen and Deidre McFadden, 141–50. New York: Monthly Review Press.

Fernández-Kelly, Maria Patricia. 1983. *For We Are Sold, I and My People: Women and Industry in Mexico's Frontier.* Albany: State University of New York Press.

Foff Paules, Greta. 1991. *Dishing It Out: Power and Resistance among Waitresses in a New Jersey Restaurant.* Philadelphia: Temple University Press.

Foucault, Michel. 1985. *History of Sexuality.* New York: Vintage.

———. 1986. "Of Other Spaces." *Diacritics* 16:22–27.

———. 1990 [1977]. *Discipline and Punish: The Birth of the Prison.* New York: Pantheon.

French, W. 1992. "Prostitutes and Guardian Angels: Women, Work, and the Family in Porfirian Mexico." *Hispanic American Historical Review* 72(4): 529–53.

Galeano, Eduardo. 1991. *The Book of Embraces.* New York: W. W. Norton.

García, María Cristina. 2006. *Seeking Refuge: Central American Migration to Mexico, the United States, and Canada.* Berkeley: University of California Press.

Gay Mexico News and Reports. 2000–2003, www.globalgayz.com/mexico-news-00–03.html. Accessed April 6, 2005.

Genet, Jean. 1966 [1958]. *The Balcony.* New York: Grove Press.

Gilfoyle, Timothy. 1992. *City of Eros: New York City, Prostitution, and the Commercialization of Sex, 1790–1920.* New York: W. W. Norton.

Gill, Leslie. 1994. *Precarious Dependencies: Gender, Class, and Domestic Service in Bolivia.* New York: Columbia University Press.

Gledhill, John. 1995. *Neoliberalism, Transnationalization, and Rural Poverty: A Case Study.* Boulder, CO: Westview Press.

Gobierno del Estado de Chiapas. 1995. *Plan estatal de desarrollo, 1995–2000.* Tuxtla Gutiérrez: Talleres Gráficos del Estado.

Goffman, Erving. 1963. *Stigma: Notes on the Management of Spoiled Identity.* Englewood Cliffs, NJ: Prentice-Hall.

Goode, Erich, and Nachman Ben-Yehuda. 1994. *Moral Panics: The Social Construction of Deviance.* Oxford: Blackwell.

Gossen, Gary. 1974. *Chamulas in the World of the Sun: Time and Space in a Maya Oral Tradition.* Cambridge: Harvard University Press.

Greene, Graham. 1939. *The Lawless Roads.* London: Penguin.

Gutmann, Matthew. 1996. *The Meanings of Macho: Being a Man in Mexico City.* Berkeley: University of California Press.

Guy, Donna. 1988. "White Slavery, Public Health, and the Socialist Position on Legalized Prostitution in Argentina." *Latin American Research Review* 23(3): 60–80.

———. 1990. *Sex and Danger in Buenos Aires: Prostitution, Family, and Nation in Argentina.* Lincoln: University of Nebraska Press.

Haber, Stephen. 1999. "Anything Goes: Mexico's 'New' Cultural History." *Hispanic American Historical Review* 79(2): 309–30.

Harvey, David. 2005. *A Brief History of Neoliberalism.* Oxford: Oxford University Press.

Harvey, Neil. 1994. *Rebellion in Chiapas: Rural Reforms, Campesino Radicalism, and the Limits to Salinismo.* San Diego: Center for U.S.–Mexican Studies, University of California.

———. 1998. *The Chiapas Rebellion: The Struggle for Land and Democracy.* Durham, NC: Duke University.

H. Ayuntamiento de Tuxtla Gutiérrez. 1988. *Monografía del Municipio de Tuxtla Gutiérrez.* Mexico, DF: Ediciones y Publicaciones IDEART.

Held, David, Anthony McGrew, David Goldblatt, and Jonathan Perraton. 1999. *Global Transformations: Politics, Economics, and Culture.* Cambridge, U.K.: Polity Press.

Higgins, Michael James, and Tanya Coen. 2000. *Streets, Bedrooms, and Patios: The Ordinariness of Diversity in Urban Oaxaca.* Austin: University of Texas Press.

Hochschild, Arlie. 1983. *The Managed Heart: Commercialization of Human Feeling.* Berkeley: University of California Press.

Holston, James. 1989. *The Modernist City: An Anthropological Critique of Brasília.* Chicago: University of Chicago Press.

Hubbard, Philip, ed. 1999. *Sex and the City: Geographies of Prostitution in the Urban West.* Aldershot, U.K.: Ashgate.

Human Rights Watch. 1997. *Implausible Deniability: State Responsibility for Rural Violence in Mexico.* New York: Human Rights Watch.

———. 2006. *The Second Assault: Obstructing Access to Legal Abortion after Rape in Mexico,* http://hrw.org/reports/2006/mexico0306. Accessed June 14, 2006.

Hyam, R. 1990. *Empire and Sexuality: The British Experience.* Manchester: Manchester University Press.

Iglesias Prieto, Norma. 1997. *Beautiful Flowers of the Maquiladora: Life Histories of Women Workers in Tijuana.* Austin: University of Texas Press.

Instituto Nacional de Estadística, Geografía, e Informática (INEGI). 1993. *Tuxtla*

Gutiérrez, *Estado de Chiapas: Cuaderno estadístico municipal*. Tuxtla Gutiérrez: INEGI, Gobierno del Estado de Chiapas, H. Ayuntamiento Constitutional de Tuxtla Gutiérrez.

Jefferson, LaShawn R. 1996. *Mexico: No Guarantees: Sex Discrimination in Mexico's Maquiladora Sector*. New York: Human Rights Watch.

Jelin, Elizabeth, ed. 1990. *Women and Social Change in Latin America*. London: Zed.

Jensen, Derrick. 2000. *A Language Older Than Words*. New York: Context Books.

———. 2006. *Endgame*. Volume 1: *The Problem of Civilization*. New York: Seven Stories Press.

Joseph, Gilbert, and Daniel Nugent. 1994. *Everyday Forms of State Formation: Revolution and the Negotiation of Rule in Modern Mexico*. Durham: Duke University Press.

Kamel, Rachel, and Anya Hoffman, eds. 1999. *The Maquiladora Reader: Cross-Border Organizing since NAFTA*. Philadelphia: American Friends Service Committee.

Kappeler, Susanne. 1986. *The Pornography of Representation*. Minneapolis: University of Minnesota Press.

Kelly, Patty. 2004. "Awkward Intimacies: Prostitution, Politics, and Fieldwork in Urban Mexico." In *Anthropologists in the Field: Cases in Participant Observation*, ed. Lynne Hume and Jane Mulcock, 3–17. New York: Columbia University Press.

Kempadoo, Kamala, ed. 1999. *Sun, Sex, and Gold: Tourism and Sex Work in the Caribbean*. Lanham, MD: Rowan and Littlefield.

Kempadoo, Kamala, and Jo Doezema, eds. 1998. *Global Sex Workers: Rights, Resistance, and Redefinition*. New York: Routledge.

Khan, Shivananda. 1999. "Through a Window Darkly: Men Who Sell Sex to Men in India and Bangladesh." In *Men Who Sell Sex: International Perspectives on Male Prostitution and HIV/AIDS*, ed. Peter Aggleton, 195–212. London: UCL Press.

Knight, Alan. 2002. "Subalterns, Signifiers, and Statistics: Perspectives on Mexican Historiography." *Latin American Research Review* 37(2): 136–58.

Kovic, Christine, and Patty Kelly. 2005. "A Just Cause: Central American Migrants and Mexico's Southern Border." *Catholic Worker* 25(6): 1, 6, 7.

———. 2006. "Fronteras seguras, cuerpos vulnerables: Migración y género en la frontera sur." *Debate Feminista* 33:69–83.

Kulick, Don. 1998. *Travesti: Sex, Gender, and Culture among Brazilian Transgendered Prostitutes*. Chicago: University of Chicago Press.

Lancaster, Roger. 1992. *Life Is Hard: Machismo, Danger, and the Intimacy of Power in Nicaragua*. Berkeley: University of California Press.

———. 2003. *The Trouble with Nature: Sex in Science and Popular Culture*. Berkeley: University of California Press.

————. 2005. "Tolerance and Intolerance in Sexual Cultures in Latin America." In *Passing Lines: Sexuality and Immigration*, ed. Brad Epps, Keja Valens, and Bill Johnson González, 255–74. Cambridge, MA: Harvard University Press.

Lavrín, Asunción, ed. 1978. *Latin American Women: Historical Perspectives*. Westport, CT: Greenwood Press.

Leon-Portilla, Miguel. 1967. *Trece poemas del mundo Azteca*. Mexico City: UNAM.

LeVine, Sarah, with Clara Sunderland Correa. 1993. *Dolor y Alegría: Women and Social Change in Urban Mexico*. Madison: University of Wisconsin.

Liguori, Ana Luisa, and Peter Aggleton. 1999. "Aspects of Male Sex Work in Mexico City." In *Men Who Sell Sex: International Perspectives on Male Prostitution and HIV/AIDS*. Peter Aggleton, 103–26. London: UCL Press.

Lim, Lin Lean, ed. 1998. *The Sex Sector: The Economic and Social Bases of Prostitution in Southeast Asia*. Geneva, Switzerland: International Labour Office.

Lopez-Jones, Nina. 1987. "Workers: Introducing the English Collective of Prostitutes." In *Sex Work: Writings by Women in the Sex Industry*, ed. Frédérique Delacoste and Priscilla Alexander, 271–78. Pittsburgh: Cleiss.

Macdonald, Cameron Lynne, and Carmen Sirianni. 1996. "The Service Society and the Changing Experience of Work." In *Working in the Service Society*, ed. Cameron Lynne Macdonaldo and Carmen Sirianni, 1–28. Philadelphia: Temple University Press.

Mallon, Florencia. 1999. "Time on the Wheel: Cycles of Revisionism and the 'New Cultural History of Mexico.'" *Hispanic American Historical Review* 79(2): 367–83.

Marichal, Carlos. 1997. "The Rapid Rise of the Neobanqueros: Mexico's New Financial Elite." *NACLA: Report on the Americas* 30(6), May.

Marín Hernández, J. J. 1994. "Prostitución y pecado en la bella y próspera ciudad de San José (1850–1930)." In *El Paso del Cometa: Estado, política social y culturas populares en Costa Rica (1800–1950)*, ed. I. Molina Jiménez and S. Palmer, 47–80. San Jose, Costa Rica: Editorial Porvenir and Plumsock Mesoamerican Studies.

McClintock, Anne, ed. 1993. "Sex and Sex Workers." *Social Text* 11(4), Winter.

McCreery, David. 1987. "This Life of Misery and Shame: Female Prostitution in Guatemala City, 1880–1920." *Journal of Latin American Studies* 18:333–53.

McKinley, James C. 2005. "A New Law in Tijuana Regulates the Oldest Profession." *New York Times*, December 13, www.nytimes.com/2005/12/13/international/americas/13prostitutes.html. Accessed December 18, 2005.

Meil Hobson, Barbara. 1987. *Uneasy Virtue: The Politics of Prostitution and American Reform*. New York: Basic Books.

Menjívar, Cecilia. 2000. *Fragmented Ties: Salvadoran Immigrant Networks in America*. Berkeley: University of California Press.

Mérida Mancilla, Arturo. 1995. "Evolución urbano-arquitectónica de la ciudad de Tuxtla Gutiérrez, Chiapas." In *Cuadernos de arquitectura y urbanismo: Espacio y poder*, ed. Carlos Uriel del Carpio Penagos, 69–89. Tuxtla Gutiérrez: Universidad Autónoma de Chiapas.

Mies, Maria. 1986. *Patriarchy and Accumulation on a World Scale: Women in the International Division of Labor*. London: Zed.

Mirandé, Alfredo. 1997. *Hombres y Machos: Masculinity and Latino Culture*. Boulder, CO: Westview Press.

Montgomery, Heather. 2001. *Modern Babylon: Prostituting Children in Thailand*. New York: Berghahn Books.

Monto, Martin A. 2000. "Why Men Seek Out Prostitutes." In *Sex for Sale: Prostitution, Pornography, and the Sex Industry*, ed. Ronald Weitzer, 67–84. New York: Routledge.

Muriel, Josefina. 1974. *Los recogimientos de mujeres: Respuesta a una problematica social Novohispana*. Mexico City: UNAM.

Najar, Alberto. 2003. "El costo de cuidar el patio trasero." *La Jornada*, www .jornada.unam.mx/2003/02/09/mas-najar.html. Accessed June 14, 2006.

Nash, June. 1990. "Latin American Women in the World Capitalist Crisis." *Gender and Society* 4(3): 338–53.

———, ed. 1993. *Crafts in the World Market: The Impact of Global Exchange on Middle American Artisans*. Albany: State University of New York Press.

———. 1994. "Global Integration and Subsistence Insecurity." *American Anthropologist* 97(1): 7–30.

———. 1997. "Press Reports on the Chiapas Uprising: Towards a Transnationalized Communication." *Journal of Latin American Anthropology* 2(2): 42–47.

———. 2001. *Mayan Visions: The Quest for Autonomy in an Age of Globalization*. New York: Routledge.

Nash, June, and María Patricia Fernández-Kelly. 1983. *Women, Men, and the International Division of Labor*. Albany: State University of New York Press.

National Catholic Reporter OnLine. 2005. "CAFTA Likely to Hurt Poor Central Americans," November. http://ncronline.org/NCR_Online/archives2/2005d/111105/111105w.php. Accessed April 18, 2006.

Nencel, Lorraine. 2001. *Ethnography and Prostitution in Peru*. London: Pluto Press.

North American Congress on Latin America (NACLA). 1997. "Latin America in the Age of the Billionaires." *NACLA: Report on the Americas* 30(6) (May–June).

O'Connell Davidson, Julia. 1998. *Prostitution, Power, and Freedom*. Ann Arbor: University of Michigan Press.

Odzer, Cleo. 1994. *Patpong Sisters: An American Woman's View of the Bangkok Sex World*. New York: Arcade Publishing.

Ong, Aihwa. 1987. *Spirits of Resistance and Capitalist Discipline: Factory Women in Malaysia*. Albany: State University of New York Press.

Ortiz, Maritza, Alicia Zamora, Ana Rodríguez, Laura Chacón, and Ana Lucía Gutiérrez. 1998. *"Soy una mujer de ambiente . . . ": Las mujeres en prostitución y la prevención del VIH/sida*. San Jose: Editorial de la Universidad de Costa Rica.

Otero, Gerardo. 1996. "Neoliberal Reform and Politics in Mexico: An Overview." In *Neoliberalism Revisited: Economic Restructuring and Mexico's Political Future*, ed. Gerardo Otero, 1–26. Boulder, CO: Westview Press.

———, ed. 2004. *Mexico in Transition: Neoliberal Globalism, the State, and Civil Society*. London: Zed.

Overall, Claire. 1992. "What's Wrong with Prostitution? Evaluating Sex Work." *Signs* 17(4): 705–25.

Paglia, Camille. 1994. *Vamps and Tramps*. New York: Vintage Books.

Palmer, Steven. 1994. "Pánico en San José. El consumo de heroína, la cultura plebeya, y la política social en 1929." In *El Paso del Cometa: Estado, política social y culturas populares en Costa Rica (1800–1950)*, ed. I. Molina Jiménez and S. Palmer, 47–80. San Jose: Editorial Porvenir and Plumsock Mesoamerican Studies.

Parker, Richard. 1991. *Bodies, Pleasures, and Passions: Sexual Culture in Contemporary Brazil*. Boston: Beacon Press.

Parker, Richard, Regina Maria Barbosa, and Peter Aggleton, eds. 2000. *Framing the Sexual Subject: The Politics of Gender, Sexuality, and Power*. Berkeley: University of California Press.

Paz, Octavio. 1985. *The Labyrinth of Solitude and Other Writings*. New York: Grove Weidenfeld.

Penyak, Lee Michael. 1993. "Criminal Sexuality in Central Mexico, 1750–1850." PhD diss., University of Connecticut.

Pheterson, Gail, ed. 1989. *A Vindication of the Rights of Whores*. Seattle: Seal.

Phongpaichit, Pasuk. 1982. *From Peasant Girls to Bangkok Masseuses*. Geneva, Switzerland: International Labor Office.

Pollock Sturdevant, Saundra, and Brenda Stoltzfus. 1992. *Let the Good Times Roll: Prostitution and the U.S. Military in Asia*. New York: New Press.

Portelli, Alessandro. 1991. *The Death of Luigi Trastulli and Other Stories: Form and Meaning in Oral History*. Albany: State University of New York Press.

Prieur, Annick. 1998. *Mema's House, Mexico City: On Transvestites, Queens, and Machos*. Chicago: University of Chicago Press.

Public Citizen. n.d. "NAFTA Truth and Consequences: Corn," www.citizen .org/trade/nafta/agriculture/articles.cfm?ID = 11330. Accessed April 10, 2007.

Rabinow, Paul, ed. 1984. *The Foucault Reader*. New York: Pantheon.

Reding, Andrew. 1998. *Mexico: Treatment of Homosexuals*. Washington, DC: INS Resource Information Center.

Rivera, George Jr., Hugo Vicente-Ralde, and Aileen F. Lucero. 1992. "Knowledge about AIDS among Mexican Prostitutes." In *Sociology and Social Research* 76(2): 74–80.

Rojas Wiesner, Martha Luz, and Esperanza Tuñon Pablos. 2001. "Situación demográfica y ocupacional de las mujeres del estado de Chiapas en los años noventa." In *Mujeres en las fronteras: Trabajo, salud, y migración*, ed. Esperanza Tuñon Pablos, 77–120. Mexico City: ECOSUR-COLSON-COLEF.

Rosenbaum, B. 1993. *With Our Heads Bowed: The Dynamics of Gender in a Maya Community*. Albany: State University of New York Press.

Ross, John. 2005. "Teoti-Wal-Mart." *The Progressive* 69(3), www.findarticles .com/p/articles/mi_m1295/is_3_69/ai_n13251106. Accessed May 28, 2006.

Rubin, Gayle. 1984. "Thinking Sex: Notes for a Radical Theory of the Politics of Sexuality." In *Pleasure and Danger: Exploring Female Sexuality*, ed. Carol S. Vance, 267–319. Boston: Routledge.

Rus, Diane. 1997. *Mujeres de tierra fría: Conversacions con las coletas*. Chiapas: UNACH.

Russell, Philip. 1994. *Solidarity: Mexico under Salinas*. Austin, TX: Mexico Resource Center.

Safa, Helen. 1994. *The Myth of the Male Breadwinner*. Boulder, CO: Westview Press.

———. 1995. "The New Women Workers: Does Money Equal Power?" In *Free Trade and Economic Restructuring in Latin America*, ed. Fred Rosen and Deidre McFadden, 39–43. New York: Monthly Review Press.

Scheper-Hughes, Nancy. 1992. *Death without Weeping: The Violence of Everyday Life in Brazil*. Berkeley: University of California Press.

Schifter, Jacobo. 1998. *Lila's House: Male Prostitution in Latin America*. New York: Haworth Press.

Schneider, Cathy. 1995. "Chile: The Underside of the Miracle." In *Free Trade and Economic Restructuring in Latin America*, ed. Fred Rosen and Deidre McFadden, 151–55. New York: Monthly Review Press.

Scott, James C. 1998. *Seeing Like a State: How Certain Schemes to Improve the Human Condition Have Failed*. New Haven: Yale University Press.

Secretaría de Gobernación. 1873. *Memorias de la Secretaría de Gobernación*. Mexico City.

Selby, Henry. 1997. Foreword to *Beautiful Flowers of the Maquiladora: Life Histories of Women Workers in Tijuana*, ed. Norma Iglesias Prieto, ix–xii. Austin: University of Texas Press.

Senzek, Alva. 1997. "The Entrepreneurs Who Became Radicals." *NACLA: Report on the Americas*. 30(4): 28–29.

Shrage, Laurie. 1994. "Comment on Overall's "What's Wrong with Prostitution? Evaluating Sex Work." *Signs* 19(2): 564–70.

Siverts, Hennings, ed. 1973. *Drinking Patterns in Highland Chiapas: A Teamwork Approach to the Study of Semantics through Ethnography.* Bergen, Norway: Universitetsforlaget.

Soja, Edward. 1989. *Postmodern Geographies: The Reassertion of Space in Critical Social Theory.* London: Verso.

Sparr, Pam, ed. 1994. *Mortgaging Women's Lives: Feminist Critiques of Structural Adjustment.* London: Zed Books.

Stacey, Judith. 1988. "Can There Be a Feminist Ethnography?" *Women's Studies International Forum* 11(1): 21–27.

Stoler, Anne. 1991. "Carnal Knowledge and Imperial Power: Gender, Race, and Morality in Colonial Asia." In *Gender at the Crossroads of Knowledge: Feminist Anthropology in the Postmodern Era,* ed. Micaela DiLeonardo, 51–101. Berkeley: University of California Press.

———. 1995. *Race and the Education of Desire: Foucault's History of Sexuality and the Colonial Order of Things.* Durham: Duke University Press.

Strauss, Anselm, and Juliet Corbin. 1990. *Basics of Qualitative Research: Grounded Theory Procedures and Techniques.* Newbury Park: Sage.

Sturdevant, Saundra, and Brenda Stoltzfus. 1992. *Let the Good Times Roll: Prostitution and the U.S. Military in Asia.* New York: New Press.

Suárez Findlay, Eileen. 1999. *Imposing Decency: The Politics of Sexuality and Race in Puerto Rico, 1870–1920.* Durham, NC: Duke University Press.

Subcomandante Marcos. 1994. "Chiapas: The Southeast in Two Winds." In *¡Zapatistas! Documents of the New Mexican Revolution,* ed. The Editorial Collective, 25–46. Brooklyn, NY: Autonomedia.

Symanski, R. 1981. *Immoral Landscape: Female Prostitution in Western Societies.* Toronto: Butterworth.

Teichman, Judith. 1988. *Policymaking in Mexico: From Boom to Crisis.* Boston: Allen and Unwin.

———. 1993. "Dismantling the Mexican State and the Role of the Private Sector." In *The Political Economy of North American Free Trade,* ed. Ricardo Grinspun and Maxwell Cameron, 177–92. New York: St. Martin's Press.

———. 1996. "Economic Restructuring, State-Labor Relations, and the Transformation of Mexican Corporatism." In *Neoliberalism Revisited: Economic Restructuring and Mexico's Political Future,* ed. Gerardo Otero, 149–66. Boulder, CO: Westview Press.

Truong, Thanh-Dam. 1990. *Sex, Money, and Morality: Prostitution and Tourism in South-East Asia.* London: Zed Books.

UNAIDS. 2004. *Report on the Global AIDS Epidemic: Fourth Global Report,*

www.unaids.org/bangkok2004/GAR2004-html/GAR2004_00_en.htm.
Accessed June 27, 2005.

UNICEF. 2005. *Child Poverty in Rich Countries*. Innocenti Report Card no. 6. Florence, Italy: UNICEF Innocenti Research Center, www.unicef.org/irc.

Uribe, Patricia, and Mario Bronfman. 1997. "Frontera sur: Comercio sexual y prevención del VIH." *La Jornada en Internet*, Letra S, July 3, www.jornada .unam.mx/1997/ago97/970814/ls-texto2.html. Accessed April 18, 2005.

Uribe, Patricia, Laura Elena de Caso, Victor Aguirre, and Mauricio Hernández. 1998. "Prostitución en México." In *Mujer: Sexualidad y salud reproductiva en México*, ed. Ana Langer and Kathryn Tolbert, 179–206. New York: Population Council and EDAMEX.

Vance, Carol, ed. 1984. *Pleasure and Danger: Exploring Female Sexuality*. Boston: Routledge and Kegan Paul.

van den Berghe, Pierre, and George P. Primov. 1977. *Inequality in the Peruvian Andes*. Columbia: University of Missouri Press.

Van Young, Eric. 1999. "The New Cultural History Comes to Old Mexico." *Hispanic American Historical Review* 79(2): 211–47.

Veselka, Vanessa. 2006. "The Collapsible Woman: Cultural Response to Rape and Sexual Abuse." In *Bitchfest: Ten Years of Cultural Criticism from the Pages of Bitch Magazine*, ed. Lisa Jervis and Andi Zeisler, 56–61. New York: Farrar, Straus, Giroux.

Vilas, Carlos. 1993. "The Hour of Civil Society." *NACLA: Report on the Americas* 27(2): 38–43.

———. 1996. "Neoliberal Social Policy: Managing Poverty (Somehow)." *NACLA: Report on the Americas* 29(6): 16–25.

Vogt, Evan. 1970. *The Zinacantecos of Mexico: A Modern Maya Way of Life*. New York: Holt, Rinehart, and Winston.

Walkowitz, Judith. 1980. *Prostitution and Victorian Society: Women, Class, and the State*. Cambridge: Cambridge University Press.

———. 1992. *City of Dreadful Delight: Narratives of Sexual Danger in Late-Victorian London*. Chicago: University of Chicago Press.

Ward, Colleen A. 1995. *Attitudes Towards Rape: Feminist and Social Psychological Perspectives*. London: Sage.

Wardlow, Holly. 1998. "Changing Sexuality, Changing Self: The Huli Dawe Anda as Contemporary Male Ritual." Paper prepared for the meetings of the Association for Social Anthropology in Oceania, Pensecola, FL.

Warman, Arturo. 1980. *We Come to Object: The Peasants of Morelos and the National State*. Baltimore: Johns Hopkins University Press.

Wasserstrom, Robert. 1976. "El bracerismo guatemalteco en Chiapas: Un motivo de orgullo para el pueblo mexicano?" *Punto Critico* 5(62): 11–12.

————. 1983. *Clase y sociedad en el centro de Chiapas*. Mexico City: Fondo de Cultura Económica.

Weeks, Jeffrey. 1981. *Sex, Politics, and Society: The Regulation of Sexuality since 1800*. London: Longman.

————. 1985. *Sexuality and Its Discontents: Meanings, Myths, and Modern Sexualities*. London: Routledge and Keegan Paul.

Weitzer, Ronald, ed. 2000. *Sex for Sale: Prostitution, Pornography, and the Sex Industry*. New York: Routledge.

White, Louise. 1990. *The Comforts of Home: Prostitution in Colonial Nairobi*. Chicago: University of Chicago Press.

White, Marceline, Carlos Salas, and Sarah Gammage. 2003. *Trade Impact Review: Mexico Case Study. NAFTA and the FTAA: A Gender Analysis of Employment and Poverty Impacts in Agriculture*. Washington, DC: Women's Edge Coalition.

Wilson, Ara. 1997. "Women in the City of Consumption: Markets and the Construction of Gender in Bangkok, Thailand." PhD diss., City University of New York.

————. 2004. *The Intimate Economies of Bangkok: Tomboys, Tycoons, and Avon Ladies in the Global City*. Berkeley: University of California Press.

Witness for Peace. n.d. "Behind the Seams: Maquilas and Development in Nicaragua," www.witnessforpeace.org/pdf.seams.pdf. Accessed April 10, 2007.

Womack, John. 1999. *Rebellion in Chiapas: An Historical Reader*. New York: New Press.

Wright, Melissa. 2001. "Feminine Villains, Masculine Heroes, and the Reproduction of Ciudad Juárez." *Social Text* 19(4): 93–113.

Wynter Sarah. 1987. "WHISPER: Women Hurt in Systems of Prostitution Engaged in Revolt." In *Sex Work: Writings by Women in the Sex Industry*, ed. Frédérique Delacoste and Priscilla Alexander, 266–70. Pittsburgh: Cleiss.

Zukin, Sharon. 1991. *Landscapes of Power*. Berkeley: University of California Press.

Index

abortion, 224n54
Aceituna, La (The Olive), 56
Adriana (pseud.), 195–96
advertisements, 38, 105, 172
age: of clients, 155, 162, 175, 176; of workers, 92, 161–62
Agee, James, 29, 204
Aggleton, Peter, 69, 74
agrarian activists: context of protests, 102–4; military force used against, 17–18; murders of, 14–15, 224n43; penal code and, 17, 224n48. *See also* ejidatarios; Zapatista uprising (1994)
Agrarian Law, 106–7
agriculture: campesino movements and, 14–15, 224n43; corn prices and, 222n5; declining crop prices in, 16; land redistribution and, 9; modernization of, 7, 76; for sale and subsistence, 131; undocumented migrants in, 135–36

AIDS. *See* HIV / AIDS
Albert, Alexa, 114, 168–69
alcohol: afternoon rituals and, 178–80; problems with selling, 50–51; strikers and, 97
Alejandra (pseud.), 127, 169–70
Alianza por Chiapas, 13
Alicia (pseud.), 147, 218–19
Altamirano, prostitutes in, 66–67
Amalia (pseud.), 57
ambiente (milieu or scene): academic discourse on, 121–22; contradictions and complexities of, 205–9; decisions to enter, 122–34, 185, 204–5, 206–7; independientes in, 146–47, 148, 149–50; leaving work in, 190–91; national identity and, 134–45; obligadas in, 131–34, 145–46, 147, 148, 150, 235n27; self-worth in, 189–90; signs of embeddedness in, 163–64; use of term, 233n. *See also* Galactic Zone (Zona Galáctica)
Amnesty International, 71

Text:	10/14 Palatino
Display:	Univers Condensed Light 47, Bauer Bodoni
Compositor:	BookMatters, Berkeley
Cartographer:	Bill Nelson
Indexer:	Margie Towery
Printer and binder:	Maple-Vail Manufacturing Group